PRAISE FOR SELF-PUBLISHING BOOT CAMP

Carla King is a self-publishing guru and her *Self-Publishing Boot Camp Guide for Authors* proves just that. Filled with real-life advice for every step of the publishing process, this book is highly recommended for anyone looking to jump into the self-publishing game.

— Fauzia Burke, author of *Online Marketing for Busy Authors*

There is no facet of publishing evolving faster than self-publishing and somehow, Carla King manages to stay one step ahead. Now in its fifth edition, King delivers sage advice to all types of writers, on every step of the process. Whether you are planning to DIY, or simply want to be an informed purchaser of publishing services, you'll find yourself returning to the *Self-Publishing Boot Camp Guide for Authors* for each new chapter of your journey.

— David Wogahn, founder of AuthorImprints.com and author, *Register Your Book: The Essential Guide to ISBNs, Barcodes, Copyright, and LCCNs*

Carla King's *Self-Publishing Boot Camp Guide for Authors* continues to be the most comprehensive and up-to-date guide for anyone new to self-publishing. It contains help for authors from writing your book to getting distribution, to selling books from your own site, as well as specific recommendations for today's best service providers and software solutions for indie authors. Highly recommended.

Carla King's excellent guide is a must-read for anyone thinking about publishing their own work. I beg you to read this book before you even write your first word and you'll have a better understanding of how to bring a book to fruition and then to be successful in the marketplace. She's a great friend to the Indie community and provides this valuable resource as a gift of love.

SELF-PUBLISHING BOOT CAMP GUIDE FOR INDEPENDENT AUTHORS

SELF-PUBLISHING BOOT CAMP GUIDE FOR INDEPENDENT AUTHORS

5TH EDITION: HOW TO CREATE, PUBLISH, MARKET, AND SELL YOUR BOOK LIKE A PRO

CARLA KING

Published 2020
Printed in the United States of America
ISBN 978-1-945703-16-4 Paperback
ISBN 978-1-945703-15-7 Kindle
ISBN 978-1-945703-17-1 EPUB

Library of Congress Control Number: 2019916007

For information, address:
Misadventures Media
Kalispell, MT
hello@misadventuresmedia.com
(510) 230.4262

For all the writers.

CONTENTS

FREE READER UPDATES

Staying up-to-date can be challenging. The good news is that this is my passion and I've created a simple way to keep you informed. If you subscribe to my readers list, I'll tell you all about the updates and changes to this guide.

www.selfpubbootcamp.com/readers

In addition, the *Consumer's Guide* in Part VII of this guide is available as separate ebook that I constantly update. You have access to it at no charge.

You also get bonuses like a metadata cheatsheet, a book launch check-list, and whatever else I cook up for you that eases your publishing journey.

Please join it!

PART I

PREPARING FOR SUCCESS

Welcome to the first and most important part of this guide. Many authors write a book and want to get on with the publishing part, and that is very easy to do these days. What takes the most effort is validating your book idea and developing your manuscript into a professionally produced book readers want to buy.

The only way to do this is to find early readers and invite them to help guide your writing journey. This means putting your work out into the world before it's finished, taking reader feedback to heart, and polishing your manuscript with a professional edit.

Here's a list of the chapters in this first part of the guide.

The Publishing Journey
Foundational Advice for Beginners
The Importance of Beta Publishing
The Importance of Editing

I hope these four chapters will encourage you to reach out to readers now. Please don't skip these steps. You'll miss out on a lot of fun and valuable feedback on your stories.

1

THE PUBLISHING JOURNEY

This is the 5th edition of the *Self-Publishing Boot Camp Guide for Authors*. It consolidates my firsthand experience and that of the hundreds of students, clients, and colleagues I've helped over the years. It was also shaped by all of authors who gave me feedback on the previous four editions, including a great team of beta readers eager to learn how to publish and willing to tell me what they wanted to know.

This guide is designed to help you in every stage of the publishing journey. Maybe you're just thinking about writing a book, or you've got a first draft from NaNoWriMo, or a completed manuscript that's been sitting in a folder for too long. Perhaps you're writing a book proposal because you hope to find an agent and a traditional publishing deal. Or maybe you're a published author with a small book that will promote your brand or a book that your publisher rejected.

Whatever stage you are in, however you're thinking about publishing, I'm glad you're here. I created this guide for authors who want to publish professionally and remain free to do what you like with your book, including attracting an agent and a publisher.

I don't want you to be trapped with a service or to wreck your chances of success with a hastily distributed book of low quality. Anyone can upload a book for sale but it takes time to publish a professionally produced book that readers will buy.

This guide is a shortcut to your learning process so you can skip all the experimentation and follow the path to a satisfying completion. I took the long way around, self-publishing my first book in 1994. I was working in the hi-tech industry so the tools were easy for me to learn, but after book production, wow, getting it into stores was a challenge. It's easier today.

But still, I've made just about every mistake there is to make, and yes, I've suffered the consequences. With these experiences and a lot of learning by trial and error in the 20+ years since then, I've developed a system.

The system demands that you slow down, set goals, create realistic expectations, connect with readers, and do all the things a publishing house does, especially getting professional editing and design.

Today, publishing is the easy part. It is very easy to upload a book for distribution to the online retailers. It's everything that happens before distribution that's time consuming. It takes time to produce a book that sells.

Are you looking to publish just one book or do you hope to make a career as an author? Are you publishing for fun, to promote a business, get a message to the world, express your ideas through fiction?

There are many paths in the journey to publishing professionally. Whether you aim to publish just one book or form a small press, to use do-it-yourself tools or hire it all out, I'll be here with you on the journey to producing a book you can be proud of.

You can read this guide from front to back or dive in to the various parts as you need them. I've tried to make each part as complete as possible. You may occasionally find repetition where information was relevant in more than once section. I centralized writing and publishing products, tools, and services reviewed in *Part VII, Consumer's Guide*, because I refer to them so often. Additionally, I've given you access to a constantly updated digital version of the guide so please sign up for the reader's updates.

The self-publishing industry is always innovating but there is a proven strategy which can assure your success. I want to help you achieve this success. I will help you slow down, follow this proven process, and proudly publish to five-star reviews.

2

FOUNDATIONAL ADVICE FOR BEGINNERS

Ride along with me for a minute. In 1995, I set out across America on a Russian sidecar and posted dispatches to the web, which is now called blogging. My fans were the 500 people who were on the internet at the time and they gave me immediate feedback on my stories, which was surprising and a little scary.

Some posts didn't get many responses, but others inspired a flurry of emails. I quickly learned what readers wanted, and that was even more scary because they wanted more intimacy, more risk, more expression of fears and hopes and dreams, of prejudices and preconceived notions. I took the risk and I received a lot of emails saying, *I hear you! I have felt exactly the same way.*

And I hear *you*. Writing is a scary, intimate act. You write to connect, to touch, to send a message, to make others feel as you do, or to teach, or to get lost in a new world. Whether you're writing fiction or nonfiction you're revealing yourself to hundreds, thousands, millions, the whole world. So you want it to be good.

Connect with your readers

On that journey, I learned to listen to my readers, to make friends with them, and to take what they had to say to heart. I learned to interpret silence as an indication of ambivalence. So I sought feedback from critique partners and editors to help me discover the why behind that resounding silence and to help me develop a style, to take risks and stretch my boundaries. And, to my surprise, I gathered a fan base. True fans. People who would shriek and hug me and buy five books to give away to their friends. It's a crazy feeling to be loved by strangers. It's weird and thrilling and awesome all at the same time.

And I love them. They read my drafts and will let me know what's boring and what they wanted more of. I'm always surprised at how deep they encourage me to go in my writing. They tell me to write more about this, less about that, and always go deeper emotionally, to slow down and tell them every little detail.

Publish to five-star reviews

I want you to find your true fans, the people who will keep you motivated and who will review your book on launch day and share it with their friends on social media.

Don't wait to share your work until after you've paid for expensive editing and design. Do it now, when it's still raw and a little painful to read. Sharing your early writing will force you to create something great. This is the step that guarantees five-star reviews.

Slow down

By now you may be starting to realize your deadline may be unrealistic. It's true that publishing a quality book and doing the advance marketing necessary to succeed with reviews and word-of-mouth recommendations takes time. So ask yourself, is your deadline real or self-imposed? Is your book tied to an event? Could you release it next year instead? I know many authors who have been sorry they rushed through the process. My best advice, and theirs (in retrospect), is to slow down.

One of my authors was rushing through a series to release for Black History Month. But after some tough deliberation she decided to wait a year. This decision relieved a lot of her stress. She also had time to market her book by publishing stories and gathering new fans. Then she sent her book to reviewers, got some great ones, and built a better foundation for her platform.

Does the idea of waiting make you breathe a little easier?

Follow the proven process

Again, you can slap your book up on Amazon today and say you're an author. But you know it's not a formula for success, which is why you're reading this guide. I wrote this guide because I want your book to look as professional as any book published by the big publishing houses.

Think about it. You can simply publish. Or you can publish well. Because you invested in this guide and are taking the time to learn about publishing, I know you aim to publish well. You're not wasting your time.

Publishing is a business like any other with rules and procedures and expectations from colleagues, vendors, and customers. There is a certain way things are done.

When self-publishing emerged as an alternative the world was flooded with new books. Hundreds of thousands of ISBNs a year are now assigned to self-published titles; but since many authors who publish on Amazon don't use ISBNs, there's no way to pin down how many books are self-published.

Few of those books have sold beyond the author's immediate network. Many are personal books, many are vanity projects, and many have not been edited. But there are many other reasons books fail.

- The author didn't do the market research and competitive analysis to make sure the book fits into a category that sells.
- The author did not share the book with early readers to get feedback and reviews, nor with a critique group or an editor knowledgeable enough to guide it in the right direction.
- The book cover or title didn't fit the standards of the category so people didn't realize they wanted to read it.
- The book description and author bio were uninspiring.
- The author didn't produce the book professionally to industry standards, with margins and leading, headers and footers, typography, and design elements readers expect in the genre.
- The author published without letting anyone know.

I hope to help you overcome your publishing challenges, starting with publishing professionally.

Beyond writing a story readers want, doing the research and sharing early work with readers, publishing professionally means learning about the business. It means doing all the things that make your book look exactly like a book released by a Big 5 publishing house.

That means that when someone in the book industry looks at your book they're going to see a copyright page with the ISBNs, an LCCN, a logo and publisher name. They're going to see that the headers, footers, and page numbers are printed on each page according to standards. They can't help it, and we all do some version of this. Do you do see typos on billboards, restaurant menus, real estate listings? This is the same thing. They see inappropriate fonts, a footer on a blank page, a self-publishing company logo, and a cover that doesn't match the genre.

To help you, the Independent Book Publishers Association offers a free *Industry Standards Checklist for a Professionally Published Book*. You can find it at the IBPA website under their *Resources* tab.

So write a great story readers want. Do all the things listed in the IBPA standards checklist. Keep learning about the publishing business. Stick with me. We'll take it one step at a time.

Work with the right tools

Choosing among the array of tools that help you write, edit, format, and publish can be overwhelming. Maybe that's why you bought this guide. That's good, because as you read through each step you'll find out which tools and services can help you. You'll be able to narrow down your choices and assemble a toolbox that suits your publishing project.

Parts I through IV of this guide step you through the process of self-publishing. The *Consumer's Guide* in Part VII provides detailed reviews of products, tools, and services you may use in your publishing journey. Because these companies improve their services so often, I maintain a digital version which you can access by subscribing to reader updates.

www.selfpubbootcamp.com/readers

I also interview the people behind these companies in the Author Friendly podcast, which you can find on Apple Podcasts, YouTube, SoundCloud, and wherever podcasts are published. Find more information and subscription links here.

www.authorfriendly.com

My toolbox

To give you an idea of the role of some of the tools I recommend, I'd like to share my personal process with you here. You'll develop your own process so this is just to give you an idea of the options and the tools that can help. You'll find them reviewed in *Part VII, Consumer's Guide.*

First, I use Scrivener to organize my thoughts, develop ideas and organize them into sections, scenes, blog posts, and stories to get ready to collect them all in a book.

I share my writing with early readers by blogging or sending them to my email list. I post stories on Facebook Notes, Wattpad, and forums.

If I don't get any feedback, I ask myself why. Is it because my readers aren't in the place I'm looking for them or they're just not interested? To help with this question I ask my critique partners, friends, and family, who I know will give me honest answers.

When I have a manuscript I think will work as a first draft, I export the book into Microsoft Word so my sister and my mom can edit it using the Track Changes feature. Both are avid readers (two book clubs each) and their critiques are usually right on.

Next, I begin editing and shaping the story. I recently began using Fictionary to identify narrative arc, plot holes, and other difficulties within my story. I guess you'd call it artificial intelligence. It's one of the coolest tools I know for fiction and creative nonfiction authors (like memoirists). Find out more about Fictionary in my talk with co-founder Kristina Stanley on the Author Friendly Podcast at www.authorfriendly.com.

After story editing, I check my manuscript using an electronic editor. I use ProWritingAid, which identifies my lazy writing habits (adverbs), long sentences, overused words and clichés. Things like that.

When I get stuck finding alternatives to my overused words, or if I find a place that needs a richer description, I use MasterWriter, a thesaurus on steroids.

Now it's time to share formally with critique partners and early readers. For that, I use BetaBooks, an online tool which lets everybody comment (privately or publicly) in the same place.

During all this time I'm still beta publishing, sending stories to my email newsletter subscribers (I use ConvertKit), and sharing with influencers in my genre, even though I know there are errors. That's okay. I'm getting lots of great feedback.

When I've had enough feedback, it goes to a copyeditor. There's really no substitute for a good human editor. I've used a number of copyeditors depending on genre and the editor's availability. The best copyeditors are often booked up in advance.

Finally, after I incorporate the edits, it's time to format the book. I have used Word, Pages, InDesign, Vellum, Pressbooks, Leanpub, Scrivener, and even Keynote (Mac's version of PowerPoint) to format my book. It just depends on the project.

Then, it's time for a final proofread (to "read your proof") and check for errors introduced during formatting. Hire this out!

Finally, it's time to distribute. I've tried most of the distribution companies by now. I always like to publish directly to Amazon using Amazon KDP for digital and print. Then I'll use either Smashwords, Draft2Digital, PublishDrive, or StreetLib to distribute the ebook everywhere else.

For print, I'll use Amazon KDP for print and IngramSpark to distribute everywhere else.

I've also printed large quantities of books with an offset press to sell at events. Earlier in my career I used Small Press United, a traditional-style wholesale distributor, to get books into stores.

For my website I use WordPress and a premium theme which includes a page builder, landing pages and many other perks. And for my email marketing newsletter I use ConvertKit. (Though MailChimp is more popular.)

For direct sales, I use an e-commerce widget to sell my books directly to readers from my website.

So you see, there are a lot of choices, and every author's path will differ, maybe slightly, maybe radically. As someone who has made her living by writing about technology and the internet and who is curious about all the new ways to share stories, make books, and publish, I enjoy exploring, testing, and making recommendations. So let me provide you with the information you need to choose the tools that work best for your particular book project and skillset.

You'll find out much more about these tools in the context of learning how to publish, so please be patient but don't be afraid to try things. Paralysis by analysis can be more destructive than taking the wrong step. As long as you own your ISBN you will be free to back up and switch tools and tactics anytime you like.

Again, look to the *Consumer's Guide* in Part VII for reviews of the products, tools, and services available to you. I obsessively update this part of the guide in the form of a web book titled the *Consumer's Guide for Self-Publishers*. Get free access to it by subscribing to the reader's updates.

www.selfpubbootcamp.com/readers

Here's a list of the tools I mentioned above.

- Scrivener
- Facebook Notes
- Wattpad
- ConvertKit
- Microsoft Word
- Apple Pages
- Adobe InDesign
- Pressbooks
- Vellum
- Keynote
- Leanpub
- Fictionary
- ProWritingAid
- MasterWriter

- BetaBooks
- Amazon KDP
- Kobo
- PublishDrive
- Smashwords
- IngramSpark
- Small Press United
- WordPress
- Thrive Themes
- Draft2Digital
- Books2Read
- Gumroad
- PayPal

Now, let's move on to the process of beta publishing and editing your book. These are two absolutely foundational activities that most authors skip. Don't miss out. Find your readers and talk with them. Let them help you reach the right audience and get those five-star reviews you're looking for. Bonus: these relationships work well on social media, so you can start having fun with Facebook, Instagram, Twitter, LinkedIn, or whatever platform you like using.

3

THE IMPORTANCE OF BETA PUBLISHING

PUTTING YOUR WRITING OUT THERE IN ITS UNFINISHED FORM can keep you energized, make sure you're writing to the audience you think you're writing to, and collect early readers to cultivate as super-fans and your street team. Getting feedback from early readers is the only way, in my experience, to make sure you launch your book to five-star reviews.

Pre-publishing or beta publishing is publishing "small," before you distribute "big." This happens long before you upload your finished book to online retailers, bookstores, and libraries. It happens long before you've even finished your book.

There's a difference between beta readers and beta publishing. You should only have a few beta readers, but you can publish your book in beta to hundreds of readers. Critique partners are different still—these are people who know writing, editing, publishing—probably other authors like you.

The beta-publishing process can give you insights about your market, your genre, and your audience. You'll get to know your readers and what they expect from the book.

As you learned in the previous chapter, I beta published by blogging, and you can too. But if you're not a blogger, there are many other ways to share your early writing with readers.

Free beta-publishing tools, besides your own blog, include your Facebook page (using Facebook Notes), and document sharing sites (Wattpad, Scribd), along with sites which enable you to sell or give away your book directly (Gumroad, Scribd, Patreon, BookFunnel, Prolific Works). Two paid critique and beta publishing tools I think are pretty awesome are BetaBooks, who I interviewed on the Author Friendly Podcast at www.authorfriendly.com.

You can also beta publish to other people's blogs, e-zines, and anthologies that publish stories like yours. Don't be afraid to reach out to them. Editors always need content and are happy to find a talented, hardworking writer who meets deadlines.

Stuart Horwitz protean excellent guide, *Finish Your Book in Three Drafts: How to Write a Book, Revise a Book, and Complete a Book While You Still Love It.* In it, he advises authors to gather between three and seven beta readers and reward them for their efforts.

> Make sure you are giving something of value in return to your beta readers because you are going to ask something of substance from them. Maybe you are beta reading their books, or you are offering free PR or SEO expertise, or you are dog sitting for them next week, or you are paying them. You can't afford to be unappreciative of your beta readers, so ask them how you can best return the favor.

To find critique partners and beta readers you'll need to connect with them where they hang out. It's pretty easy to figure that out these days just by doing a web search. Find out where your tribes hang out and join the crowd.

Also in Horowitz's book, you'll find tools like a beta reader questionnaire and sample questions to ask your beta readers about content, pacing, and marketing.

Avoid embarrassing mistakes

In case you're not completely sold on the idea of beta readers, let me tell you that many authors who publish too quickly are sorry later when they read in the Amazon reviews that their main character is too young or too old or just plain unlikable. They may have made some cultural, historical, or linguistic errors. There may be too much dialogue or not enough. Characters may appear and disappear without closure or their names misspelled or their hair color changes. These kinds of consistency problems are easily solved with beta reader feedback.

Beta readers can also help you with copyediting and proofreading. Reviewers on Amazon aren't shy about complaining. One author I know has a great book with excellent reviews, but there are lots of comments in the Amazon reviews about copyediting errors.

Early readers and content editing

In Chapter 1, I mentioned how the Fictionary story editing tool helps you identify story structure problems. Beta publishing is also a great way to get content editing (also called structural or developmental editing).

Your early readers will let you know about plot holes, theme breaks, and problems with the narrative arc. They'll ask you about that character you dropped halfway through the book. They won't say it the way an editor would, but if you have a compelling story and they want more, they'll let you know what's stopping them from having a great reading experience.

There's always an expert out there to correct you. I had a reader point out there wasn't a full moon on a certain date when I said I was looking at a full moon. Another corrected me on the population of a town, and another on the cubic inches of a particular model of motorcycle.

I had many beta readers for this guide. The first set were publishing pros, the founders of many of the self-publishing services companies listed here, longtime colleagues, people I met at conferences, or people I interviewed for articles and blogs. The second set of beta readers were self-publishing authors, many from my courses and workshops. Their feedback helped me decide to restructure this 5th edition of the guide into seven parts.

I. Preparing for Success
II. Your Publishing Business
III. Book Design and Production
IV. Distributing Your Book
V. Selling Your Book Direct
VI. Book Marketing and Promotion
VII. Consumer's Guide

Though there is some repetition and cross-referencing, I think this works really well. In fact, I've been told I should really be selling seven books. I may take their advice, but at this point, I'm arguing the steps are too interconnected to separate.

If you're a nonfiction author with a business or how-to book, I hope you find your colleagues just as helpful. There's no harm in asking. If you're a fiction author, connect with other authors and readers of your genre. Connect with your tribes in person and online.

Connecting with your tribes

To beta publish you'll need to connect with your tribes. Your fellow author tribe and your reader tribe are two of these. You might be writing for a community or a targeted segment of the population.

For example, one of my tribes are made up of authors and publishing professionals who have consulting, design, and editing businesses.

Another tribe I belong to are adventure travelers. I write specifically for several different niches in this broader category: solo women travelers, solo women motorcycle travelers, and people who are considering traveling to Baja.

Another group I write for are armchair travelers. People like my mom and my sister who don't do adventure travel themselves but like to read about it. (They're great beta readers.)

I find these people in many places online, but I am in my happiest place at adventure-travel events where I connect with readers and with other adventure travelers who want to publish their books.

Where is your happiest place?

How to identify your tribes

It's much easier to connect with existing tribes rather than create one of your own. Do a web search using keywords to research potential tribes:

- Regency romance writers and readers
- Cowboy romance writers and readers
- Holistic health educators and cancer patients
- Science fiction and fantasy writers
- Car racing fans
- Women who have waited almost too late to have children

- Readers of Celtic fairy tales
- Yogis
- Owners of long-haired-cats
- Gardeners who live in the desert

The more specific you can be, the better.

Is your tribe on Facebook? In a forum somewhere? Out in the Nevada desert building a big wooden man to burn down? Are they on LinkedIn or Instagram? Hiking in the Sierras? Cozied up by the fire with their cats?

Are they single, married with two children, Christian, Buddhist, Hindu, Jewish, agnostic, atheist? College educated? Are they 30 or 60? Are they on dating sites searching for the love of their lives? Looking to retire in another country? Concerned about climate change? Fans of *The Hunger Games*?

Connecting with your tribe should be fun and rewarding and not work you dread.

How to identify your audience

Who is your audience? Do you have beta readers that you think typify your audience? Sketch out a few profiles of people who you expect to be in your various tribes. These are called "customer avatars." Write character sketches of three ideal readers. Be as specific as possible. Maybe they're real people.

I know some of my readers pretty well. Sometimes I even tape their photos to my computer screen when I'm writing. This helps so much. It makes it easier to write for Lynn and Tom and not just authors in general.

If you don't know any of your biggest fans or ideal readers in real life, make them up. However, there's nothing like connecting with real people, and it takes basic research to find them.

Dan Blank, in his book *Be the Gateway: A Practical Guide to Sharing Your Creative Work and Engaging an Audience* talks a lot about how to identify your audience and grow it, one person at a time. I really like his approach:

> Opening the gate is about finding your people. Knowing what resonates with them, where they hang out, and who reaches them. Then, one by one, bringing them through the gate.

He emphasizes the value of slow, organic growth, as opposed to the unrealistic expectation of creating a sudden rush to your book with an ad or PR campaign. There are many valuable exercises in this book that can help you identify and engage your audience, focus on individuals, and craft an author bio that attracts readers.

Who do you think you're writing for?

When I set out on my *American Borders* motorcycle journey in 1995, I thought I was blogging to women my age who wanted to travel solo on a motorcycle. During my trip, I did receive a few emails from women, but mostly my readers were middle-aged-to-older men who loved motorcycling. I got a lot of emails that read like this:

> Dear Carla,
>
> I really admire what you're doing and your skills as a mechanic. I've always wanted to take a motorcycle trip around the US, and I don't know what has been stopping me, but I guess now I figure that if you can do it, I can do it.
>
> Thank you for the inspiration. And if you pass through Boise my wife and I would be happy to give you dinner and a place to sleep.

Jake

I have to admit this threw me for a loop as I assumed men just got up and went exploring the world on a whim. Clearly, this wasn't the case.

Also, this was 1995, so the internet was new. Mostly my readers were on BBSs—Bulletin Board System—at work in science, academic, and government institutions. Most people didn't have computers at home. This also explained why most of my readers were men.

What was really interesting though was the burgeoning growth of women in technology. It was a small but passionate group, and many of these women lived in developing countries. I visited one of these women on my motorcycle trip to India five years later.

Who do you want to write for?

To continue my story, my tribe—the tribe I was aiming to reach—was not on the internet yet. How could I reach them? Years later, I turned my blog posts into a book, but I made a critical mistake. The cover image was a photograph of me on my big hulking sidecar motorcycle. Very intimidating to women. But intriguing to men.

Today, because everybody is on the internet and social media tools are so much better than those old BBSs, my female readership comprises almost half of my audience. Still, I don't stop striving to reach more women.

You're in control

I'm in the process of rereleasing *American Borders* under a new name and a new cover that will do a better job to attract the readership I targeted and missed on first publication.

That's the beauty of self-publishing. All of this is completely under my control.

Many authors go through a similar struggle. That is, the difference between who you think your audience is and who it really is. The only way to know in advance of your book launch is by beta publishing.

If you're a fiction author, you may even need to adjust the traits of your main character. One author friend who writes historical fiction was told her character was too old, so she made her ten years younger and, voila, it became a bestseller.

Use your early readers to figure all this out.

How to communicate with your readers

Once you've found interested readers, communicate with them a lot. Ask them questions. Answer their questions. Give them writing they love.

Your email newsletter is a great place to interact. I always ask people what they're doing—what books they're reading, what books they're writing, what is their most urgent question about publishing, what is their dream trip, what is their dream motorcycle, or what's stopping them from going.

I invite them to "Just hit the reply button to send me a quick note." Over half of my "adventure travel interest" subscribers open the email and between five and 10 percent of them actually send me a note. Many are a sentence or two long, but a few will go on for a couple of pages. This is the kind of engagement you're looking for. It takes a lot of time, but it's the best way to figure out what they care about.

Once you've connected with your tribe, gotten to know them, joined forces, helped out, answered questions, offered advice, engaged in conversations, and have become a part of the community, then you can start testing your book with them. Offer them stories and invite feedback. Invite your super-fans to join your street team and spread the word when you launch your book.

How to ask busy influencers for feedback

Be especially mindful of asking influencers for feedback.

Influencers are colleagues, fellow authors, bloggers, editors, and anybody with a large audience. They're busy and get a lot of requests, so it takes longer to get to know them and create a know-like-trust relationship.

You'll find a story about how one author reached out to me in *Chapter 37, Book Reviews.*

It may be difficult for you to get up the nerve to ask people you admire to blurb your book or give you feedback. But if you are sincere, respectful of their time, and give them feedback, you may make a friend. And you may find this lonely life of writing not so lonely after all.

> Writers improve over time by practicing their craft in addition to getting focused feedback from experienced people who push them to improve and do better. - Jane Friedman, *The Business of Being a Writer*

How to create a giveaway or ethical bribe

Beta publishing can also help you fund your book as you grow your platform. For example, you can provide a small ebook as a giveaway when someone signs up for your email newsletter. This is also called an ethical bribe. You'll learn about this in the chapter on websites.

Grow awareness of your writing by contributing articles to magazines and submitting stories to anthologies. You can even create an anthology and recruit other authors who write in your genre to contribute.

So think of ebooks or booklets, anthologies, and articles as marketing tools.

Where to beta publish

You don't need to have a perfectly edited and formatted book to beta publish. Simply copy and paste your document to a place where the public can read it and give you feedback.

Use any of the tools I've mentioned so far. Or choose a dedicated social publishing website like Wattpad, or a fan-fiction website like, well, FanFiction.net.

For example, the E.L. James *50 Shades of Grey* phenom was developed on a fan-fiction website where the author revealed the book chapter by chapter over several months. She received instant feedback in the comments. A UK native, she also used her tribe on Twitter to fact check American English words.

Hugh Howey's *Silo* series began as a short story, titled *Wool,* on Amazon KDP. It became a series of books when readers clamored for more. It was already a polished story when he published it as an experiment on Amazon.

Please don't worry about people copying your writing. The fear of being copied prevents many authors from sharing their writing, and they miss out on attracting readers and succeeding as authors. Anyway, the chances of copyright infringement are pretty slim for an unknown author. Copyright is set as soon as you publish any writing anywhere. So please don't let it stop you from publishing your stories.

How to beta publish

Today's tools enable you to upload documents and collect feedback from early readers. A safe and easy place to dip your toe in is to use Facebook's "Notes" feature. After all, Facebook is already populated with your friends, family, and people who like you.

One of my favorite tools is Leanpub, an iterative book-publishing platform with a sliding-scale payment option and the ability to update your readers. It offers readers "pay what you want" pricing, so you can offer your book for free while giving them the opportunity to donate cash.

Wattpad is the world's largest and fastest-growing social publishing site and is popular with young authors. Most Wattpad users read stories on their mobile devices so keep your stories short and keep them coming fast. It's also a multimedia property with Wattpad developing television series and movies from popular stories published on Wattpad.

Forums are also great places to post stories. Join the community and post your work. (I publish many of my stories on ADVRider, a network for adventure travel motorcyclists.)

But you won't receive much feedback if you simply post your story and leave it there. Commit to being social, otherwise, it doesn't work.

Though not "social publishing" per se, Gumroad is an online store where you can offer your book for free. And it collects the email addresses of people who download it. You can offer your book in Word, PDF, EPUB, Kindle, even audio format, here. You can also use Prolific Works to offer advanced and sneak peeks and collect email addresses. (Find out more in *Chapter 33, Advertising and Giveaways*.)

Blog your book. Whether fiction or nonfiction, you can serialize your book on your own blog, creating a fan base and providing a comments area where people can give you feedback. (Check out Nina Amir's *How to Blog a Book* for everything you need to know to create a popular blog.)

How to test your book

I'm often amazed to find most authors skip doing market research. This means when it comes time to publish, they don't know what Amazon category and themes apply to their book or what BISAC codes they should use. It's not a good idea to rush into publishing before you know where your book belongs on the virtual shelves. Only then can you create a successful format and design so it competes with others in the genre.

You'll need to be sure your book fits in, yet stands out, in the sea of other books people search for on Amazon and Google.

A few authors I've worked with have insisted that their book is unique. They tell me proudly that there's nothing like it.

That's bad. Because if there are no books like yours on the market there probably isn't a market for it. So keep doing your market research to see where your book belongs. You may have to make adjustments to your main character or another aspect of your story to make it fit into a category that exists.

Use your community

Test your book with friends, communities, and editors. Solicit honest feedback. Make sure people can read it all the way through without putting it down. Make sure they're excited about it and want to tell their friends.

Use the search engines, especially Amazon Advanced Search, to figure out what category fits your book. Identify color choices, typography, use of graphics versus photography, and other trends used by top sellers. Use keywords and the date field to narrow your search. You may also want to specify format such as "paperback," and "bestselling" to display the best of the best books, and "latest" to display recently published books.

. . .

Use Amazon's Advanced Search for books

The tool readers use to find books they love is your most important competitive analysis and market research tool.

Use Amazon's Advanced Search for your market research.

Look for books like yours published recently and study the bestsellers to figure out what they're doing right. Look at their book descriptions, categories, book covers, everything about their listing. Make notes as you study:

- Save the bestselling book covers in a folder on your computer or a tool like Pinterest and, when it's time, hand them over to your cover designer.
- Remember, your cover should fit in with others in the genre so readers recognize your book, in just one glance, as the kind they like to read.
- Figure out which Amazon category, themes, and keywords similar books are shelved in.
- Follow your fellow authors on social media and begin conversations with them. There may be opportunities to co-promote down the road, or create an anthology, or begin a writing group.

It's good business to know as much as you can about your competition. I've found most authors to be more cooperative than competitive.

How to sell your book before you've finished it

A lot of the platforms I have mentioned enable you to sell directly to your fans and keep 100 percent of the profit. Leanpub, Gumroad, and Patreon are especially good for this. Get more information on how to use these tools for selling and crowdfunding your work in *Chapter 9, Fund Your Book*. See also *Chapter 54, Crowdfunding Tools and Services* and *Chapter 55, Direct Sales Tools*.

How to know when you're done

How many drafts do you have of your book? When is enough, enough? There's a concept in business called a minimum viable product (MVP), a product with sufficient features to satisfy early adopters. These early adopters provide feedback that affects the development of the final product. In authorship, that's a beta book.

Once your beta book is out there, you get feedback and incorporate those changes. Ideally, you'll get a manuscript review or a content editor (or a writing group) to look over your book and you'll also incorporate those changes. Get it copyedited, proofread, designed, and then publish. Let it fly away and get to work on your next book.

4

THE IMPORTANCE OF EDITING

Before you send your book to a human editor, first do some self-editing and run it through a few electronic editing tools. The three I recommend most often are ProWritingAid, MasterWriter, and Fictionary. (You can find reviews of these and alternatives in *Chapter 46, Writing and Editing Tools*.)

Fictionary identifies your story structure, plot holes, character arc, and other elements of story. ProWritingAid offers copyediting help by identifying style, grammar, readability, cliches, overused words, and repeats. MasterWriter is a thesaurus on steroids, giving you ideas on how to improve your word choices.

You'll save money and your human editor will be grateful to work on a manuscript that's been crafted with care.

There are lots of methods of self-editing, one of which is to tinker with your manuscript until you're sick of it. That's why I recommend Stuart Horwitz's book, *Finish Your Book in Three Drafts: How to Write a Book, Revise a Book, and Complete a Book While You Still Love It.* Here's his description of the three drafts:

We'll call the first draft the messy draft, which is all about getting it down. We'll call the second draft the method draft, which is all about making sense. And we'll call the third draft the polished draft, which is all about making it good. We could also call the third draft the design draft if you are publishing independently or the agent draft if you are seeking traditional publication.

Run Fictionary at the second and third draft stages to catch story errors. Then clean up or enhance your language in the final draft using ProWritingAid and MasterWriter.

The importance of mutual respect

Professional editing will cost you money and may also cost some emotional stress. Some authors find a great editor and then resent and resist all of their suggestions. Please don't do that. Take the time to choose an industry professional you respect. Ask for a sample edit. They also need to know if they want to work with you. The editor-writer relationship is an intimate one. A good outcome counts on good communication, respect, open-mindedness, kindness, honesty, and trust.

As an editor of travel stories, I love helping writers enrich their prose, pare down and tighten their writing, incorporate sensual detail, pick up the pace, and hone a narrative arc that takes the reader on a compelling and emotional journey. As an author, I've learned to seek out honest critiques. This makes me a better writer and makes my articles, stories, and books more marketable.

Cutting costs

Editing is expensive, and most experts agree it's the single most important item to budget for whether self-publishing or seeking an agent and a traditional publishing deal.

To cut costs, you can use writing groups and beta readers to help you validate your book's viability, improve its structure and language, and correct errors.

Traditional publishing companies have eliminated a lot of jobs and processes in the past decade. But there's a reason they have not eliminated the editing process. Follow their lead and have your work edited.

The different kinds of editors

There are many levels of editing and some editors do more than one kind. I'll start with the acquisitions editor, whose role you mimic when you do your market research and competitive analysis as described in *Part II, Your Publishing Business.* Then we'll discuss manuscript reviews, content editing, copyediting, and proofreading.

The acquisitions editor

First, before you even write your book, try to think like an acquisitions editor—that is, if you want to sell your book. This is the person in a traditional publishing company with the crystal ball. Acquisitions editors are the gatekeepers. They're the editors who say yes or no to agents. Their decisions are based on market trends and the author's ability to deliver a book that meets the publisher's standards.

This task will require you get to work with your market research and competitive analysis. Wait (you might be thinking), this isn't an editing topic, but it is, especially for authors whose genre is dominated by a bestselling author. You may find you need to approach your book differently so you're not directly competing with these superstars. (Find out about tools that can help in *Chapter 50, Market Research and Competitive Analysis Tools.*)

Because you don't have the experience of an acquisitions editor, you'll need to get up to speed by studying the bestselling books on Amazon. I'll show you how later in this guide. It's also a good idea to start beta publishing now to connect with readers and get their feedback. (You'll find places to beta publish in *Chapter 47, Social Publishing Tools and Sites.*)

Also connect with other authors in your genre. Team up with them for brainstorming sessions, masterminding, creating anthologies, group blogs, and editing. These activities will not only educate you about your market but will inject much-needed socialization and community in what can be an isolated writer's life.

Manuscript reviewers

If you have written a book with no outside input and think it's ready for the market, I implore you to get a manuscript review from a qualified book editor. A manuscript review identifies your book's strengths and weaknesses, plot holes, adherence to themes, pacing, character development, non-essential sections, repetitions, nonsensical verb tense changes, narrative arc, dialogue, point-of-view (POV), and narrative (author) voice.

Editors often receive submissions in which the author believes their manuscript is one genre when in fact it's not. This often occurs with authors who don't seek support from critique partners and beta readers.

Expect an editorial memo that opens with broad impressions of your book and becomes increasingly more detailed, providing specific advice for specific sections and pages. You'll pay between $500 and $2,500 for this service.

Lucky for you, there is a tool for that, which uses artificial intelligence. As I've mentioned a couple of times already, Fictionary will do the structural editing work for you, saving you a lot of time and money. It's still no substitute for a human editor, but consider it a good first step.

Content editing

A content edit (also called a developmental, substantive, or compre-hensive edit) addresses the art and craft of storytelling. Expect comments on your prose and language issues like word choice, sensual detail, dialogue, voice, style, and general readability. You may be able to skip hiring a content editor if you've done extensive beta publishing or workshopped your book with a writing group.

A content editor should be familiar with your market and be aware of trends in the genre. Your editor will provide a manuscript review and take it many steps further by working closely with you during the rewriting process until the manuscript is finished.

Content editing is time-consuming and priced accordingly. I've seen pricing as low as $2,000 and as high as $20,000. I'll bet a writing group and the Fictionary tool are looking pretty good to you right now.

Copyediting

Make sure you know exactly what you're getting when you hire a copyeditor. Some copyeditors limit their scope to a technical check and correction of your manuscript, addressing grammatical and spelling errors, typos and punctuation, consistency issues (place and people names, tense, times, dates, and seasons). They'll check facts and legal issues like libel and copyright infringement (such as the inclusion of song lyrics without permission). They may check for storyline consistency, make sure characters stay in character, and ensure landscapes and cityscapes remain stable.

A copyedit is not a content edit even though the jobs overlap somewhat, and they may indeed be the same person. A copyeditor may charge by the word, the page, or the hour. I've seen fees range from about $1,500 up to $7,000, depending on the length of your book, quality of your writing, and the caliber of the editor. Expect your copyedit to take from two to five weeks.

This is really an essential step, and I highly recommend using a professional copyeditor. But if you simply cannot afford one, please hire at least three people highly recommended by an English department or trusted source. You'll probably find they catch different errors. Hopefully, with three sets of eyes you'll end up with a clean manuscript.

Proofreading

Many authors revise the manuscript after the copyedit. This phase of the process usually has authors rethinking sections of their book and often opens a rabbit hole of additional revisions. So you need another round of copyediting, or at least a thorough proofread. If you've done any rewriting at all, it's smart to get a light copyedit before a final proofread. Even if you've barely touched the dang thing, typos will inevitably creep in, so get it proofed. After the "typesetting," which is called "formatting" today, you're smart to go over it a couple of times more yourself. A final proofread is $300 to $500 well spent.

How to approach an editor

Find an editor who specializes in your genre and who is qualified to do the level of editing you seek. Take the time to look through the list of books they have edited (check their website). I would then check out all of their books on Amazon and look through the reviews and read all the "look inside" content to make sure you like the sentence structure and flow of the book. When hiring, do your due diligence. Are certifications and education important to you? How many books have they edited? How many years have they been doing this? Search social media sites for reviews and feedback on other people's experience with the editor.

One of the best ways to find an editor is by asking for recommendations from other authors who have published quality, successful books in your genre. The best editors are busy and can afford to be picky about who they work with. They usually want to see a sample of your book to see if they want to work with you, but you also have the right to request a small sample from them to make sure you like what they do with your words. This stage is very important for both parties to make sure you are a match.

The second best way to find an editor is to hire a respected editing service. Some of these services will charge a nominal fee for a trial or test edit before you commit, to match you with an appropriate editor and gauge your suitability for working together. For example, NY Book Editors' trial edit includes a 2,500-word read-through, 1,500-word content edit, a short memo, and a twenty-minute phone call for a very reasonable $165.

Content editing is highly subjective. An experienced editor who is expert in your genre can be priceless. Once you've polished your story, hire a copyeditor or proofreader to handle the last, technical check of your manuscript before it goes to print.

Writing groups

Writing groups come in all flavors, so select yours carefully. To state the obvious, if you are writing a business book, you're not likely to get constructive feedback from a group of romance writers. Your writing group should also consist of people who are as committed to their projects as you are to yours. They should be able to give you constructive suggestions delivered in a positive tone.

I'm lucky to have lived in areas with high concentrations of professional writers, and I've belonged to three writing groups. My first group was a mix of fiction and creative nonfiction writers in Santa Cruz, California. We met for a weekly *al fresco* lunch at the picnic table on my lawn and read to each other in a leisurely fashion. Sometimes we swapped printed stories in advance.

The second group was twelve professional women travel writers and editors in San Francisco. Anywhere between five and eight of us would show up for our monthly meeting, hosted at one of our homes with a lavish dinner and often rather too much wine, which would extend the meeting into a slumber party. We handed out printed stories and read them aloud as the others made notes and offered criticism after the reading. Though we met too infrequently to work on books, we worked on each other's book proposals and query letters as well as our travel articles and stories.

This group also produced a multimedia ebook about a trip to Ireland and self-published an anthology titled *Wild Writing Women: Stories of World Travel*, which sold out in a week. Unfortunately, the group voted (seven to five) to sign it over to a New York publishing house, where it languishes today.

The third group I belonged to was the most successful in helping each other complete our books. All three of us were writers, but also worked as professional editors at technology companies. Our stated goal was to motivate each other by providing a weekly editing deadline to finish our books in three months.

We handed out our chapters in advance to be reviewed, and critiqued them carefully. We met every Tuesday evening at a bright, noisy Indian restaurant on Haight Street in San Francisco where we spread out our papers on a large, linoleum-topped table to discuss our books as we took advantage of the bottomless chai.

Two of us did finish our books, and the third member almost finished. My book, *American Borders*, went straight to the copyeditor after our last meeting, then to the proofreader, and then I published it.

How do you find writing groups? Search the web, Craigslist, and Meetup. Scour the social media sites like Facebook. Look for regional NaNoWriMo groups. Query local writing and publishing organizations, or check your library and local bookstores. If you can't find one in your area, then consider starting your own. You might be surprised how many people are seeking the same thing and just need a leader. Meetup is a great place to start. You can also post notices at local libraries, bookstores, and coffee shops. If you live in a remote area you may form a virtual writing group. Google Hangouts on YouTube, Skype, and Zoom are all good and free tools for virtual "in person" meetings.

Decide what level of critique is appropriate in the group. You might just want encouragement or more of a support group for freewriting, or the pressure of a deadline. You might, like me, want the straight, unvarnished truth. I started writing for technology in the '80s, and have formed a pretty tough shell. I have known a writer or two to dissolve in tears in critique groups, even when valid comments were delivered with kindness. This type of author needs to join a group for encouragement, not critique.

Electronic editing programs and apps

Because professional editors are so expensive, it's smart to invest in electronic editing software. Fictionary is a tool that analyzes your manuscript and can be used to identify plot holes, narrative and character arcs, and other issues. (Learn about it in my interview with Kristina Stanley, co-founder of Fictionary, on the Author Friendly Podcast at www.authorfriendly.com.

Choose ProWritingAid, Grammarly or AutoCrit to analyze your language, grammar, and spelling. Add MasterWriter, which is amazing for finding synonyms, word families, and alliterations. See *Chapter 46, Writing and Editing Software,* for detailed reviews of both free and paid tools.

These tools do much more work than the built-in spelling and grammar checkers in your word processing program. They alert you to overuse of adverbs, clichés, redundancies, overlong sentences, sticky sentences, glue words, vague and abstract words, diction, and misuse of dialog tags, to name just a few. Some will even connect you to a human editor with a click of a button.

Electronic editing apps are great for "first-pass" and "last-pass" editing to clean up mistakes in spelling, grammar, and punctuation. I love that these tools even follow me around the web to prevent errors in my social media posts, blog, and other places online.

When you clean up your manuscript before handing it over to a human editor, you get a lot more for your money.

Book consultants

Some people hire a book coach, book shepherd, or production assistant at the very beginning of their project to make sure the project is viable. These professionals will be able to help you succeed. If you don't have the luxury of a budget for this task, a writing group can help.

I've coached authors on both writing and publishing for years, and it's a difficult job. Make sure you're compatible with your book coach or consultant, that you respect their knowledge, and are open to taking their advice. Make sure to put everything in writing—what they promise to do for you, how much it will cost, how many times a week you'll talk, and hours of work (whether via email or phone/Skype).

Nail down a deliverable. It can help to outline both what is included and what is not included. For example, I discovered (the hard way) that I needed to spell out certain aspects of my publishing plan service. For example, that I will I show authors *how to* do market research and competitive analysis, but I do not actually *do* the market research and competitive analysis for them.

A book coach is your guide to quality writing or publishing, not a ghostwriter or a publisher. Make sure you know what you're paying for. Probably it's guidance, expertise, and accountability, not services (unless specified) like uploading manuscripts, creating cover files, researching the market, choosing BISAC codes, categories, and keywords.

A consultant can provide worksheets, talk over ideas, and connect you with trusted professionals. A consultant can also keep you from making very expensive mistakes.

Find more about working with professional author assistants, coaches, and book packagers in *Chapter 26, Custom Book Publishing.*

Finishing your book

Are you working toward a goal? Want to finish your book fast? Team up. The three members of my third writing group made a commitment to finish our books in three months. We calculated that if we gave each other fifty pages (double-spaced) each week, we'd be done in eight weeks. It worked! At the end of the process, we each had a solidly developed book with good story structure, character development, and narrative arc. Basically, this served as a developmental peer edit. After we finished we just needed to hire our copyeditors.

If you're one of those writers who works best on a deadline, make one up for yourself. Calculate the time it should take to finish your book and create a set of milestones. Schedule reminders on your mobile device or a calendar app. Set up a regular writing schedule to complete each chapter. If you keep a steady pace, you should be able to calculate how much time it will take to complete.

You might also commit to publishing your book on a social platform so your fans, even if it's just your family and friends on Facebook, can hold you to a deadline. Facebook Notes is a great publishing tool for this. You can also blog your book, use Pressbooks, or publish with Leanpub or on Scribd.

Research shows people who set goals—whether it's writing or weight-loss—are 30 to 50 percent more likely to reach them. When we share our goals with other people, we are over 75 percent more likely to succeed. This is also called "accountability."

Online communities for writers and readers

There are many online communities for writers and readers. Explore them to cultivate writing friends, reading friends, and beta readers who will encourage you (and vice-versa). Examples are WattPad, FanFiction, Daily Science Fiction, Men with Pens, Mythic Scribes, Hatrack, Figment, Absolute Writer, Critique Circle, Mibba, Reddit Write and Reddit Writing. The list goes on and on. Express your desire to the Great Google and see what pops up.

Preparing for success

This is the end of *Part I, Preparing for Success*. I hope you feel empowered to publish well whether you end up doing it on your own, with an agent book proposal, or by negotiating a hybrid deal with a distribution company.

Remember to slow down, set goals, create realistic expectations, connect with readers, and do all the things a publishing house does so you can publish to five-star reviews. You really can do this.

Let's start by creating your publishing business, setting goals, and working out a strategy for getting your book to market.

PART II

YOUR PUBLISHING BUSINESS

In this part of the guide you'll learn all about doing business as an independent author and publisher. Here are the chapters that will guide you through the process.

Create Your Publishing Business
Your Book Budget
Choose Your Tools
Your Sales Strategy
Fund Your Book
Copyright, Pirating, and DRM
Developing Your Brand
All about ISBNs

If you've ever run a small business, some of this will be familiar to you. If you haven't, don't worry, it's really not that difficult. I know you'd rather be writing, that you may not enjoy creating a business plan or budget. But you'll definitely enjoy the benefits these activities reap.

The most important thing, in my opinion, is your freedom. When you have a plan, when you figure out how you're going to get the money for your book, when you know how you're going to sell, how to build a brand, and what it takes to keep your rights and your freedom to publish as you wish, you have the power to succeed.

5

CREATE YOUR PUBLISHING BUSINESS

Self-publishers wear many hats, including that of a small-business owner. This role can be rewarding for many authors once they realize how much more control they have over their book than if they had sold it to a publishing company.

Creating a successful business with your writing requires you to spend time not writing. It may also necessitate writing articles and stories for pay, which also takes away from writing your book.

You may find you can create a media property based on your writing using a platform like Patreon, by selling related products using Gumroad, or to crowdfund your writing with a tool like Kickstarter or PubLaunch.

You'll need to decide if you want to keep your day job and write on the side or live modestly and work hard to create a profitable business. It is also possible to live well on a fraction of the cost of living in the US or the EU in by relocating to South America or Asia.

Whether you're writing full time or part time, if you're spending money on your writing and publishing efforts, it pays to create a small business. Here are the essentials of creating and building a small publishing business as an independent author.

Developing a business plan

A business plan, even a short one, will help you with goals and expectations as it requires market research, competitive analysis, and creating realistic financial projections.

If you plan to publish only a single book, your business plan might consist of a simple document stating your mission, goals, and budget. (However, most of the one-book authors I know have gone on to write two and more.)

If you plan to publish many books, or if your book is tied to a business, product, or service, you already have a business plan (I hope), so just add your book to it and specify its role in your business.

There are many business plan templates on the web and lots of books to guide you through the process. I like Business Plan in a Day by Rhonda Abrams.

Your mission and goals

A business plan can help you to articulate your mission. Whenever you have to make a decision, you can return to this mission statement to figure out if the action you are about to take serves it. You may be tempted to skip this step and blindly jump into publishing your book, but it's better to think it out, write it down, and modify it as you become more aware of the challenges of this business.

Authors have told me this simple step of writing down their mission and goals has helped them every day. Some have even pinned their mission statements to their walls.

Jane Friedman, in *The Business of Being a Writer*, states that, "Most writers, in their desire to get published, put the cart before the horse: They want to see their work accepted and validated before they've thought through what their larger goals are."

What is your larger goal? So it helps to step back and consider what writing and publishing have to do with your life goals. Why are you writing this particular book? Is your mission to change the world, to make money, to support your business, to leave a family legacy? Is your goal to entertain or inform a small audience—family or community— or a larger audience in a geographic area, profession, lifestyle, or interest group? Perhaps you are writing to establish yourself as an expert in your field or to promote other products and services you offer. (Do you envision spinoff media, workshops, a product line?)

Perhaps you are among the many traditionally published authors disillusioned with the industry who are turning to self-publishing. Or will you use your book as part of a book proposal to try to attract an agent and publisher? The mission and goals section of your business plan is the place to spell it out in both broad and fine strokes.

Business tasks and timeline

Your bookselling journey may be a short one, or it might be a long, fluid, and creative process. It can sometimes take years for a book to take off, so set up good social media channels, good relationships, and good communities. Never stop marketing.

Below is a starter list of items for your timeline with an estimated time to complete provided. Adjust tasks to suit your project. For example, if you are formatting your book in Word, it won't take nearly as long as it would to format it using InDesign.

If you want it to compete alongside books published by the big publishers, you'll need to do what they do. Here are some items to put in your timeline:

- Purchase a set of ten or 100 ISBNs from Bowker (immediate)
- Get a tax ID to separate your business from your personal tax records (immediate)
- Choose your publisher name and get a DBA (two weeks)
- Create a publisher logo or type treatment (one day/week)
- Create good metadata – this is an important marketing tool and can (and should) take a long time. You can continue to refine it.
- Open a Library of Congress (LoC) PCN account to get an LCCN and PCIP block for the copyright page (three to six weeks)
- Set a price for your book (market research competing books using Amazon Advanced Search)
- File reseller certificates with the POD services you use
- Register your copyright (after publishing)

This business timeline does not include book production and marketing tasks.

Get a federal tax ID for your business

The simplest way to separate your publishing business and finances is to have two separate tax IDs.

In the US your business tax ID will be an EIN (Employee Identifier Number) and you can get it online in just a few minutes. An EIN replaces your Social Security Number wherever an SSN is required. Though it's called an Employer Identifier, you don't need to have employees to get one.

Like your SSN, the EIN is just another TIN (Taxpayer Identification Number). When you use an EIN for your publishing business, it makes it very easy to separate business from personal expenses at tax time. Yay! For a thorough description of the EIN see IRS publication 1635.pdf.

Where to apply for a free EIN

In the US, go to IRS.gov to get your EIN. Predictably, there are several unscrupulous agencies who offer to save you the trouble of getting an EIN by doing it for you, for a price. Ha. You can't fool me! These agencies have great SEO (Search Engine Optimization) and they often appear above results for the IRS website. They also mimic the look and feel of the IRS site. They lure many unsuspecting small-business owners into their clutches. Don't be one of them.

For authors living outside of the US

Until recently, authors living outside of the US had to get an EIN to avoid being taxed 30 percent on royalties earned in the US. That's no longer the case.

If you want to sell books in the US, but you don't live in the country, you do not need an EIN. Instead, apply for an ITIN (Individual Tax Identification Number) using Form W-7.

You also need to complete a W-8BEN form. This allows distributors to pay your royalties without withholding taxes as specified in the tax treaty for your country.

Some companies will automatically pop the W-8BEN form up when you need it during the publishing process. With others you need to do it as an extra step.

For more information, see UK-based author Catherine Ryan Howard's blog post and Smashwords' checklist of the steps you need to take.

Why obtaining a business tax ID is important

Just in case you're not already convinced, let me count the reasons you should get a separate tax identification number for your business.

- You can avoid spreading your personal tax ID (SSN) around the internet.
- It enables you to separate your business expenses from your personal expenses.
- You need one if you are ever going to employ somebody.
- It's easy and fast using the online forms.
- Your accountant will love you.
- It's free.

Getting a separate tax ID is a good first step to doing business as a publisher. When tax time comes around, you'll be ready to present your case as a small business with Schedule C (in the US). If you want to formalize your business by creating your own imprint, getting a DBA, setting up an LLC, or even incorporating, you can do it under this tax ID. You may also need to pay for a business license depending on the area you live in.

Until recently, authors living outside of the US had to obtain an EIN to avoid being taxed 30% on royalties earned in the US. The rules have changed, so now if you are selling books in the US but you don't live in the country, you do not need an EIN but you do need to apply for a ITIN (Individual Tax Identification Number) using Form W-7. You'll also need to complete a W-8BEN form, which allows distributors to pay your royalties without withholding taxes as specified in the tax treaty for your country. Some companies, such as IngramSpark and Amazon, have systems that are smart enough to automatically display the W-8BEN form up when you need it during the publishing process. For details on how this works, search for Smashwords' checklist of the steps you need to take. (It's in the Smashwords support FAQs, just search for ITIN.) You can use roughly the same procedure for other distributors and vendors.

Use your name or a business name

Create a business or publishing house name (your publisher imprint). You don't need to file for a Fictitious Business Name (FBN) to get a DBA (Doing Business As), but it's not expensive and it's worth protecting your brand.

With a DBA and a business bank account you can accept checks made out to your company name. It will make you look more professional and it will separate your business from your personal finances.

You don't need to form a business to get a tax ID. You can get the tax ID first, and apply it to the business later. The sooner you start separating your business finances, the better.

You can get DBA forms and procedures for free from your local city hall. Just fill out the forms, advertise your DBA in a local newspaper as instructed, and then take your DBA paperwork to the bank to open a business bank account.

It's easy but rather tedious so I often recommend a service called Legal Zoom to handle it for you.

Choose a publishing house name and logo

Your publisher name or imprint will be displayed on your title page and the spine of your book, in your Bowker ISBN record, and in your book distribution accounts.

You'll also need a logo. Make sure it's legible in a very small size, because this will go on the spine of your book cover. It can even be an image or a type treatment.

Your imprint name and logo shouldn't scream "self-published" but it doesn't need to sound stodgy or corporate, either. Solicit input from your friends, family, colleagues, members of your writing groups, and anyone else whose opinion you value. Search the web to make sure your publisher name isn't already taken.

Think about your company description—is it a press, a media company, or a business? I named my publishing company Misadventures Media instead of Misadventures Press because I also create multimedia products.

Publisher name of record

If you use a free ISBN from one of the self-publishing companies rather than your own, your books will be listed as published by that company.

Even if you use your own ISBN and one of the self-publishing companies to distribute your book (which most of us do including me), your book will be listed as published by your publisher name. However, the book industry will be able to see it is distributed by the self-publishing company.

How can they tell? Well, they can look it up in the *Books In Print* database, which is the leading bibliographic database for libraries, publishers, and retailers around the world. Your book is listed in *Books In Print* with the data from your ISBN record.

In your ISBN record you list your distributor—because it's necessary to know who will print and fulfill your book. This happens in the SALES & PRICING section of the record. Here's the HELP text for the Distributor field.

Distributor
Choose one Distributor from the drop-down list.
If no selection is made, the Publisher will be entered on our file as the Distributor.
If your distributor is not listed, click the Help link below the field to

contact us.
If you wish to add a "Distributor", it must be a name other than the name
of your publishing company name.

This isn't usually a barrier to entry for bookstores (with a published-by-Amazon status a notable exception) so most authors shouldn't worry about this.

If you want your book to be completely free of any association with self-publishing companies you can use a traditional-style wholesale distribution company like SPU (see chapter 23), a custom publishing company (see chapter 25) or a self-publishing services company like Gatekeeper Press (see chapter 42) who will set up your book data for you without their branding. This will cost an extra $100 or more because it takes extra time. (Gatekeeper Press has offered to waive the fee for my readers when you use code *carlaking*.)

Again, for the great majority of authors this is not an issue. I have used many of these self-publishing companies as my distributor to reach retailers without feeling the need to take this extra step.

Get your resale certificate

If you sell physical books at an event, like a conference or book show, you're legally obligated to obtain a seller's permit, which is also called a resale certificate. To find out how to register your permit search for "sellers permit" in your area for instructions.

Before you purchase your own books from POD distribution company IngramSpark you should file a resale certificate with them. Otherwise you'll pay tax when you purchase your own books and then you'll be taxed again on the same books when you sell them at an event.

Amazon used to have a resale certification registration page but since they moved from CreateSpace to KDP for print that feature has disappeared. (I hope they reinstate it, it's needed! So keep checking and sign up for my readers updates so I can let you know if it happens.)

Don't pay tax twice when you order copies from IngramSpark. Obtain the permit and then login to your account and find the resellers permit filing area. (If you can't find it, just google it and the page will usually show up.)

If you sell books at a show or conference or even mail a book to a customer you are supposed to pay taxes in the state where it's sold. For example, I live in California but when I spoke at a conference in Philadelphia I had to pay Philadelphia taxes on the books I shipped there for sale. (This isn't true when a bookstore handles sales at an event.)

Most conference and show organizers will provide you with the proper forms, but if they don't, it's your responsibility. So make sure to search for the forms for the place you're selling in and file them yourself. You can register for a seller's permit online and click "Temporary Seller's Permit."

Include sales tax when selling at a show or conference. I round up the price of my books to an even number so I don't have to make change.

It's up to you to keep track of all the physical books you sell so you can report and pay sales tax on them. So set money aside from each sale and make sure to charge sales tax on top of your selling price so you're not surprised come tax time.

Legal help for authors

There's a lot more legal and financial stuff to know, and it can fill an entire book. Lucky for us, lawyer and self-published author Helen Sedwick has provided us with this information in her excellent resource, *Self-Publisher's Legal Handbook, 2nd Edition*.

When you become a member of the Authors Guild you'll get free legal assistance, from contract reviews to advising on and intervening in legal disputes. Joining the Authors Guild essentially provides an author with a free attorney on retainer. Find out more about the organization in *Chapter 62, Professional Organizations.*

More business resources

Please see *Chapter 49, Business and Productivity Tools* for reviews of the tools and services available for you to do business as an independent author. I also offer a course on doing business as an independent author at selfpubbootcampcourses.com.

For a deep dive in to the business aspects of this career, look to Jane Friedman's excellent guide, *The Business of Being a Writer.* This guide, as she puts it, takes a "strategic, high-level look at how writers can establish a lifelong writing career."

I'd also like to recommend a book that will clarify how the publishing industry works, including hybrid publishing. Take a look at Brooke Warner's *Green-Light Your Book: How Writers Can Succeed in the New Era of Publishing.*

Both of these books are also very interesting reads. You won't be bored!

6

YOUR BOOK BUDGET

CREATING A REALISTIC BUDGET IS ESSENTIAL FOR THE SUCCESS OF any business. In it, you'll figure out what you can afford to invest in publishing your book. Set your first goals by answering the question, "Will I support the book or will the book support me?"

Here are some general considerations budgeting your book-publishing journey.

Distribution

You can get ebook and print book distribution for free with some services because they take a percentage of sales, usually between 10 percent and 15 percent.

Print-book distributors include IngramSpark, Draft2Digital, and StreetLib. These three services also act as ebook aggregators who distribute your ebook to the online retailers.

Smashwords is an ebook aggregator, and some authors like to use the combination of Smashwords with Amazon KDP to distribute their ebook and for their print book, use IngramSpark. That's just one of the many combinations available to you.

Companies that charge fees up-front instead of taking a percentage of books sold include BookBaby and Gatekeeper Press. Find a summary of these and other full-service companies in *Chapter 39, Distribution Tools and Services.*

Interior formatting and design

Determine the level of professionalism you desire and can afford. It's super easy to use a template (free to $60) and do it yourself if you know how to use Microsoft Word Styles or InDesign. But if you want to compete in the general marketplace alongside authors who are published by the big houses, you'll want to hire a pro.

Why pay a pro?

In my experience, professional interior design and formatting using InDesign costs about $2,000 though you might get lucky and spend half that. This produces the kind of book that truly competes with any published by the Big Five publishers.

Here's the process. Somebody comes to me with a book project. I help hire the right professional book designer for the project. Typically, it's an InDesign pro who charges around $1,500. During the process, the three of us—author, designer, and I—constantly check in with each other. There's a lot of conversation about the copyright page with the LCCN and PCIP block, how to get the type treatment from the cover designer for the half-title and title pages in the interior, and creating a logo or type treatment for the publishing house name. More talk about including testimonials in the front of the print book. And about whether or not to start each chapter on a right-facing page, leaving the left-facing page blank. About moving the acknowledgments, testimonials, and other front matter to the back for the ebook version. Typically, there are adjustments to the table of contents because lots of authors mix capitalization and don't realize it until they've seen the automatically generated contents. Then they proof the book and find typos in it they didn't see before it was printed.

All this takes a lot of my time and the designer's time, and there are lots of picky little things to rework. After the print proof is done, then the EPUB and MOBI ebook files are created, which requires checking them in the Adobe Reader and Kindle apps. (Check the copyright page, especially. For some reason, the formatting often produces gobbledygook on that page.)

If all goes well, the professionals you hire make a living wage. Often, however, they end up making $5 an hour and call it a learning process. More and more often, professional designers charge a fixed price with a menu of charges for changes.

The thing is, we are all invested in making your book look amazing. Nobody would be in the business if they didn't love it. I love creating a professional publishing plan for authors who had no idea they could compete with Big Pub titles. Designers love making beautiful books. Editors love perfecting prose. Copywriters get a lot of satisfaction from creating an exciting, compelling description and author bio. Website designers have fun with technology and design. Every single person you hire is invested in the beauty and professionalism of your book and author presence, and I have seen most go over and above the call of duty, often sacrificing valuable time and money to do a good job. Most authors see it and appreciate it and are happy to compensate these professionals fairly.

Templates

An interior design template from Amazon is free, but it's not beautiful. So buy a professional Book Design Template for between $37 and $57 and make a great-looking book almost effortlessly.

If your book is simple and you don't want to do it yourself, you can hire somebody to do it for you for $100 or less. They will use their own template and customize it for you, but you can ask them to use one you bought. Another option is to use WordPress-based Pressbooks to create and format your books (ebook $20 and ebook-plus-print for $100).

A lot of people go to Fiverr and other cheap places to get their books formatted, but often these people make mistakes like putting headers and footers on opening chapter pages and blank pages, or not starting chapters on odd pages. Refer to *Chapter 14, Book Production Basics*, for a list of front and back matter and standards for headers, footers, and pagination.

Get more information on Book Design Templates, Pressbooks, and many other formatting tools in *Design and Formatting Tools*.

Fanciness

Want fancy flourishes, drop caps, pull quotes, and other design elements? You can do it yourself, but if you're hiring it out, the more complicated it all gets, the higher the price. The price goes way up if you need tables and columns and also if you want to include images and text boxes such as in a cookbook.

Ebook first?

There are arguments for and against publishing your ebook first. Ideally, you will have beta published your book and if you used a tool like LeanPub, the formatting will already be done. So you can upload it for ebook distribution or direct sales to each store.

I recommend publishing your ebook first, perhaps to Kobo Writing Life because of their marketing perks, or Amazon KDP Select because of theirs. Study the opportunities. This is really a marketing decision. Do you want to grow your readership using their tools or do you want to come out of the gate with full distribution to all the retailers in digital and print?

Some experts recommend designing your print book first, correctly pointing out you'll find all kinds of crazy, unexpected text that looks wrong when you look at the printed proof in your hand. (Special characters that didn't translate, missing fonts, unnumbered chapters, missing chapter names, and style issues.)

Based on these common problems, they recommend you use your print book as the basis for all other versions. Most authors I've worked with use their ebook to grow their audience and then release the print edition. Some launch in both print and digital at the same time. (I actually released this guide in print format first, using my *Consumer's Guide for Self-Publishers* as a giveaway to grow my audience.)

Book cover design

You can hire a book cover designer for as little as $50, but they will probably use stock photos, which may also appear on many other book covers.

Since book cover design is such an important investment in your sales, pay as much as you can for a professional designer. Make sure they use original art and photography, licensed images, and professional, licensed fonts.

If you insist on creating your own cover, or are paying someone on Fiverr, make sure to pay attention to the licensing details. Most of the time you will need to pay more for an extended license for book covers and interiors. Also make sure you have the license to use the fonts for book covers.

A professional cover designer knows the market and has had success with books like yours. Budget between $100 and $1,500 for cover design, remembering you get what you pay for. See *Chapter 14, Book Production Basics*, for details on what you need for front, back, interior flaps, and spine.

Editing

As discussed in previous chapters, your book needs professional editing. For budget purposes, a manuscript review can cost $500, content editing up to $5,000. Final copyediting, another $500 to $1,500. If you can get content editing taken care of by writing groups and beta readers, budget $500 to $1,500 for copyediting and possibly another $500 for final proofreading.

Domain names and website

Domain names at GoDaddy cost under $10 per year when purchased in two-year blocks, and a managed self-hosted website with a blog can cost anywhere between $12 and $60 per year.

Popular domain names or short names that a seller perceives as valuable can cost hundreds and even thousands of dollars. (For example, Patrick Collison, the founder of Stripe, felt lucky to purchase the company domain name for $20,000.) But your name probably isn't up for auction at that kind of price.

As discussed in *Chapter 34, Your Website and Blog*, it's critical to pay for a self-hosted website so you don't have to worry about security and you always have a backup. I like tinkering with WordPress, but many authors want to hand it off to someone else. If you're that person, check out Pub Site's excellent service. I make specific recommendations for website tools in *Chapter 57, Website and Blog Tools*.

Miscellaneous costs

It's tough to nail down a price for stock photography, font licenses, membership in writing organizations, Advanced Reader Copies (ARCs), paid reviews ($500), consultant and coaching fees, bookkeeping, and Facebook advertising. These things add up, but they're spread over a long period of time.

The real cost of self-publishing

As an example, if you publish an ebook with no ISBNs, a $70 interior design, a $50 cover, and $500 for editing, you'll spend $620.

But I strongly recommend you obtain a set of at least ten ISBNs, which costs $295 in the US. Total so far: $915. This assures your freedom to publish using any service you like and not end up with duplicate ISBNs.

Get professional formatting. For a simple book I'll estimate $100 for a Word document and $1,000 for an InDesign document. The cost now ranges between $1015 and $1915.

Add $1,000 more for editing and another $500 to $1,000 for cover design, bump up the interior design with a professional touch for yet another $50 to $1,000, to bring your book up to professional standards. Cost so far: Just shy of $3000.

By the time you've touched all your files, you'll need another proofread, so add another $500. Let's round up to $3500.

Add a web pro to design your website for $500 and, if you are clueless about social media, another $500 for someone to establish your presence and get you started with a few posts on each platform. Your total now is around $4500.

This is not surprising. Most successful authors I work with do most of the work themselves and still spend $5,000 to publish, which does not include consulting fees, training, or services. Authors who are committed to success and to making money from their book pay double and triple that, and many even pay quadruple that.

Few authors realize how much it costs to publish when they begin. Later they tell me it didn't hurt so much, as the process was spread out over time. So I hope the information here helps you make smart decisions, avoid paying too much, or expecting too much for too little.

Fast, easy, and cheap

There's nothing wrong with test-driving your book using a fast, cheap, and easy method. By test-driving, though, I mean beta publishing, discussed in Chapter 3. Please don't distribute your book before it's been fully edited and designed.

Budget checklist

Here's a starter list of budget items you should be aware of. All of these expenses can be written off on your taxes, so hire a tax accountant who is familiar with publishing.

Here are some items you may pay for in your business as an independent author-publisher:

- Equipment (laptop and other hardware)
- Software and apps (Word, Scrivener, InDesign, Photoshop, etc.)
- Domain name purchases ($10 each per year)
- Website hosting services ($50 per year+)
- Website development ($500 average)
- Social media establishment ($500)
- Mailing list management (to $50 per month)

- DropBox subscription ($100)
- Author photo ($200–$500)
- Other photography
- Images and graphics (stock photos or commissioned)
- Editing and proofreading ($1,000+)
- DBA (fictitious business name)
- Advanced Reader Copies (ARCs)
- Giveaways
- Bowker: ISBNs ($295 in US)
- PCIP block ($160)
- MARC record ($20)
- Cover design ($100-$1500)
- Interior design (to $50-$1500)
- Logo design ($100)
- Copyright ($35-$55)
- Office supplies
- Travel expenses
- Telephone and internet expenses
- Contest entries
- Memberships, dues, and subscriptions (IBPA, $129)
- Advertising (business cards, Amazon and Facebook ads)
- Promotional materials (bookmarks, postcards)
- Copywriting services
- Review services (Foreword, PW, etc.)
- Vendor fees (setup fees)
- Printing

7

CHOOSE YOUR TOOLS

In this chapter, I want to talk about the tools I recommend most often to my clients and why. Choosing the tools you'll use is one of your most important business decisions. Independent authors should maintain control of every aspect of the publishing process so you'll either need to learn how to use these tools or how to hire professionals to do it for you. In this guide I aim to help you decide what to do yourself and what to hire out.

Refer to the extensive *Consumer's Guide* in Part VII where these tools and many others I recommend are described in detail. And don't forget to subscribe for updates.

selfpubbootcamp.com/readers

Book creation tools

Here are the tools I like most for creating novels and creative nonfiction books. These tools are discussed further in *Chapter 15, Interior Book Design*, and *Chapter 16, Book Cover Design*.

- Microsoft Word with Book Design Templates
- Pressbooks
- Vellum
- InDesign

You may also opt to create your beta books in an easy-to-use cloud-based tool by Draft2Digital, PublishDrive, or Reedsy, and that's okay. But for a truly professional interior book design with the ability to customize your book so it looks different than everybody else's, try using one of the tools listed above.

I don't list tools used to create book covers because I believe you should always hire this task out. If you're a designer, then you know what tools to use—probably Adobe Photoshop, Illustrator, and InDesign. Authors: Find out what you need to know to hire a cover designer in *Chapter 16, Book Cover Design*.

Distribution tools and services

These are my go-to tools for getting books in the stores. Find details on how distribution works in *Part IV, Distributing Your Book*, and details on the tools and services available in *Chapter 39, Distribution Tools and Services*.

It's smart to use Amazon KDP Print to sell books in the Amazon store because if you don't, your book page may list your book as out of stock. You can exclude Amazon distribution from IngramSpark, Draft2Digital, and other distribution services.

Do not use Amazon's Expanded Distribution Program. They don't offer the discounts or returns program bookstores require.

For ebooks, use Amazon KDP plus Smashwords for the widest distribution. Draft2Digital, PublishDrive, and StreetLib are also popular choices, depending on your goals or the territories you want to reach. Check the *Consumer's Guide* in Part VII for details on these aggregators and distributors, and also the Author Friendly podcast where I interview a lot of the founders of these companies.

Full-service book creation and distribution services

Full-service book creation and distribution companies like Gatekeeper Press will help you with every aspect of publishing.

There is another in-between option I also recommend. It's a company called Blurb whose DIY tools help full-color book authors tinker with design by providing easy-to-use tools and templates. Find out more in *Chapter 42, Full-Service Companies.*

When I recommend full service

So why, since I tout the DIY option, do I send business to full service companies? Two reasons:

First, lots of authors just want to publish a single book and don't need to make the investment in skills and education.

Then there are the authors who lack a desire to be hands-on with the publishing tasks, and want to offload all the book production to a reputable company.

Those are great reasons to go full-service.

Positives and negatives of full service

As is typical with most things, there are positives and negatives to hiring an all-inclusive publishing service. The positive is they handle everything for you including distributing your books to all the major resellers so you don't have to lift a finger.

But if you want to make changes or corrections to the book or to the metadata, you'll pay. Typical fees are $40 to $90 for ten to fifty changes. To avoid fees, perfect your manuscript before you hand it over to them.

Ditto for the cover. You get a couple of iterations for free and then you'll need to pay about $25 per batch of changes.

Neither of these companies charge distribution fees, so you'll earn 100 percent of the royalty after the retailer takes their 30 to 53 percent cut.

Direct sales tools

I like Gumroad best for selling books directly from my own website, but you could use PayPal or a number of other tools.

What you'll need to do is create your book files (PDF, EPUB, MOBI). Upload them to Gumroad, add the book descriptions, cover, and price. Gumroad creates a widget you can grab for your website. It's easy to add the widget to your sales page or a sidebar. Readers who purchase the book will not leave your website to do so. This creates a seamless experience readers love.

Find out more about direct sales in *Part V, Selling Direct*. You can find reviews of Gumroad and other e-commerce tools in *Chapter 55, Direct Sales Tools*.

Book printing services

There are also printing costs to take into consideration when choosing a distribution tool, though you can print with a digital or offset print company instead. (See *Chapter 17, Create Your Print PDF*, for details.)

Find details on print book pricing in *Part III, Book Design and Production*.

8

YOUR SALES STRATEGY

YOU CAN SELL YOUR BOOK IN MANY DIFFERENT WAYS: BY PRE-selling or crowdfunding, and then distributing using one of the Print On Demand (POD) vendors.

If you are printing over 300 copies for an event or sales directly from your own website (or via a widget from a company like Gumroad), it may be more cost-effective to use an offset printer.

A few authors—especially those who write books to increase business or support a public-speaking career—like the convenience of an exclusive distribution service, even though the service takes 65 percent or more of the profits.

Beta publishing and pre-sales

Include beta publishing in your sales strategy and timeline. That way you can get to know your market at the same time as you're setting up your business correctly and learning about the publishing process. Use free tools like Gumroad, Leanpub, Wattpad, Scribd, your Facebook

Notes pages, Pressbooks, your website and blog to pre-publish and even collect money for your book-in-progress.

The impact of pre-orders

When you set your book up for online sales before your book is released, you can create a nice buzz about your book. Pre-orders count toward first-week sales and can increase your chances of being on a bestseller list, placing your book higher in customer search results. Bookstores look at pre-order sales as an indication of what books are hot and may even stock your book at their store. The longer your book is available for pre-order, the more time your book has to accumulate orders. So use social media marketing, giveaways, and leverage influencers to do whatever you can to point readers to your pre-order pages. See *Chapter 8, Your Sales Strategy*, for ideas on how to set this up.

Your book distribution strategy

It can be confusing to choose between services to distribute your book to online retailers and bookstores. I've reviewed each of them in *Chapter 39, Distribution Tools and Services*.

Your direct sales strategy

When you sell your books using an intermediary like the distribution services mentioned above, you have no idea who your readers are. When you sell direct, you get the email addresses of your customers and the ability to take advantage of the incredibly valuable "permission marketing" that goes along with it. You can also manually add email addresses to your list and welcome them to your community. If you use Gumroad to sell direct—and I think you should—you can use their integration with MailChimp to automatically add buyers to your email newsletter. Refer to *Chapter 8, Your Sales Strategy*, for a more in-depth exploration of this topic.

Mailing books

Books fit nicely in a free USPS Priority Mail envelope for about $6 in the US. You can charge the customer for shipping. Customers will receive the book in two days, which makes them very happy, especially during the holidays, and especially if it's autographed. Do send your books Priority or First-Class mail. The drastically lower cost of media mail might be tempting, but it can take a long time to deliver, and sometimes—especially during the holidays—your book is likely to be delivered too late. It also may be damaged as media mail gets banged around at the bottom of the pile. I've had envelopes returned to me, torn and empty.

Back-of-room sales

Take advantage of back-of-room sales at personal appearances to earn 100 percent of the profits. At some events, you may be asked to pay a small percentage to the organization or tip a cashier. Find out more in *Chapter 8, Your Sales Strategy*.

Choosing an exclusive distribution service

If you've written a book to boost your business, you might offload sales and distribution to a company who specializes in these tasks. These kinds of companies only take on books they think they can sell, so you'll need to pitch the book. They also take a lot of your profits, 65 percent and up.

The most popular solution for indie authors with commercially viable projects is IPG's Small Press United (SPU). SPU was formed as a branch of IPG's distribution service for traditional publishers to serve self-publishers. All the authors I know who have used them like them a lot.

An alternative is to find a small press to serve as your distributor. The sooner in the book creation process you can make contact, the better. They will have valuable insights and advice on editing, design, and production.

Your pricing strategy

You may be tempted to calculate the price of your book based on what it cost to produce it. That doesn't work; you need to price your book to compete in the marketplace. Ebook prices are all over the place, but are becoming standardized at 20–25 percent less than the least expensive print edition. A price of $9.99 also seems to be a consumer-accepted price-point for ebooks, though $4.99 is the ebook sweet-spot.

Some marketers will tell you that to succeed, you should price your first ebook at free and subsequent books at 99 cents or $1.99 or $2.99. This works well for authors in particular genres, but it is probably not a good model for business books or books which are also available in print. Study your competition to see what the market will bear and price accordingly. Don't be afraid to experiment with pricing or offer discounts and freebies to your social media followers and newsletter subscribers.

Working with a publishing partner

The defining fact about publishing partners is they vet their work, whereas POD author services companies will print and distribute almost anything. A reputable publishing partner has a track record. Their reputation is on the line, and they want to work with like-minded independent publishers dedicated to your success. Consider them a partner and not just a sales team.

Do not dismiss the fact that, whatever route you take, you are responsible for the marketing and promotion to create buzz and sell your book. That is, you can't just send the books to your distributor and expect them to sell magically. It can take years for even a very good book to rise to the top. Persistence pays off.

Find out more about publishing partners in *Chapter 25, Custom Book Publishing.*

9

FUND YOUR BOOK

In any business plan, there's that pesky "funding" section to work out. How will you pay these expenses? Besides sweat equity, you'll need to spend money for ISBNs, editing, and design if you want to create a professional-quality book.

Do you have a day job? Did you get a bonus? Inherit some money? Get a loan? Maybe the cost of this guide is the only expense you can afford. (That would be unfortunate, but books can be written and published for nothing, though it's rare that it will get noticed.)

You may despair you will never raise enough money to distribute and market your book. But there's hope. Have you ever considered leveraging the crowd—your fans—to fund, finish, and publish your book? While you can make some money beta publishing your book, crowdfunding might be the way to go. This allows you to set goals and generate enough money to publish your book and make it look as good as the Big Five.

Crowdfunding Platforms

PubLaunch, Inkshares, and Unbound are book-specific crowdfunding platforms for authors, but Kickstarter also has a very strong record of success with books.

Leanpub, Gumroad, and Patreon are not crowdfunding platforms per se, but, as I described in the previous section on beta publishing, you can use them to collect email addresses and solicit real cash from enthusiastic fans. (Find out how to use these tools in *Part V: Selling Your Book Direct.*)

Inkshares (based in San Francisco) and Unbound (in London), are unique because, if you meet your goal, they take on the editing, design, distribution, and publication of your book.

Greg Ioannou, the founder of PubLaunch, had a lot of insights about crowdfunding when we talked on the Author Friendly Podcast at www.authorfriendly.com.

Crowdfunding is hard work

Crowdfunding is hard work and takes determination, communication, constant enthusiasm, time, and energy to create marketing materials, videos, and social media posts. See *Chapter 52, Social Media Marketing Tools,* for tools that can help.

To successfully fund your book, you'll need to leverage your crowd and you should have a significant number of people who will back you.

Look up Kevin Kelly's *1,000 True Fans*, and I think you'll be inspired to work on building your tribe.

Find out more about funding solutions and crowdfunding platforms in *Chapter 54, Crowdfunding Sites.*

10

COPYRIGHT, PIRACY, AND DRM

With the perceived risk among writers of copyright infringement and book pirating so high, it's no wonder you're concerned about copyright. Digital Rights Management (DRM) protects files from infringement but the music industry gave up DRM for a reason—file encoding makes it difficult for the purchaser to transfer it between devices they own. Let's delve into these topics one by one.

***

Copyright is automatic

In reality, you don't need to register copyright. US copyright law states copyright exists from the moment the work is created, "without any action taken by the author, the moment it is fixed in a tangible form so it is perceptible either directly or with the aid of a machine or device."

You don't even have to put a copyright notice on your work, though it wards off potential word thieves. However, registration creates a legal record of your ownership that will help you in court, should there ever be an issue with someone copying your work or claiming you have used theirs.

In the US you can register your copyright for thirty-five dollars in thirty-five steps and, coincidentally, it took me about thirty-five minutes. I wrote a lengthy blog post detailing this step-by-step process, with screenshots. The US Government Copyright Registration site provides very detailed instructions. Do take a look at the post before you start so you can prepare all your materials and gather your information. There's a lot of it.

You can file your copyright electronically with the US Copyright eCO Online System.

You should receive a confirmation of your copyright in about four months. Each country has its own copyright office and the process is similar.

The take-down notice for pirates

After you publish your book, you will eventually find it listed on a bunch of free ebook websites. In your justified outrage, you may be tempted to sign up for a free account at the infringing site to investigate. Do. Not. Do. This.

Many of these sites are pirates doing something called phishing. They probably don't have your book files at all.

They're phishing for data

Phishing is an attempt to collect information like usernames, passwords, social security and credit card numbers, or even to launch malware on your computer. They look like legitimate sites, even going so far as to post comments from fake users. Your book cover and description are used as bait to the phish, otherwise known as people who are looking for free books, music, movies, software, and games.

You may have seen phishing in the form of an email that urges you to change the password on your banking site. It looks like it's from your bank, but it isn't. This is the same kind of thing, just on the web.

These free ebook websites scrape public information from the book sales websites such as book cover and description (easy to do) and place bogus awards icons at the bottom. The site tempts the potential phish with lots of bait: the available status, read now, and full version buttons. (Yes, they may have grabbed sample pages from Amazon's "Look Inside.") They promise unlimited book downloads; just sign up for a free one-month trial and cancel at any time. This is very tempting to a lot of unfortunate folks.

Some phishing sites are designed to phish for outraged copyright owners. That would be you.

The solution

Blasty is an online tool that monitors Google for illegal copies of your content. With just one click you can remove the listing from Google search engine results. Blasty's system will alert you by email when it finds a Google search engine entry for your book.

Blasty has an arrangement with Google to take down your listing when you click the orange Blast button next to an infringing site. The listing will disappear, often in a few hours. Removing search results from Google means people will not see them offered for free.

This is convenient, because otherwise you'd need to contact Google directly to remove each website from their search engine results.

Next to each suspected entry you'll be able to click Forbidden (trusted by Google site), Whitelisted, or Blast.

Sites trusted by Google are retailers like Amazon, who may indeed be offering your ebook for free, with your permission. Whitelist the entries you recognize as blogs, excerpts, and interviews for which you've given permission by clicking the white flag. For infringing sites, click Blast.

The rules of copyright and the DMCA

If the website is not a phishing website and your book has been pirated, you have recourse. The 1998 Digital Millennium Copyright Act (DMCA) criminalized copyright infringement and provided a way to order your copyrighted content to be taken down. You can contact the editor or webmaster of the offending site. If you get no results, file a takedown notice with their internet service provider (ISP).

Filing a takedown notice

To get your work removed from the infringing site, find it by visiting whois.net or a DNS lookup tool like DomainTools. The site's managing ISP and its associated IP address will be listed there.

Now you're ready to send the information to the hosting ISP with the domain name and IP address plus your DMCA "Notice to Host." Find a sample takedown notice on the Plagiarism Today website.

Right now, a Blast will remove the infringement from the site itself. I don't know if you'll have to pay for this service in the future, but I think it's likely they'll leave it free for self-publishers and charge a fee to the publishing companies.

Most of the sites advertising your books for free are phishing sites that don't really have your book. Personally, I'm happy to remove these listings from Google results. I may change my mind later if I see there's real piracy happening and that I'm losing a significant amount of income.

How concerned should you be about piracy, anyway?

You've probably heard the maxim, "Information wants to be free." It's attributed to Stewart Brand, who founded the Whole Earth Catalog in the 1960s. This misquote was oft quoted, with a shrug, by a generation of internet users who didn't see anything wrong with downloading copyrighted music on Napster. That is, until A&R Music sued in 2000. The outcome of the seven-year case helped to bring about rules about online sharing for all information online.

About fair use

What Brand really said, though, was this:

> I believe that all generally useful information should be free. By "free" I am not referring to price, but rather to the freedom to copy the information and to adapt it to one's own uses... When information is generally useful, redistributing it makes humanity wealthier no matter who is distributing and no matter who is receiving.

This is the idea behind fair use. There is a big difference between fair use and infringement so be aware of it before you take action. Personally, I love to see my work quoted in other works as educational content and referred to in Wikipedia. I consider it free publicity.

A lesson from the music industry

The music industry tried to protect songs from being shared by using DRM (Digital Rights Management). It didn't work. Buyers were prevented from moving songs from their computer to their mobile device without a lot of hassle. It was a customer service nightmare and made users so angry the industry dropped it.

DRM (Digital Rights Management

Like music, DRM-free books are becoming the standard, with some exceptions. Your EPUB for Apple will be wrapped in DRM. And the Amazon KDP format can be delivered in a DRM-protected MOBI format if you choose. You don't have to worry about this as a separate step; the DRM is embedded in the formatting. But people dislike DRM. It makes it difficult to read your book on various devices or to loan it.

Companies who deliver digital files are constantly experimenting with ways to prevent abusive sharing. It's a tradeoff between convenience and customer support versus artist rights.

Remember…

For a typical author, obscurity is a far greater threat than piracy.

—Tim O'Reilly, founder of O'Reilly Media

Watermarking and social DRM

Photographers have long watermarked online images to discourage sharing, and this can also be done with digital files. The file can still be read and shared, but the source will be visible.

Social DRM hopes to discourage the purchaser from sharing or copying too freely by embedding their name and perhaps even their credit card number to make the file traceable.

Gumroad, a company I use to sell books directly to my customers, uses PDF Stamping to discourage over-sharing or pirating, but just on the first page of the book. They also let you password-protect your files. I wouldn't recommend it for the aforementioned customer-service nightmare reason. Imagine getting emails a year later from customers who lost the password. Or they had a system crash, and the email with the password in it was deleted. Or something…there's always something.

Got a legal question?

For more information on copyright, fair use, and any legal question an author will ever think of asking, refer to Helen Sedwick's excellent *Self-Publishers Legal Handbook*. Though slanted toward authors in the United States, it includes a lot of good information for authors worldwide.

11

DEVELOPING YOUR BRAND

Now's the time to create your author brand. Your brand is your unique expression of you as a public persona, including identifying images, graphics, words, and photographs to work in harmony with your author voice.

Understanding brand

Your author brand is a big part of your author platform. It defines the way people perceive you in the marketplace. While brand may not be as important to you as it is to Dove or Nike, it warrants conscious consideration. Most authors don't think of brand at all, but creating and leveraging your brand can help you market yourself and your books.

An author's brand is largely about "voice." Deliver an emotional experience to your readers with visuals like your author photo, book covers, and website.

First tip: Create a plain, simple website instead of rushing through a poorly designed, ad hoc site with clashing and confusing colors, typography, and images. Try to build a consistent and recognizable presence, and keep at it for long enough people start to recognize you. Use WordPress if you can. It's arguably the best platform with the most people designing for it than any other.

A great alternative is Pub Site. This is a very quick and easy tool to build your author website in just a couple of hours. You can use it forever or as a stopgap while you're designing your WordPress site. Find out more in *Chapter 57, Website and Blog Tools*.

An example

I like Isabel Allende's website and have followed its evolution. It used to be quite busy, but these days it's very simple, in keeping with current trends. Take a look.

Note how clean and simple it is, with lots of white space. It is also "responsive" for mobile devices, which is a requirement for Google to index websites. It's important to follow both trends and requirements for websites, so use a reputable service and keep your WordPress versions updated.

Elusive and subjective

Brand is subjective and elusive, and it appears everywhere. It appears in your writing, on your website, your book covers, and even your hair and your clothes, your house, and the car you drive. I struggle with brand—with my adventure-travel-writer persona versus my self-publishing-geek persona. Which one is me? Well, that's why I have two websites. Brand is style and, like many authors, I find I cannot reconcile the two in one place.

Brand and author platform

Here is an attempt to nail the visual and style aspects of brand into manageable chunks you can use consistently so readers recognize you.

Your brand is made up of solid and recognizable trademark items like your author name, publisher or company name, photography, logo, colors, images, even typography.

In your author photo, elements of your brand might be considered personal style: a feather boa, a motorcycle, a hat, red lipstick, tweed jacket, your cat.

Brand is communicated on your website, social media profiles, stationery, posters, and other print materials.

Brand creates the feeling people have about you—the thing you are known for. This is also called author platform.

Brand is reflected in your writing style, your media personality, your expertise or niche, and your overall image as reflected by your activities in person and on social media.

What makes a brand?

To organize elements of your brand, you might want to create a brand worksheet or idea folder on your computer to collect images of visual brands which attract you.

You can save web pages by printing to PDF and organizing them in a folder. Or using a tool like Evernote's web clipper. (I love Evernote.)

Professional designers love getting this kind of detailed input. It saves them from having to try to read your mind and therefore will cost you less. Apply your brand to your web pages, social media sites, and book covers. Elements of brand include:

- Graphics
- Author photos
- Color schemes
- Typography

Publisher name

The first thing to do is to decide on your publishing house name. You may choose a version of your name or something more descriptive. As you read a few chapters back, I opted for Misadventures Media, which I think sounds fun and adventurous, instead of using my last name and choosing King Press or King Media, which sound a bit stodgy and traditional. Besides, somebody else is already using them. I also didn't want to look self-published by using my author name as a publisher name.

Publisher logo

A logo is an essential element of your media presence. Use it long enough, and people will begin to recognize and trust it. Develop a simple and effective logo that looks good in various sizes. It should look great both in color and grayscale. Your logo might incorporate your company (publishing house) name, or it may be a standalone graphic or type treatment.

Take a look at the spine and title pages of books at a library or bookstore and note which publisher logos are effective and why. Sketch out some ideas for your logo and collect examples of logos you like before contacting a designer.

Your author name is your strongest brand

Try to get your author name for your domain name. Luckily I was able to buy CarlaKing.com early on. But if someone else with your name has already claimed yours, you may need to use your middle initial or incorporate the word "author" in your domain name.

Your author bio

Your biographical description should be crafted to affirm your author brand. Information you share about yourself may include your education, accomplishments, professional qualifications, awards, titles, prior publications, media appearances, location, and family information.

Like an elevator speech, your author bio should be entertaining and informative, not dry and boring. Also convey how you are uniquely qualified, talented, or fascinating enough that anyone will want to read your book.

Place your bio on the back of the book (nonfiction) or inside the book (fiction), on your website, on other people's websites, in press and news releases, in magazine articles, in advertisements, during speeches, at dinners, and as introductions by interviewers. A good test is to read it out loud, just like the host of a radio show would. Would the listener change the channel or stay tuned?

Create several different bios to apply to different media, from long to short: between 30 and 250 words for various websites and social media, and just 140 characters for Twitter. Write your bio in the appropriate tone. If you're writing nonfiction, consider a tagline or a title to describe your expertise. Also, make sure your bios are keyword-rich, so search engines can help you market (as explained in *Chapter 36, Metadata and Discovery*).

In my workshops, I like to divide authors into groups of three authors who don't know each other. Each author is interviewed by the other two for five minutes. Those two people then write the bio of the author interviewed. Then we switch, and everybody gets two bios to use as source material for their own author bio. It works because most of us are too shy to brag about our accomplishments and, besides, it's difficult to know what's interesting about ourselves. Lots of great bios have come out of these exercises. Maybe you can find two strangers who are authors to share this exercise with you. And, who knows, it may be the beginning of a writing group.

Your author photo

Your photo is a recognizable part of your author brand, so make sure it is fairly recent, or at least still looks like you. It should sharply frame your head and neck and look good in both color and grayscale.

Avoid shots with a lot of competing activity in the background or one where you've Photoshopped out your ex. You will need to be clearly recognized, even when the photo is reduced to the size of a postage stamp, because that's about all the space some social media sites give you.

Decide what you want to convey to readers about you in your author headshot and collect some examples for your photographer.

How to hire a photographer

How do you hire a good photographer? Well, it probably should not be the gal at the drugstore who snapped your passport photo. Maybe you're lucky enough to have a talented photographer in your circle of friends or family. You may find one at a writer's conference. Look for portrait photographers in your area. You see them all over the place, parading families into scenic settings, coaxing smiles from cranky toddlers. Expect to pay between $50 and $500 for a session depending on how much time they spend with you in various settings, plus an order minimum.

At the San Francisco Writers Conference, an entrepreneurial photographer offers author headshots for $50, which is a great deal. I was referred to my photographer by my yoga teacher. When I went to his site, I found out he rides motorcycles and travels to Baja. We connected instantly, and it shows in the results.

12

ALL ABOUT ISBNS

THE INTERNATIONAL STANDARD BOOK NUMBER (ISBN) SYSTEM was created to track books. Without an ISBN, your book cannot be tracked and compared with other books to rank, for instance, as a bestseller.

Many authors who self-publish use the free ISBNs owned by retailers and distribution companies. Many authors who publish to Amazon don't use an ISBN at all, so they're essentially off the record.

All this makes it difficult for researchers to figure out how many books are published each year, but it doesn't stop them from making estimates. So when you read something about the growth of books, remember, books without ISBNs are not counted.

What do the numbers mean?

An International Standard Book Number (ISBN) consists of thirteen numbers that identify the book to book systems worldwide. Here's what the numbers mean.

Parts of the ISBN

Most important is the publisher number, which you'll need when applying for an LCCN. You can only obtain a publisher number when you by 10 or more ISBNs.

- **EAN**: Either 978 or 979. Identifies the EAN element (European/International Article Number).
- **Group**: Identifies the country or language agency.
- **Publisher**: Numbers six through nine make up the four numbers of your publisher identifier, which means you and your publishing company. (You need this number when applying for an LCCN.)
- **Title**: The title or specific edition of your book.
- **Check digit**: The check digit validates the ISBN.

That's really all you need to know, but if you want to get geeky, look it up in Wikipedia.

Do you really need to purchase ISBNs?

No. Yes. Maybe. Bear with me.

ISBNs in the US are expensive—$295 for a set of ten. In most other countries, they are much more affordable, and even free.

Many younger, hipper authors than I bypass the formal book publication process entirely by uploading their ebooks directly to the online retailers, none of which require ISBNs.

Some of these authors make significant money on their ebooks, but their books aren't counted in the book systems. If they print, they use Amazon's free ISBNs. They don't care if the publisher is listed as Amazon.

But what if they start to experience success, and they want their book in stores? There's no obligation to publish within the system, to stand up and be counted. But there's no way for bookstores and libraries to find your books if you do not have an ISBN.

Without an ISBN or a publishing house name and logo your book won't look professional. Are being counted, being found, and looking professional important to you?

If you're reading this guide, you're probably serious about becoming an independent publisher and aspire to make a business of writing and publishing. So invest in a set of at least ten ISBNs. Think of it as a $295 insurance package.

To stand up and be counted is a good reason to use an ISBN, but also remember, whoever buys your ISBN controls your book data—so it should be you. You'll also be recognized as a publisher and not a self-published author. Keep reading, there are more reasons to purchase your own set of 10 or more rather than using a company's free ISBN.

Where to buy ISBNs

To buy ISBNs, visit the ISBN agency in your country. The "I" in ISBN stands for "International" and it will identify your book in every country where your book is sold. One ISBN identifies your book worldwide.

If you live in Canada or another country that offers free ISBNs, you're in luck. But here in the US, and in the UK, and Australia, we pay. That's because the ISBN system has been privatized. In Canada, New Zealand, and South Africa, ISBNs are assigned by the government or library systems and paid for by the taxpayers.

If you know you're going to write more than two books or you want to look like a modest publishing house and not a self-published author, buy a block of 100 ISBNs for $575. (By the way, 1,000 ISBNs cost $1,000.)

If you write more than two books, consider buying the pack of 100. You'll need more than ten ISBNs if you are publishing in paperback, hardcover, EPUB, MOBI, and audiobook formats, and even more for translations and special editions.

In the US, members of IBPA enjoy a 15 percent discount on ISBNs. You can also sign up for the Bowker mailing list and wait around for a sale. They discount them fairly often.

When your book is ready to publish, log into your identifiers account and fill out all the metadata in your ISBN record. This makes your book discoverable to distributors and retailers, which in turn makes it discoverable to readers. Metadata is important for categorization and marketing and is described in more detail in *Chapter 36, Metadata and Discovery*.

Do you need a SAN?

When you purchase your ISBNs, you may be asked if you want to add a SAN (Standard Address Number). Most self-publishers and small presses don't need one. A SAN is used by big, complicated publishing companies to reduce billing errors, books shipped to the wrong points, and errors in payments and returns.

What formats need separate ISBNs?

The International ISBN agency states you need one ISBN per format. That means you need an ISBN for each of these formats (and formats within editions).

- Hardcover (casebound)
- Paperback
- EPUB
- MOBI/KF8 for Kindle
- PDF
- Audio
- Fixed-layout EPUB (can be multimedia)
- Fixed-layout for Kindle (also multimedia-capable)
- Repeat above for each language translation (Spanish edition ebook, paperback, etc.)

If you use a distributor to reach Amazon they will send Amazon an EPUB. The EPUB will be automatically converted to a Kindle format for sale in the Kindle store.

You should still assign a Kindle ISBN to your book so you can track Amazon sales. You will also need it for the Kindle edition books you sell directly from your website. (See *Part V: Selling Your Book Direct.*)

How to list ISBNs on your copyright page

Don't make yourself crazy by changing the ISBN in each version of your manuscript. Simply list all the ISBNs on the copyright page so your copyright page is universal to all versions of your book. This has the added benefit of letting people know your book is available in other formats.

When you need a new ISBN

Typos and insignificant updates a reader probably wouldn't notice when comparing the book side-by-side do not need a new ISBN.

A new cover does not warrant a new ISBN.

Significant changes to a book or a new edition of your book will need a new ISBN. For example, this is the 5th edition of this guide, and it has a different ISBN than the first four editions.

There are no ISBN police, so this is really up to you.

How to replace an old ISBN with a new one

Did you publish with a traditional press and win your rights back?

Did you accidentally publish with a predatory vanity press?

Did you create a new edition of your book?

If you own the ISBN, simply retire and replace it with the new edition in the identifier record for your book. If another company owns the ISBN you don't have access to their record, but that's okay. Indicate in your new ISBN record that it replaces the old one.

If your book is trapped with a vanity press, telephone their customer service and ask for all of your original files—the Adobe InDesign files for your interior and cover, the EPUB files, the PDFs, the Photoshop images, the fonts, the graphics—the whole package.

Don't let them tell you no. You paid for all of this, and you have the right to demand these files.

Now, after you have all your files, give them another ring and tell them to "retire" your book. If they don't, don't worry. You can indicate that it's retired in the new ISBN record. In other words, that the new ISBN replaces an old one.

Now, what to do with your original book files? You need to edit the copyright page to list your new ISBNs, your publisher name, and logo. If you registered for a PCIP block for library sales and the appearance of professionalism, add that, too.

Can't figure out how to edit your files? You should be able to outsource this affordably, depending on the complexity of your book.

The Books In Print database

The Books In Print database supplies libraries, booksellers, publishers, and other information professionals with the details you provided about your book.

In the US, it used to be necessary to manually add your book to the Books In Print database, but no longer. Now Bowker automatically adds your listing based on your ISBN record.

This does not mean bookstores will stock your book—you'll need to market to them—but it does mean they can find it in the system.

Barcodes are free

You need a barcode for the print edition of your book, so make room for it on the back cover. Each vendor supplies specific instructions on where to leave space for it.

Don't buy barcodes. Bowker in the US will upsell barcodes to you when you buy your ISBNs. Instead, use IngramSpark's cover template generator to automatically create a barcode.

Find the IngramSpark cover template generator for paperback and hardback books along with a print and ship calculator (royalty calculator), and weight and spine width calculator.

Even if you're printing a book elsewhere, you can get a free barcode from IngramSpark by visiting their site and generating a book cover template. You don't have to use the template; you can just send the template to your book designer, or you can ask your designer to supply one. (Your designer probably already knows about this tool. If not, I'd consider hiring someone else.)

Find these and other tools by visiting IngramSpark and click RESOURCES > TOOLS.

Include the ISBN (though you can enter 13 zeros if you're just experimenting) and also include the price in the barcode. It makes your book appear much more professional.

Professionalism matters.

Managing your ISBN records

Once you assign an ISBN to your book you'll see how much data it provides to distributors, wholesalers, libraries, and retailers (online and brick-and-mortar) so they can convey it to readers.

You'll fill in your book's title, subtitle, author, description, number of pages, size, language, copyright year, date of publication, contributors, category, title status (out-of-print, active, etc.), price, currency, book cover, interior (to index keywords), dimensions, weight, and so on.

Because you'll need three or four records—hardcover, paperback, EPUB, Kindle—it's a good idea to fill out one record as best you can, and then use their CLONE function to create the other records. There are four pages of data, so it pays to get the first one right. You don't want to spend time correcting each version.

It's a tedious process here in the US, though Bowker has improved their website significantly since I started using it in 1995.

Find out how to create good metadata in the correct word and character counts for Bowker and each retailer in *Chapter 36, Metadata and Discovery.*

For the ebook, it's important to fill out the ***file size*** field so retailers and customers can tell how much time it might take to download your book, and how much space on their device it will use.

Find the file size by using the *Properties* or *Get Info* function on your ebook file on your computer.

For the hardcover and paperback, you'll need to enter the ***weight and dimensions*** (width, height, and depth). But how do you know what that will be until you get the book? Guess what? IngramSpark has a weight and spine-width calculator. Just go to their site and choose RESOURCES > TOOLS.

The ***medium*** will be either print or ebook. For ebook the format will be set as "electronic book text," but for print, you'll be asked to select from a dizzying number of print format types. Just scroll down until you find the correct format.

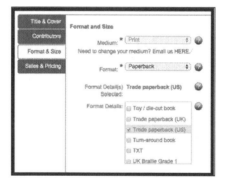

Identify your book as a paperback, hardcover, EPUB, or Kindle in the ISBN record for each format of your book.

In the **Sales and Pricing** menu, you'll be asked to specify who is distributing the book. If you don't see the distributor in the list, you can add yours by emailing Bowker. (There's an email link hidden under the drop-down menu, below.)

Specify the price, currency, and distributor for the format
assigned to this particular ISBN.

Don't forget to update your ISBN data once you've chosen (or changed) a distributor, when you've determined the file size, and whenever you change your book description.

That's a wrap!

Okay, maybe not quite a wrap. I figure you're going to come back to this part of the guide again and again. I really don't expect you to do it all in one shot. It's a process.

Where are you in the process now? Do you need to check in with your beta readers and revise your draft? Is your book ready for editing and design? If so, let's move on to *Part III, Book Design and Production.*

PART III

BOOK DESIGN AND PRODUCTION

So you're ready to create your book. You have a lot of choices when it comes to designing and formatting your book interior and there are things you need to know whether you're hiring it out or doing it yourself. Here's what you'll learn.

The Different Book Formats
Book Production Basics
Interior Book Design
Book Cover Design
Creating Your Print PDF
Creating Your Ebook
Creating Advanced Reader Copies (ARCs)

Before you start, I hope that you've had lots of great feedback from beta readers. If you've skipped beta publishing, please look back at *Chapter 3, The Importance of Beta Publishing*, for a review of the benefits of that process. I think it's the very most important part of the writing and publishing process and it's arguably the only way to assure five-star reviews on launch day.

Also before producing your final book, editing is key. Go take a look at *Chapter 4, The Importance of Editing*. Already did? Okay, then. Your final copyedit is done. So let's move on to understanding the book formats and how to design, format, and produce your ebook and print book.

If you don't want to do all this yourself, you can outsource it to a full-service self-publishing company, a custom book publisher, or a hybrid publishing service. These options are provided in *Part IV, Distributing Your Book*. Even if you plan to hire it out, I think it's useful to know how book design and production works so you can hire the right professionals and guide the process. Let's begin by learning about the different book formats, PDF, EPUB, and MOBI.

13

THE DIFFERENT BOOK FORMATS

To understand how to make your book, it's necessary to understand the alphabet soup of book formats. So here's a short primer on PDF, EPUB, MOBI, fixed-layout formats, reading devices, and apps.

There are three types of book formats you need to know about.

1. PDF is the standard for print.
2. Standard or reflowable EPUB is the industry standard format needed for ebooks. Amazon uses a MOBI for Kindle format (which is based on EPUB).
3. Fixed-layout EPUB and MOBI (which Amazon calls Print Replica ebooks), keep their layout and are viewed on the iPad and Kindle Fire tablet computers.

PDF

PDF is the format printing companies need to print your books. It's not a good format for reading devices because it does not reflow.

PDFs delivered digitally are best for short works to promote your book and ethical bribes to encourage customers to sign up for your email newsletter.

It's easy to create PDFs. Find out how in *Chapter 18, Creating Your Print PDF.*

Standard or reflowable ebooks

EPUB for books is like MP3 is for music. EPUB is an open standard, meaning no single company can control the format. Most major devices use this format. The two types of EPUB formats are reflowable and fixed-layout.

Books in standard or reflowable EPUB reflow to fit the screen of the device, whether it is a large computer screen or a tiny mobile device. Book-buyers can set the size and even style of the font.

Amazon just has to be different. Their version of EPUB is called MOBI. You might also have heard of AZW, which is a MOBI format protected with DRM. (I don't like DRM. Find out why in *Chapter 10, Copyright, Piracy, and Digital Rights Management.*)

Many of the same tools and services that create EPUB files will also create a Kindle-formatted ebook. These include Word (saved as Filtered HTML), InDesign, Scrivener, Pressbooks, Draft2Digital, PublishDrive, and Reedsy.

If you already have an EPUB, then validate it with KindleGen or Kindle Previewer to make sure it will look great.

Find out how to create ebooks in chapter 18.

Fixed-layout EPUB and MOBI

The placement of text and images in fixed-layout EPUB or MOBI book does not reflow or change in size. When viewed on a tablet, books in fixed-layout will look much like their paper counterparts, but on smaller mobile devices like phones, the content will likely be unreadable.

Use fixed-layout formats for graphic-heavy books like comic books, graphic novels, graphically heavy textbooks, and illustrated books like children's books.

Professional book designers use InDesign and HTML to create fixed-layout ebooks, but you have several easy-to-use tools at your disposal:

- Apple iBooks Author to create fixed-layout books in EPUB format to sell in the Apple iBooks store.
- Kindle Create to sell in the Amazon Kindle store for the Kindle Fire tablet
- Blurb's proprietary BookWright tool to distribute to stores and compatible with Apple iPhone, iPad, and Amazon Kindle Fire.

You can also hire the job out to full-service companies like Gatekeeper Press and BookBaby who can create and distribute them for you. create fixed-layout books and distribute them.

Understanding reading devices and apps

Your customers will read your ebook on various devices using a variety of ebook reading apps. This may be a single-purpose device like the Kindle or the NOOK, or a multi-purpose tablet like the iPad, the Samsung Galaxy, or the Kindle Fire. People also read on their mobile devices and computer screens using an app downloaded from an app store.

Apple iPad users might buy one book from the iBook store and another from the Amazon store. The iPad will automatically open the book bought from the iBook store in the iBooks app, but the first time a customer tries to read a book they bought from Amazon they'll get a message they need to download the Kindle app.

More than a few of your potential customers have discovered they can pick up where they left off on one device and continue reading on another. Personally, I do this all the time, switching between the Kindle Paperwhite, iPhone, and a laptop.

Your book should reflow to look good on any device, and it can. Just make sure you or your designer has validated your EPUB files and, if you've converted it to MOBI/KF8, check your files using KindleGen or Kindle Previewer.

Aspect ratios: the problem of fixed-layout ebooks

The only time you have to consider which group you're targeting—Apple owners or Kindle owners—is when you want to create a fixed-layout book. Because the aspect ratio is different for these two devices you will need two different designs, two different files, and two different ISBNs. Most people choose one or the other because it's too expensive to design for both.

This is where market research comes in (again). Do people who read books like yours own an Apple iPad or a Kindle Fire? I asked this question to an author creating an art book and she answered "iPad" without any hesitation. Another author with a children's book didn't know.

The term "Kindle" may mean one of these three things

You'll hear the term "Kindle" bandied about a lot, and it can mean any of these three things:

- The Kindle ebook (document) format (MOBI/KF8)
- The Kindle reading device (Paperwhite, Kindle Fire, Oasis, etc.)
- The Kindle platform (or app)

The most popular apps for reading ebooks are Kindle, Kobo, Ibis Reader (HTML5 format), EPUB Reader for Firefox, Adobe Digital Editions, and Stanza (for Apple).

The most popular reading devices are the Apple suite (iPad, iPhone, iPod Touch), Amazon's Kindle and Kindle Fire, Android-powered mobile devices, any web browser (Firefox, IE, Safari), B&N NOOK, and Kobo.

14

BOOK PRODUCTION BASICS

Most authors think it's easy to format and upload a book for sale, and sure, it can be simple. Just look at the hundreds of thousands of books on Amazon you don't want to read. Yes, that was a little snarky, but you've invested in this guide because you want to produce a quality book that competes alongside those produced by big publishing companies. And whatever you think about big publishing, there is a reason it takes so long to get a book to market: quality.

Please don't get discouraged. There are a lot of elements that need to come together you probably haven't thought of yet. That's why I've provided checklists and cheatsheets for you.

Reality check

I hope this chapter will give you a reality check on the number of tasks to be done. It's going to take longer than you think to work with editors and cover designers. You'll need a month to get a PCIP block and you'll also want to order a proof.

When you receive your printed proof you'll find typos and other things to change because your book simply looks different in print.

You might not like the cover colors, or the spine width might be wrong. You'll make those changes, and upload it again, and again. Not to mention creating metadata (book description, author bio, keywords) required by the distributors that will help readers identify your book as one they want to read—which is arguably your most important sales tool in this era of shopping by search engine.

Goals

My goal in this chapter is to help you with these tasks:

1. Make sure you've gathered all the elements of your book.
2. Present front and back matter in the right order.
3. Gather all the information you need to create your book.
4. Gather all the information you need for the distributors to accept your book.

You may not be familiar with some of the terms right now (metadata, LCCN, PCIP block), but you'll learn about them soon.

Vendor-specific instructions

Each retailer and distributor supplies specific instructions on how to create and deliver files so their fully automated systems can check, approve, or reject them. They're not all that different though, since there are industry-wide standards. Variances are in paper weight, which affects the spine width, and the availability of trim sizes.

Your initial task list

Here's a brief review of tasks necessary to finalize your book cover and interior. It includes both book creation and data gathering tasks.

Book cover research: Start gathering book covers you like (doing competitive analysis by studying successful books in your genre), and gather cover images into a folder or in an app like Dropbox or Pinterest. Look for designers sooner rather than later. The good ones are booked up well in advance.

Branding elements: Organize your author photo and graphics like your publisher logo (or type treatments) in folders.

Metadata research: Figure out what metadata will help you sell your book (description, author bio, keywords). This is very important and you should start earlier than you think. When you upload your book, you need to include compelling, keyword-rich description that will sell the book. Don't just make up a description on the fly. Read more about this in *Chapter 36, Metadata and Book Discovery*. Be sure to sign up for reader updates to get the metadata cheatsheet.

Purchase ISBNs as described in chapter 12 and assign one to each book format. You only need barcodes for printed books and you can get those free using tools described in *Chapter 49, Business and Productivity Tools*.

LCCNs and PCIP blocks: If you're marketing to libraries, or if you want your book to look like those sold by big publishing, get an LCCN, and then a PCIP block. This can take up to a month. This information will be listed on your copyright page. Refer to *Chapter 12, All About ISBNs* and *Chapter 29, Library Sales* for details.

Trim size: Choose a book trim size (see *Standard Book Sizes* in *Chapter 17, Creating Your Print PDF*) and design and properly format your book interior using a program like Word or InDesign. "Properly format" is the key phrase here. You need to assign styles to each paragraph of your book because styles are the programming language digital ebook readers understand. Find details in *Chapter 15, Interior Book Design.*

Cover design: Work with your cover designer to finalize your book cover design, including the spine, by getting a template from Ingram-Spark. (You'll find out more about this, later.) And make sure your cover, and all art, including logos and other graphics, are created in Adobe InDesign, Photoshop, or Illustrator (not an obscure or little-used program like CorelDRAW), so you can hire someone to take over if your first designer doesn't work out. Once it's finished, you'll need to export your cover to PDF and JPG formats in the book size you've chosen. It also doesn't hurt to create poster-sized covers for events. This is all covered in *Chapter 16, Book Cover Design.*

Formatting: Now you'll need to export the interior and cover files to formats the distributors use to make your book available to customers. PDF format is necessary for print. For ebooks you must create either EPUB and MOBI files (for IngramSpark and Amazon KDP) or, instead, you can upload a Word document file (for Smashwords and Amazon KDP). Find more about these tasks in *Chapter 17, Creating Your Print PDF* and *Chapter 18, Creating Your Ebook.*

Choose a distribution vendor: Sign up for distribution services. Each retailer and distributor supplies specific instructions on how to create and deliver files so their fully automated systems can check, approve, or reject them. Upload the files to their sites, providing banking, tax information, and all the metadata they require.

Order a printed proof: Get a proof of your book, make any adjustments, upload, and proof again until it is perfect and ready to publish.

Publish: Upload your book to the retailers individually or use a distribution service.

You can hire a lot of these tasks out or do it yourself. See *Chapter 6, Your Book Budget,* for costs associated with these tasks and services.

Vendor tools and templates

No matter where you print and distribute—with Amazon, Ingram-Spark, or an offset printer—you'll need to create a PDF with a front, back, and spine. Each company has its own book cover and interior creation specifications so look for guidelines on each of their websites.

IngramSpark cover template generator

You can use the IngramSpark cover template generator as a template for most of the other vendors. Create templates for paperbacks and hardcover books using their online tool which emails you either a PDF file (which you can open using Photoshop and other programs) or an Adobe InDesign file.

An added benefit to using the IngramSpark template is it comes with a free barcode.

Other tools IngramSpark offers include a spine width calculator, publisher compensation calculator, and weight and spine width calculator.

Find the IngramSpark tools here

http://www.ingramspark.com/resources/tools

Even if you're printing with Amazon or another company, you can use the barcode art included with the IngramSpark template to paste into your design.

About the IngramSpark cover template generator

Here's the cover template generator on the IngramSpark site.

Click image to go to IngramSpark's Cover Template Generator.

Here's some explanation about the fields you'll need to fill out.

- Enter your thirteen-digit ISBN. This is important because the ISBN will be coded into the barcode. (See also *Chapter 12, All About ISBNs.*)
- Choose your trim size and paper color according to genre standards and page count of your book. The next chapter, on interior book design, will walk you through this process.
- For paper color, choose crème for immersive reading such as fiction and creative nonfiction because it's easy on reader's eyes, and white for nonfiction and color books.

- The page count is the total number of single pages in the book, including front and back matter and blank pages, and it must be an even number. Open your PDF file with the free Adobe Acrobat Reader app and click VIEW in the toolbar, then NAVIGATION PANEL > PAGES as shown in the screenshot below this list. Scroll to the bottom and you'll see how many pages are in your book.
- Choose the file type you want to work with (InDesign or PDF to open in Photoshop).
- Enter your book price and do include the price in the barcode, especially if you want to sell to bookstores. Don't worry if you don't have the exact page count or your ISBN yet. You can download another later. (Adding more than four pages or switching between white and crème colored paper can result in a larger spine, so if you do add pages, download a new template.)

How to find the number of pages in your print book

Use the free Adobe PDF reader to view previews of the pages in your book. Page thumbnails appear in the navigation pane and you'll be able to scroll down to see how many actual pages (not how many page numbers) are actually in your book.

How to find the number of actual pages in your book
using the free Adobe Acrobat Reader app.

If the last page of your book is an odd page, then round up to the next even page. So if your book is 235 pages, indicate to the printer it's 236. You don't need to add a page to the document itself.

Some authors are confused about the number of pages versus the number of pieces of paper in a book. To clarify, yes, the book will be printed on both sides of the paper. However, use the number of single pages to specify page count. In other words, if the book is 200 pages long, specify 200 pages, not 100 pieces of paper.

The Amazon book cover design template

The IngramSpark template also works for your Amazon book but you can use an Amazon template. Find it by searching for "KDP print template."

You can import your Amazon cover templates into Photoshop or InDesign as a layer to guide your cover design. Your book designer knows how to design covers with layers.

Remember to obtain all of the files your designer uses to create your cover, including the InDesign files, Photoshop files, licensed fonts, licensed images, and graphics.

15

INTERIOR BOOK DESIGN

Give your customer a great reading experience by using fonts and white space that are easy on the eyes. Fonts, leading, margins, and paper color choices all work to make reading effortless. Choose crème paper for immersive reading like novels and creative nonfiction to ease eyestrain. Use white for nonfiction to make it easier for readers to pick out the information they want.

Professional interior tinker with fonts, leading, and ligature to ease the reader's journey through the story in a relaxing manner, without undue eyestrain, to convey information and orient them with page numbers, captions, and chapter and section titles, in as unobtrusive a way as possible.

To handle interior design, you can use a tool, a template, or hire a professional interior book designer.

Here's what you'll learn in this chapter.

- How ebooks are different
- Front matter
- Headers and footers
- Body

- Back matter
- How to decide which tool to use
- The importance of styles
- Microsoft Word and Book Design Templates
- Interior typography and flourishes
- Scanning a book
- Setting the begin-reading point in ebooks
- Creating print and ebook ready files
- Hiring a professional

How ebooks are different

If you read ebooks you know the experience is much different from reading a print book. The most obvious difference is there are no page numbers and no headers and footers. Fonts and font sizes can be adjusted by the reader. Even the background color can be set to light or dark. Here's a list of the differences to keep in mind when you're designing your ebook.

Begin reading point: Where should your ebook begin? Do you want the reader to have to scroll through the cover and pages and pages of front matter? Probably not. So just in case the ebook reader or app does not start the reader off where you've correctly set the start bookmark, move the bulk of the front matter to the back.

Pages: Ebooks don't have page numbers. The page view will depend on each reader's preferred font and font size and the size of the device they're reading on.

Image quality: To print true, images need to be 300 dpi (dots per inch) and color needs to be CMYK. For an ebook, images should be 72 dpi and color should be RGB.

File size: You want to keep your file size small for several reasons: to avoid Amazon download fees, and to provide quick downloads even if your customer has a slow internet connection. That is why you use 72-

dpi images for ebooks. You should also embed non-standard fonts. Formatting mistakes can also bloat the file size.

Font choices: Ebook reading devices allow readers to choose what fonts and font sizes they like to read in, and even the color of their fonts and background. So only use one font in your book and make it a standard one like Times New Roman or Arial. Use 12-point font for body text and 14-18 pt fonts for chapter titles. Any bigger and it may overwhelm the screen in a smaller device like a smartphone.

Back matter: You have a great opportunity to add pages to the back of your book to give the reader more information about your other books and stories. Include links to social media pages, invitations to beta read your next book, discounts on your products and services (if you're a nonfiction author), or anything you like. In an ebook, links can be live.

Links: Do not embed a link to a particular vendor like Amazon or B&N because other vendors will reject the book. Instead, lead them to a page on your website where you might offer them a free story in exchange for their email address and links to places they can review the book. This is a marketing opportunity you should not miss.

Formatting: Sloppy formatting can bloat the size of your ebook, so if you're using Microsoft Word to create a doc file make sure you've used styles consistently. (Find my free ebook, *What Every Author Needs to Know About Microsoft Word Styles* in *Chapter 63, Your Publishers Bookshelf.*)

See *Chapter 18, Creating Your Ebook,* to understand more about formatting tools and procedures.

―――――――――――

Front matter

There are many ways to create your print and ebook interior as you'll see in this chapter. In this section, I just wanted to provide a list of information and assets you'll need to gather to create a book interior.

This will serve as a checklist for you and any book production pro you have hired.

Look at traditionally published books in your genre for examples of how you might format your book.

A book's front matter can include any of the following material, and should appear on odd (right-hand) or even (left-hand) pages as noted:

1. First odd page—can optionally include advance praise for your book—quotes, testimonials, and blurbs. You'll find several pages of these in some books.
2. Second odd page—half title—this is simply the title of your book printed on the page. Give it the same type treatment as the book cover if you want your book to look like those coming from the big publishing houses. (Ask your cover designer to provide a 300 dpi image in grayscale for this purpose.) You may leave this page out of your ebook editions.
3. First even page—Frontispiece—an illustration, map, or photograph, if you have one. This can be left out of your ebook editions.
4. Next odd page—Title page—is the title and subtitle. As with the half-title, it looks much more professional if the page has the same type treatment and artistic elements as the book cover. Also include the author name, publisher name, and logo. (Read more about getting a publisher name in the business section of this guide.)
5. Next even page—Copyright page—includes the copyright, ISBNs (list all ISBNs for the book formats here), publisher name and logo, city and state (for the US), LCCN and PCIP block if you want to sell to libraries (or make your book look like those from big publishing houses), plus credits for editing, design, production, and any artwork. If your book has been previously published by someone else or under a different title, add a "previously published as" note on the copyright page.
6. Next odd page—Dedication

7. Next even page—Epigraph (quotation)
8. Next odd page—Table of Contents. Make sure you generate these automatically using proper Styles.
9. If you have lists of tables and figures, these can go on the next even and odd pages. You may consider moving these to the back pages of your ebook edition.
10. Next odd page—Acknowledgments. However, more and more often you'll find acknowledgments at the back of both the print and ebook editions, where readers are more likely to read them.

These pages are optional:

1. Introduction
2. Prologue
3. A second half-title, but only if you feel there is so much information in your front matter that your book needs a break before diving into the first chapter.

Headers and footers

Headers and footers exist so readers do not get lost in your book. A book of fiction or creative nonfiction meant for immersive reading needs fewer clues for navigation than a nonfiction how-to or reference book such as this one, where readers may flip through it to find information.

Think carefully about your header and footer content. Standards vary by genre and market trends so look at a lot of recent books in your genre for guidance. Follow these rules.

- Never print headers on the opening pages of a chapter or part.
- Never print either headers or footers on blank pages. In other words, there should be no type on blank pages.

Now onto the tough decisions:

- Print the author name on the left (even) pages and the book title on the right (odd) pages in the header or footer.
- Or print the book title on the even pages and the chapter title on the odd pages in the header or footer.
- Print page numbers on the outside edge of the header or footer content.
- Or place the author name and title in the header and place the page numbers by themselves in the footer.
- Print page numbers on the opening pages of a chapter or part, or not.

By now you probably realize you need to do a bit more research to figure out what the successful books in your genre look like.

Body

For the front matter of your book, begin pagination with the lower-case Roman numeral one (i).

Chapter One or Part One should start with the Arabic numeral one (1).

The opening part and chapter pages do not get headers. Some genres include pagination on the first page of chapters and some do not. Look at current books in your genre from the big publishing companies to see what your book should look like.

The body of your book that is paginated includes the following:

Parts—if your book is separated into parts that contain chapters.

- Chapters
- Epilogue
- Afterword

Parts and chapters can begin wherever they fall, on an even or an odd page, but many designers like to begin parts and chapters on odd pages. This will leave some even pages blank, and that's okay because it's good to give readers a pause to digest your story or information before they move on to the next chapter.

Do not put headers or footers on blank pages.

If your book is over 300 pages long, you may save on real estate by eliminating blank pages and allowing chapter openings to fall where they may.

If you want to get fancy, you may want to open chapters on even pages with decorative chapter numbering, type treatments, graphics, or pre-chapter quotes, and start the chapter text on the odd facing page.

If you want sophisticated formatting, it's best to consult a professional interior book designer and use InDesign instead of Word.

Again, check out other books in your genre for standards and inspiration.

Back matter

Your print book and ebook back matter may differ as I explained in the beginning of this chapter. For example, many authors choose to move acknowledgements to the back where readers will be able to find it, since most ebooks are set to open at the first chapter. Back matter may include the following:

- Nonfiction books may include an appendix, addendum, chronology, notes, glossary, bibliography, list of contributors, index, errata, and even a colophon.
- About the author—a bio and, optionally, a good color or grayscale image (300 dpi).
- Acknowledgments—unless, of course, they're in the front of the book.

Anything after does not get headers and footers, including pagination.

***

Marketing back matter

Here's a chance to do some book marketing, connect with your readers, and get book reviews.

Invitation to review the book—Link to a page on your website (and not to a particular retailer, because other retailers will not distribute books that lists competing services).

- Invite readers to join your email list and connect on social media.
- Also by… (to lead readers to your other books).
- Sample of your next book.
- Book club discussion questions.

Again, look at recent successful books in your genre to see what those authors are doing to attract readers to their lists and social sites.

***

Choosing an interior book design tool

Choosing an interior book design tool is critical and will affect the professionalism of your result. You can make compromises to help solve the age-old dilemma of time versus money. Can you afford to hire it out or will you have to learn how to do it yourself? How professional does your book need to be?

Suggestions follow but for detailed reviews of each tool see *Chapter 41, Design and Formatting Tools.*

If you have more time than money, and your book is fairly simple, you can use **Microsoft Word and a $50 Book Design Template** to format your ebook and print book. These look professional as long as you keep it simple.

Kindle Create is Amazon's free downloadable app for Windows and Mac for creating Kindle ebooks. You can create text-heavy books like novels and memoirs, fixed-layout ebooks (they call them *Print Replica* ebooks), and comic or graphic novels with Kindle Create. This tool is Amazon's answer to book design templates but remember that it only creates ebooks for the Amazon Kindle devices and apps.

If you're on a Mac, you can use **Pages** to create a doc file and an EPUB for free. Authors who use the Mac love **Vellum**, a $249 desktop app that makes it very easy to create beautiful books in digital and print. You can even add custom drop caps and ornamental flourishes for both formats.

If you are familiar with WordPress, you'll love the **Pressbooks** cloud-based publishing system. They have about 40 different themes to choose from. Pressbooks will also import your WordPress blog posts so you can make a first draft of a book. Rearrange and edit it, collaborate, and download to multiple formats. It costs $99 to remove the watermark from the ebook and print PDF files.

Leanpub is a freemium tool that helps you publish and sell your books that also exports your book to multiple formats.

You can **hire someone** to format your book. Hiring out formatting in Word is cheaper than hiring out formatting in InDesign, but InDesign books always look better. Expect to pay over $1,000 for InDesign help. Check out **Mark's List** on **Smashwords** for low-cost ebook formatters.

If your book requires complex styling, columns, text boxes, spreads, or bleeds, you'll need to use **InDesign**. Whether you purchase it or hire a professional is up to your skill level, patience, and budget. Expect to pay $1,000 or more if you hire it out. If you do it yourself, or plan to do edits on your own after you get the file from the designer, then purchase InDesign for $19.99 a month with Adobe's Creative Cloud service.

A good alternative is **Blurb**. Their tools are proprietary so you can't use them anywhere else, and printing prices are high. The tradeoff is it's free.

Some of the book distributors offer free book creation tools in the cloud. These include **Draft2Digital**, **PublishDrive**, and **StreetLib**. They hope you'll use their distribution service as well, but you don't have to. **Reedsy**, the author marketplace, also provides a free ebook creation tool.

Again, find detailed reviews of these and other options in *Chapter 41, Design and Formatting Tools*. If you want full service options, check them out in *Chapter 42, Full Service Companies*.

The importance of styles

Let me tell you a little story. A friend of mine was fiddling around with her chapter headings, and this was her process:

1. Highlight the chapter heading in Chapter 1
2. Change the font
3. Change the font size
4. Change the weight (bold)
5. Change the spacing before
6. Change the spacing after
7. Repeat 24 times

I begged her to learn how to use styles and she reluctantly accepted my help.

We started by using the "Select All" feature to change the entire manuscript to the standard paragraph style. Then I showed her how to create a Chapter Head style in the font she liked, centered, with lots of space above and below the heading.

We set the chapter head style to automatically create an odd section break before the heading so each chapter would begin on a right-hand page. We applied this style to each of the twenty-four chapter headings and clicked the "update automatically" checkbox.

So from then on, whenever she changed the font or size in one place, all the other chapter headings were automatically changed. She was thrilled.

So you see? Learning how to use styles will save you time. And it's also the "programming language" that tells the device how to display each paragraph of your book.

No spaces. No tabs. No hitting the return key to increase vertical space. All of this is handled with styles. That way you don't have to worry about reformatting your manuscript when you make changes. It will automatically reflow perfectly for both print and ebook readers.

Using Microsoft Word styles saves a lot of time when formatting your book.

For example, you'll be able to change all the title fonts from Arial 18 to Verdana 16, in one step, simply by modifying the style. Want to change the body text from Palatino to Georgia? Or the amount of space between the chapter titles and the first paragraphs? Use Styles. One change to the style automatically makes the change to the entire book.

Honestly, you are going to slap yourself on the forehead when you see how easy it is to use styles.

Page breaks, keep with next, and spacing

You can set your chapter head style to create a page break before it, and even set it to start on the next page. You can set images to keep with their captions, so they don't get split up in the book. Styles are also the key to generating an automatic table of contents.

Set your body text spacing to "double" for your copyeditor, to 1.5 for your final manuscript, or to 1.2 for high word-count manuscripts.

Styles are everywhere

It doesn't matter what program you use—Word, Scrivener, InDesign, Pressbooks, all of them, actually—you must apply styles to every single paragraph in your book.

The programming language for reading devices

Styles not only save you time, but they also serve as the programming for ebook reading devices. Styles get translated into the code that tells ebook reading devices how to display a paragraph versus a chapter heading versus a bulleted list versus a pull quote.

Microsoft Word

Microsoft Word is the most popular program for writing, designing, and formatting a book interior. Over the years it's evolved from a simple word-processing application to a sophisticated page-layout program. Word Styles automates character, section, and paragraph formatting. This is how Word "programs" your document to display your book correctly in all the ebook reading devices.

When you work in Word to format your book, it's essential to use styles instead of line and paragraph breaks, spaces, and tabs.

Use code EC55D to download my free how-to guide from Smashwords.

Word templates

The easiest and cheapest way to format your book in Word is by using a template. Simply choose a design you like in the appropriate book (trim) size, paste your Word document into it, and apply the appropriate predesigned style for each element of your book, such as your chapter headings and body text.

It's easy to customize the template to make it your own: simply change the fonts, leading, headers, and footers. The Book Design Templates company provides easy instructions to guide you through the entire process to make your book look beautiful and professional.

Book design templates

I highly recommend templates by Book Design Templates in Word and InDesign. This brand of templates cost from $27 to $57, and the quality is well above that of free templates provided by Amazon and others. You can download their handy Book Construction Blueprint and instructions for free. I especially recommend the 2WAY templates for simple books because they export to both print and ebook formats from the same Word file.

The guide you're reading now is actually considered a simple book—and you see how many headings and subheadings it has in it. You'll find images, right and left headers (in the print edition), italicized copy within the text, and bulleted and numbered lists. Because of these complications, my formatter charged me more than you would pay for a simple novel with chapter heads and body text.

To make your book unique, you can change the font styles, headers, and footers in a Book Design Template. Use the standard styles in the Word Styles panel, or hire someone to customize it for you.

Book Design Templates come in standard sizes for fiction and nonfiction books, children's books, and even MiniBüks (those little inspirational books you see at gift-shop check-out counters). The Book Design Templates company also provides book cover templates (though I recommend hiring a professional book cover designer instead), and templates for book proposals and media kits.

Find links to these templates and other formatting tools like Pressbooks, Word, Blurb, and InDesign, in the *Consumer's Guide, Chapter 41, Design and Formatting Tools.*

Interior typography: fonts and flourishes

From flourishes to leading, ligature, professional fonts and small graphics, you can add punch and elegance to your book design.

For the average text-heavy ebook, it doesn't pay to spend a lot of time worrying about fonts because users will set the font they like in their reading device. So do not embed fonts. In "immersive" reading—novels, memoirs, romance, and literary fiction—less is more. You want your readers to immerse themselves in the story and not be distracted by all the cool artistic elements in your formatting.

A good rule is to choose one serif font (for text) and one sans-serif font (for headings, footers, captions, and such). That may seem boring, but if you use too many variations your reader may get a headache.

For print and complex fixed-layout ebooks, you have thousands of typefaces to choose from. Don't forget, fonts are copyrighted and licensed, so make sure you buy the ones you use—and make sure your book designer sends you the licenses.

The FontSquirrel app lets you search for fonts that are approved to be used commercially. This can be very helpful with fonts for chapter titles. (Find out more about this app and others in *Chapter 41, Design and Formatting Tools*.)

Take a look at some of the "pro" fonts available from Adobe and other vendors. You'll find they offer all kinds of versions besides Regular, Bold, and Italic.

If your book is heavy on photography or art, you might want to treat typography as an artistic element, or downplay it by finding one simple font to avoid distracting the reader from the visual story. Your book's typeface will deeply, yet subconsciously, affect the reader.

Use typographical flourishes, ornaments or characters to provide graphic elements for separating chapter numbers from chapter titles or to separate sections. You might even choose a small graphic, embedded as an image.

But be sure these elements enhance, not detract from, the content.

Test your design and get input by asking your readers. You can ask on Facebook or ask people to vote on the designs by polling them using Facebook polls or a tool like Pickfu or SurveyMonkey, described in *Chapter 49, Business and Productivity*.

Scanning a book

If you have an out-of-print book to republish, you can get it scanned into a text document using OCR (optical character recognition) technology. You find places to get this done locally by typing "scanning service in *your city*" into your search engine.

If you have a PDF file, use an online tool to convert your PDF to a Word document, like OnlineOCR. It's not perfect, so proofread carefully before formatting.

If you've won rights back from your publisher, or want to create a new edition of an out-of-print book, you'll need to start over with a new

ISBN and publishing house name, as if it were a brand new book. You can make a "previously published as" note on the copyright page.

Setting the begin-reading point

When you pick up a print book, especially fiction, you're likely to flip to the first chapter or prologue and start reading. If you're reading a nonfiction book, then you aim to learn something. You will browse the table of contents to pick and choose the chapters you need. Whether fiction or nonfiction, readers are eager to start reading and skip the preface and introduction, dedications, and all the front matter so set the begin reading point of your ebook to the first chapter, foreword, table of contents, or introduction. If they want to read the copyright page and title pages they can flip backward. And move the other front matter to the back.

In Pressbooks you set the "ebook start-point" in the *Export Settings* area of their editor.

In Word, when you're formatting a book destined for Kindle and EPUB, set the start point using Word's bookmark feature. Place your cursor where you want your book to start. Click INSERT > BOOK-MARK, type the word START, and click ADD.

Creating print and ebook ready files

To create print and ebook ready files, you'll need PDFs for your print book and Word, EPUB, or MOBI files for your ebook. Refer to *Chapter 14, Book Production Basics*, for details.

Hiring a professional

Think of a professional book designer as a marketing partner. With their knowledge and expertise in your genre, your designer can help your book stand out in a crowded market. Designers also know the value of typography and how to gracefully include essential elements like your logo, the publisher name, ISBNs, and barcode.

A professional book designer will use the latest version of Adobe InDesign. Think twice about hiring a designer who uses CorelDRAW and Quark, two design programs that have fallen out of favor. If your designer ever disappears you're more likely to find a replacement at a good price if your cover was created in InDesign.

A good number of designers (and formatters) who charge very reasonable fees are listed on *Smashwords Mark's List*. Gatekeeper Press and other services also provide book cover design in their suite of services. (See *Chapter 42, Full Service Companies*.)

The best way to find a professional book designer, or a producer, coach, editor, marketer, photographer, artist, web designer, social media coach—anyone who can help you in your indie author journey —is to get a personal recommendation from another author. In the absence of a personal recommendation, check out these resources:

Independent Book Publishers Association: Annual membership pays for itself with the discounts in title uploads and revisions in IngramSpark, discounts for NetGalley and other memberships you need, not to mention the forum, webinars, and book marketing opportunities.

Mark's List at Smashwords lists ebook formatters and ebook cover designers that Smashwords authors have successfully used.

Reedsy and **PubLaunch** offer marketplaces where you can find vetted professionals. See *Chapter 44, Online Marketplaces* for more information and other marketplaces.

The Self-Publishers Ultimate Resource Guide is a book that lists publishing professionals who can help you.

Fiverr can be useful to find people to do simple jobs or fixes. I've found people to correct my website code, to remove backgrounds and touch-up photos, to create bookmarks in a very large Word file, and other tedious jobs.

Upwork is generally populated by real pros with prices to match. I hired an InDesign pro to help me out when I got stuck on a design issue and he did the job in just a couple of hours and taught me how to do it too.

16

BOOK COVER DESIGN

Your book cover is your number one marketing asset. A great cover design will grab customers' attention and compel them to buy. Leave this to the professionals, please. Cover design is not intuitive to the uninitiated. Authors make lots of mistakes in typography, color choices, and emerging trends, so it's important to hire an expert.

Professional book cover designers are current with the ever-changing trends in book covers. They understand that today's customer makes buying decisions based on the impression they get from the tiny cover displayed next to other tiny covers in a list on their computer screen. They know that the cover must fit in with others in the same genre, yet stand out enough to be noticed.

Start to gather ideas for your book cover as soon as you can. Collect ideas into a folder on your computer or Dropbox or a private Pinterest page to share with your designer.

Research books in your genre

Book buyers who are searching for something to read unconsciously expect the cover of your book to fit a particular style. So don't make the mistake of using a curlicue font for your non-fiction book, because it will look like a romance novel. Readers are subliminally confused by deviations from genre standards. Visit Amazon, Goodreads, and other book sites, or visit a bookstore or library near you to study book covers in your genre. Here is a checklist for you.

Book size: What is the most common size in your genre? (Designing a custom, non-standard book size will astronomically raise your printing costs.)

Finish: Are the covers in your genre mostly glossy or matte? Are they laminated?

Cover art: Are most of the books using graphics, photography, or a combination of the two? How about finishes?

Cover font: Look at the typography used for book titles and subtitles. Are they serif fonts with lots of curlicues (romance novels) or sans-serif fonts (non-fiction)?

Back of book: This is your chance to attract buyers. There they find out what the book is about, why the author is so fabulously interesting and/or qualified, and how many important people recommend it. Notice what is tantalizing and what is distracting, and write your copy to compete.

Do your market research and use Amazon's advanced search to study the book covers in your category.

Sketch it out

You can use Photoshop, Word, or Canva's free book cover maker for temporary covers and as sketches to give to your designer. Canva offers premade book cover templates in various genres to choose from with images and typography that work well together. I also like Canva's social media banner and blog post templates. You can even literally sketch (with pencil and paper) a book cover and take a photo to send to your cover designer. They are artists, and they're used to working with all kinds of input.

Elements of a paperback book cover

Here's what you need for the front, back, and spine of your print book. Make sure you own or have legally licensed all fonts, images, and graphics. Images for print covers and interiors should be CMYK in 300 dpi. Ebook cover and interior images should be RGB in 72 dpi

Front—title, subtitle, author name, and cover image.

Back—a short book description, maybe one testimonial, and a short author bio and image. Include a barcode with the price embedded. Get a free barcode from IngramSpark if you haven't already bought one from Bowker. You can use this barcode everywhere, no matter where you print your book.

Spine—title, author name, publishing house name (or initials) and logo (or type treatment).

Elements of a hardcover book cover

In addition to a front, back, and spine, a hardcover book also needs a front and back flap. That is, unless you're creating a case laminate cover with no dust jacket. Here's what you need to place in the different areas of a hardcover book.

Front—title, subtitle, author name, and cover image.

Back—testimonials. Distribute your ARCs early and gather reviews and testimonials well before publication. Also include a barcode with the price embedded. Get a free barcode from IngramSpark if you haven't already bought one from Bowker. You can use the same barcode on the version you upload to Amazon.

Spine—title, author name, publishing house name (or initials) and logo (or type treatment)

Front flap—book description

Back flap—author bio

Confused? Simply examine recent books in your genre to find the answers or ideas on how your book should be designed. Use *Amazon Advanced Search* to find books like yours on Amazon or visit your library or bookstore. You'll see that books in your genre are put together in much the same way and you should follow their lead.

17

CREATING YOUR PRINT PDF

ONCE YOU'VE EDITED AND FORMATTED YOUR INTERIOR AND created a cover, you'll want to order a proof to make sure your book looks great inside and out. Fortunately, Amazon Print's POD (print-on-demand) service makes this very easy. Leave the publication date blank, upload your book interior and cover files, and get an electronic proof for free. You can purchase a print proof at cost and have it sent to your home. The process takes twenty-four hours from upload to file check and approval. Even if you don't plan to use Amazon KDP Print to reach the Amazon store, their service is the easiest and fastest way to produce an unpublished proof.

Amazon will only let you order five books at a time during the pre-publication stage. So upload your files to IngramSpark to create ARCs for reviewers. IngramSpark waives their setup fee when you order at least fifty books, even before publication.

I recommend using both Amazon KDP Print and IngramSpark to distribute your book. This is because Amazon may list your book as out of stock if you don't use KDP to supply the Amazon store.

Robin Cutler at IngramSpark explains the whys and hows of distribution using Amazon and IngramSpark in Part 2 of our talk on the Author Friendly Podcast (episode #18).

Making PDFs for simple documents

It's easy to create PDFs for simple documents. Once you've formatted your document correctly choose SAVE AS PDF from your Microsoft Word (or another program) toolbar, or PRINT AS PDF or PRINT AS > ADOBE PDF. You do not need a separate PDF creation app to do this for you.

Making PDFs for book distribution

Creating PDFs for IngramSpark and Amazon is just as easy, but you have to make sure your book settings are as follows:

- Resolution: 600 ppi for 1-bit black and white line art and 300 ppi for 8-bit grayscale continuous tone images
- Color Space: Grayscale
- LPI (lines per inch): 106
- Preferred file format: PDF (.pdf) file - dimensions vary by trim size
- Bleed: 0.125" (3 mm) except on bind side
- PDF producer: Acrobat Distiller, Export from InDesign PDF/X-1a:2001 or PDF/X-3:2002

I find that if I adhere to IngramSpark's file creation guidelines, my files are universally accepted for simple, black and white books without bleeds. But if you are using bleeds (images that extend beyond the edge of the page) you'll need to study the file creation guides.

It can seem daunting at first, but plod through their instructions and you will see it's a simple but detailed process. For example, here are the basic requirements for black and white books taken from Ingram-Spark's guide:

NOTE: From Microsoft Word simply use the PRINT > SAVE AS ADOBE PDF dialog.

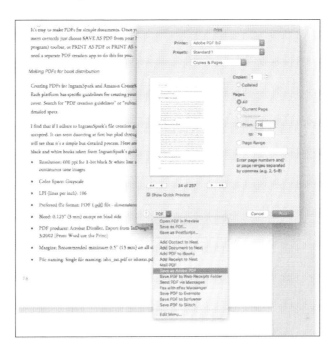

Word docs can be saved as PDFs using the Print dialog box.

All this is explained in IngramSpark's File Creation Guide, a thirty-five-page document that describes every printing situation from black and white text-only books to full-bleed color books and ebooks. Search for it on the web.

If you use a book design template (see *Chapter 41, Design and Formatting Tools*) you won't have to figure this out yourself.

Common problems

The most common problems I've seen with print books include images under 300 dpi (can be blurry), books with full bleed images (not extending at least .125" over the edge of the page), and gutter margins that are so narrow the reader struggles to flatten the book to read the text at the binding.

POD print and ship price comparison

Out of curiosity, I went to each company's print and ship calculators to do the math on how much it would cost to print and ship 50 copies of a 200-page, 6x9 trade paperback with black and white interior.

Here's what I found, listed in order of price. And I provided URLs so you can do the math on your own book. Note that vendors can change prices without notice so please just use this as a guideline. Also note there are price breaks for large quantities of books. For example, IngramSpark's price break is at 750 copies.

Amazon Print

Supply your own files. They distribute to Amazon only. (Do not use Expanded Distribution.)

https://kdp.amazon.com/en_US/help/topic/G8BKPU9AGVZSF9QF

$3.25 per book ($162.50) + $23 shipping = total print/ship 50 books for $185.50

You can see why authors like to print POD books using Amazon KDP Print. Their file upload process is also easier than IngramSpark's. However, their paper and print quality is often poorer. (It depends on timing, the machine they use and if the ink needs refilling.)

. . .

IngramSpark Print and Ship Calculator

Supply your own files. They distribute everywhere.

https://myaccount.ingramspark.com/Portal/Tools/PubCompCalculato
r

$3.58 per book ($179)+ $29.84 shipping = total print/ship 50 books for $208.84

Gatekeeper Press Printing Cost Calculator

Gatekeeper Press creates files and distributes.

https://gatekeeperpress.com/printing-costs/

$3.60 per book ($180) + 29.45 shipping = total print/ship 50 books for $209.45

This is great pricing for a full-service company.

Blurb Print Cost Calculator

Create your own files using Blurb's tools. They distribute.

http://www.blurb.com/pricing#/tab/trade-books

$3.56 per book ($178) + $65.99 shipping = total print/ship 50 books for $243.99

Blurb's cost to ship is way out of line with the others, but their print quality is superior.

BookBaby Publishing Quoter

BookBaby creates files and distributes.

https://www.bookbaby.com/quoter/

$7.58 per book ($379) + $39.50 shipping = total print/ship 50 books for $418.50

BookBaby's print quality is much higher than most due to in-house printing with quality paper and ink.

The atypical book

If you're creating an art and photography book, children's book, or workbook, do a little research and find out what size is the norm for your genre. Try to make your book fit one of the standard sizes—a custom book size is incredibly expensive to produce.

Decisions to make before printing

Before you print, you should figure the dimensions of your book along with the paper stock. This will depend on page count and type of book (do your market research).

- Book size (trim size)
- Interior paper stock
- Cover paper stock

Standard book sizes

Choose an industry-standard book size. The most common trade paperback size is 6x9. This is called the "trim" size. If your book is shorter than the norm in your genre, you might consider using a 5.5x8.5 trim size to bump up the width of the spine, or increasing the leading (space between lines) and gutter (interior margins).

Standards are different for different kinds of books. Some children's books are thirty-two pages long and 8.5" (or 8.25") square. Do the research to ensure you adhere to genre standards.

If you use Amazon to sell print books directly to Amazon customers, and IngramSpark to sell to all the other stores, choose a book size that can be produced by both vendors. You can search for the trim sizes offered by companies you are considering by typing "*company name pdf trim sizes*" into your search engine. Here are links to the three I use most often.

IngramSpark trim sizes

https://www.ingramspark.com/plan-your-book/print/trim-sizes

Amazon KDP Print trim sizes

https://kdp.amazon.com/en_US/help/topic/G201834180#trim

Interior paper stock

Most trade paperback books are printed in black and white on 50-, 55-, or 60-lb. stock in white or crème.

You can't rely on the numbers to reflect actual thickness. IngramSpark's lighter stock seems to be as thick as Amazon's heavier stock, indicating that their paper has more bulk.

The difference between IngramSpark and Amazon pricing differences to print trade paperbacks is negligible.

For color books, Amazon offers 55- and 60-lb. stock, and IngramSpark offers 70-lb. stock. Color interiors with Amazon are more affordable, but IngramSpark's 70-lb stock color printing is noticeably superior. BookBaby's color interior stock is a whopping 80 lbs.—higher quality and more expensive to print. Blurb's paper quality is even higher, with pricing to match.

Always use the print-price calculators on their sites to estimate price before you make your decision.

Paperback cover stock

Cover stock is thicker and more durable than the interior stock, and it can be treated in glossy or matte laminates or finishes.

Amazon offers cover stock in glossy or matte finish and prints paperback books only.

IngramSpark offers both paperback and hardcover (casebound) book printing and distribution. Paperback cover stock is offered in both glossy and matte.

Hardcover

IngramSpark is the only good option for hardcover book printing if you are doing it yourself; that is, managing your own book project and want to be cost effective. Amazon does not produce hardbound, but they will distribute them if you join the Amazon Advantage program.

Though other good companies can help you create hardcover books, I focus on do-it-yourself solutions in this guide. In the case of hardcover books, I recommend IngramSpark and Gatekeeper Press most often. See my discussion of full-service versus do-it-yourself tools in *Chapter 7, Choose Your Tools*, and also check the *Chapter 39, Distribution Tools and Services* and *Chapter 42, Full Service Companies*.

You'll need to decide if you want your hardcover book in 1) case laminate with no dust jacket or 2) in blue or gray cloth with or without a dust jacket. Dust jackets come in glossy and matte. Use the Ingram-Spark cover template generator to view all the choices and create a template your cover artist can use, or ask your designer to do this for you.

Use the IngramSpark cover template generator for paperback and hardback books along with a spine width calculator, print and ship calculator (royalty calculator), and weight and spine width calculator.

http://www.ingramspark.com/resources/tools

Here's the link to a set of templates for your Amazon print book cover.

https://kdp.amazon.com/en_US/cover-templates

If you've got a high-quality, arty book, then you may want to use an offset printing service in Canada or Asia and self-distribute to Amazon using Amazon Advantage, or hire a distribution partner as described in *Chapter 23, Traditional Wholesale-Style Distribution.*

Remember you are free to move the production and distribution of your books to any vendor you like, whenever you like, as long as you apply your own ISBN.

Print On Demand (POD)

POD, POD, POD, POD! Everybody is printing "on demand" these days. Why? Using a POD print and distribution service is a low-cost and risk-free way to do business because you don't hold inventory. The downside is it costs a bit more per book for POD than it does to print thousands of books with an offset press (which also prints higher-quality books, though that gap is closing as the machinery improves).

POD printing and distribution services also take care of the sales side of your business. They print the book and fulfill the order as soon as the customer pays for your book. Then they credit your bank account. It's all one efficient process.

POD print and distribution services include Amazon Kindle Direct Publishing (KDP), and you should use it to sell your book in Amazon only. Do not use their Expanded Distribution program, even though your book will be made available to other online retailers and bookstores. The problem is you need to set a 30 percent discount to sell to online retailers, and a 53 percent discount plus a returns program to sell to bookstores and Amazon does not let you do either of these things.

Amazon only offers a 40 percent discount to bookstores, and anyway, bookstores generally don't like to purchase from their competitor. If you want your book be available to a bookstore, you will need to go elsewhere.

DIY services like IngramSpark, PublishDrive, and Blurb will list your book in many online stores, including Amazon, brick and mortar bookstores, and libraries. Other services that are reaching into these markets include Draft2Digital and StreetLib. Find out about these and more in *Chapter 39, Distribution Tools and Services.* Full service companies also reach bookstore and library markets, and these are reviewed in *Chapter 42, Full Service Companies.*

Short-run printing

Short-run printing is done on digital presses, but often there is not a lot of difference in the cost and that of POD. So if you're printing a couple hundred books, it may be more efficient to order your POD books from Amazon, IngramSpark, or your POD services company.

Offset printing

Offset-print books are of higher quality and much cheaper per book than POD using "analog" type film-to-plate technology. These days you can order as few as 300 books from an offset printer. A print broker may be able to get you a better deal on offset printing than you can, even after factoring in their commission.

Authors with full-color, photography, and children's books are most likely to want to print high-quality books with an offset-print vendor, and should consult a broker (as explained in the section below).

If your book is a standard trade paperback, and you know you can sell hundreds of books at a time, then it's very cost-effective to use offset printing for special sales and events. You can use offset print brooks for direct sales at events and via your website. If you like, you can sell your offset-printed books directly to Amazon and Walmart by using their merchant programs.

Offset printing can take six to eight weeks from order to delivery—more if you are printing a full-color book overseas. Don't forget to add in the proof approval process. If you are printing a color book, check that the four-color process results in the four colors you expected. So plan ahead and schedule in double the time you think it might take.

If you're going to hire an offset printer or broker, you'll need to:

- Create a detailed book specification
- Compose a request for quote
- Hire a print broker (who can help you do the above)

Create a detailed book specification

A book specification provides details for your book designer and offset printer and print broker. Choices are dictated by the size of your book and the printer's specification. Here is the information your offset printer will need with sample information filled in:

- Quantity: 500; 750; 1,000; 2,500; 5,000…

- Number of Pages: 240
- Trim Size: 6 x 9
- Interior Copy: Black
- Illustrations: 24 grayscale
- Bleeds: Full (on cover)
- Paper: 100% recycled 50 lb. crème
- Ink: All black, soy
- Proofs: PDF
- Color Cover: four-color
- Binding: Perfect
- Lamination: Matte varnish full coverage
- Shrink Wrapping in 6s
- Delivery: Mac InDesign CS6 working files + laser proofs
- Shipping: address of location (residence or business)

Compose a Request for Quote (RFQ)

If you send out one hundred RFQs you could get one hundred different price quotes. It's much easier to enlist the help of a print broker if you're printing a full-color book. Either way, you'll need the following information.

- Your name, address, and contact information, to give your printer and their shipping company.
- Book specs: Size, number of pages, paper weight and color, recycled, soy ink, etc.
- The quantities you'd like quotes for (750; 1,000; 2,500, etc.).
- Cover lamination: Matte or glossy.
- Shrink wrapping: This helps keep books clean.
- Cover overruns: Use them for book displays at readings and expos.
- Delivery to a residence: May require delivery by small truck.
- Full bleeds on cover (probably) and interior (mostly for photography and art books).

- How you will deliver the files. For example: "PDF cover and interior created in Mac InDesign CS6."

How to hire a print broker

Print brokers know which printers are likely to give you the best price and the best quality. You may be surprised that, even with their commission, they can get lower prices than you can. That's because they have long-term relationships with printers.

Your print broker is the printing company's return customer and also your advocate and go-between. This means you won't have to navigate the process alone.

If you're a member of the Independent Book Publishers Association (IBPA) in the US, you'll find a list of printers and brokers on their site. Or get a recommendation from another author or small press. Interview as many brokers as it takes to find one you like and who likes you, who communicates well, and believes in your project. Ask for client referrals and samples of books from the printers they recommend.

18

CREATING YOUR EBOOK

IN *CHAPTER 13, THE DIFFERENT BOOK FORMATS,* YOU LEARNED that ebooks come in two basic flavors, MOBI for Amazon and EPUB for everybody else. You also learned about fixed-layout formats in EPUB and MOBI.

Before you create your ebook, you need to know a couple of things about fonts and images.

Fonts in ebooks

Readers can set a preferred font in the user preferences for their devices and apps. So don't spend any energy on imagining fonts for your ebook. To make sure the book looks great in all devices, use a standard font every device can read and translate.

- Use 12 pt Times New Roman (serif), Arial (sans serif), and Courier (even character spacing).
- Use 14-18 pt text for chapter titles.
- If you really want to use a special font for your chapter titles, embed them as images.

Images in ebooks

You can embed color images in your ebook, but they will display as black and white in devices that don't support color, so make sure the color and contrast looks good in both.

Your images should be as small as possible (in KB and MB and not dimensions) without sacrificing quality. KB stands for kilobyte (1024 bytes). MB stands for megabyte. There are 1024 KBs in one MB.

Kindle's advice is to include images at 300 pixels per inch, which is a pretty big image, but this is not common wisdom among all the ebook retailers.

See if you can get the images in the interior of your book to fit these sizes and dimensions:

- 72 to 100 dpi
- 5 inches wide (max)
- 6.9 inches high (max)

Some more tips:

If your images are in color, see how that works. You may not need to change each image to grayscale.

Make image adjustments in an image editing program and do not resize them in Word.

Import your images into Word, don't drag and drop them. Your images need to be "anchored" and drag and drop just floats them in the page.

Word doc to ebook

It's very easy to create ebooks from a doc or docx file if you've formatted your book correctly using Microsoft Word Styles (or used a template to help you).

Upload a doc or docx file to Amazon KDP and Smashwords to automatically convert your book to the formats needed by their stores. This is a one-step process.

(Note that other ebook aggregators use your doc or docx file to get your book into their ebook editing tool. These include Draft2Digital, PublishDrive, and StreetLib. Once your file is uploaded, you can make adjustments in their tools before distribution.)

My advice is to maintain a master document to use as your base document for future corrections for both print and ebook. Then create a duplicate for Smashwords and another for Kindle.

Smashwords document

Your Smashwords version must state "Smashwords Edition" on the copyright page. Upload the Word document file to Smashwords for inclusion in its Premium Catalog for distribution to all the online retailers (except for Amazon). The document must be under 15MB in size.

If you have a pretty EPUB to distribute, you can also upload it to Smashwords and it will send that out instead of the EPUB generated from your doc file. Find out more below in the EPUB section of this chapter.

Kindle document

Your Amazon KDP version does not have to state "Kindle Edition" on the copyright page, but I like to do that to differentiate it from the master document and the Smashwords document. This version will only be sold in the Amazon store. If you have a simple manuscript you can upload a doc, docx, txt, or rtf file. If your book is more complex you may need to upload a filtered HTML doc. You can also upload EPUB or MOBI if you have it. Note that they allow you to upload PDF files but don't. The formatting usually ends up looking terrible.

Check the files

Both services allow you to review your ebook before publishing. If there are any problems, fix them and reupload them.

That's it! That's a simple way to get your document file distributed as an ebook everywhere.

EPUB

If you've created your EPUB and MOBI files from InDesign or another EPUB creation service you can upload it to individual retailers (Kobo, Apple, B&N, Amazon) or reach retailers using an ebook distribution service listed in *Chapter 39, Distribution Tools and Services.*

Draft2Digital, PublishDrive, and StreetLib are ebook aggregators who offer free EPUB creation tools with no obligation to distribute with them:

You can also create an EPUB using Pressbooks, Leanpub, Scrivener, and many other tools.

IngramSpark

IngramSpark will distribute your EPUB to the online retailers, including Amazon. (Amazon sells MOBI files, but they automatically convert the EPUB they get from Ingram to MOBI for Kindle format.)

The automated process IngramSpark uses to submit an EPUB to

Amazon for Kindle book distribution may cause some confusion regarding the ISBN. Stick with me here.

The industry standard is to assign one ISBN for the MOBI for Kindle file and another for EPUB. But when you distribute to Amazon using a service, you won't need to make a MOBI for Kindle file.

So do you need an ISBN for Kindle?

Yes. Because your book will be published on Amazon and you want to track those sales.

The simple solution is to assign the EPUB ISBN to the IngramSpark ebook and list all the ISBNs on the copyright page of all versions of your book.

Smashwords

If you've used Smashwords to reach their wide network of retailers, but you have a professionally designed EPUB, you can use Smashwords Direct to replace the Smashwords-generated EPUB with the new one. Or, you can use it when uploading a new title, instead of using a Word document file. The EPUB must be under 20MB in size.

If you already have a Smashwords-generated EPUB (they will convert it for you from a Word file) but decide to use a professionally designed EPUB instead, you can use Smashwords Direct to replace the Smashwords-generated EPUB with the new one.

Amazon KDP

You may also upload your professionally designed EPUB to Amazon KDP, which will convert it to Kindle format for distribution to the Amazon store.

Pressbooks to ebooks

If you've used Pressbooks, you can export your book to PDF, EPUB, and MOBI files for distribution everywhere.

Other ebook creation tools

Draft2Digital, Reedsy, StreetLib and PublishDrive all have ebook creation tools that don't require you to use Word or InDesign, and their ease-of-use may attract you.

Depending on the complexity of your book and distribution goals, their design and distribution limitations may or may not make them the best choice for you. Get reviews of these tools in *Chapter 39, Distribution Tools and Services*.

EPUB file requirements

As soon as your EPUB is finished, validate it. EPUBs must comply with the industry IDPF spec found here:

http://idpf.org/epub

Your interior EPUB must be validated at:

http://validator.idpf.org

You can do this yourself, but if you've hired out interior book design, the designer should do this for you and guarantee their work. Do this at the very end of the formatting stage when it's ready for publication.

Ebook cover specifications

Create your ebook covers according to these specifications, which Amazon Kindle requires and which work for the other stores as well.

- a JPEG in RGB, (not CMYK, which is for print)
- less than 50MB in size
- 72 dpi
- height/width aspect ratio of at least 8:5 (1.6:1)
- dimensions of 2,560 x 1,600

Find more details on Amazon's help page:

http://bit.ly/kdpcover

All you need on your ebook cover is:

- an image
- book title and (optional) subtitle
- author name

Recommendations:

- Your ebook cover may be rejected if it has too much print on it.
- Make sure your book title matches the internal title on the title page and the metadata you entered in the distributor or retailer site.
- Get commercial rights to publish your cover image as a book cover in all the territories where you sell your book.
- You'll need to license your fonts for commercial use as well. You can purchase them in any number of places, including FontSquirrel, which also offers free fonts licensed for use in ebooks.
- Make your title font very large. Avoid Times New Roman and other free fonts used in newspapers and magazines.

- Make your author name half the size of the title.

PublishDrive offers a great post titled "A complete guide to choosing your book cover font.

More about ebook covers

Because there is no back cover on an ebook, the book description—the one that appears on the paperback back cover—lives in the metadata for the book on the retailer websites. (Find out more in *Chapter 36, Metadata and Discovery.*)

Apple wants their ebook cover images to be at least 1,400 pixels wide. Amazon wants them 2,500 pixels tall with the height 1.6 times greater than the width. B&N requires a minimum height of between 1,200 to 2,000 pixels, and so on.

It's complicated. So instead of worrying about the particular specs of each retailer, I look to Mark Coker of Smashwords to set a standard that fits everyone's needs, since they distribute so widely.

Mark figures that "good-looking covers have heights that are around 1.3 to 1.65 times greater than the width." Specifically, he recommends a "vertical rectangle of approximately 1,600 pixels wide and 2,400 pixels tall."

He also advises that covers that are mostly text and sharp lines are best saved in PNG format. Covers that contain photographs are often too large when saved in PNG, and so they will need to be saved in JPEG (JPG) format. Make sure to use a high-quality setting, he says, so the text doesn't appear fuzzy.

InDesign users should note that Creative Cloud 2015 and later have amazing PNG optimization for the web and you can get a high-quality PNG for almost the same size as a JPEG now. (This works when you export as a PNG rather than "saving as" a PNG.)

For more details and advice search for Mark Coker's blog post on ebook covers. You can also find a list of professional designers, formatters, and editors on *Mark's List* of designers.

You've got a beautiful book!

Okay, it's ready. You have a beautifully formatted book and it's ready to go out into the world. You can upload it to each of the online retailers separately or use a distribution service. The next part of the guide, *Part IV: Distributing Your Book*, will help you do that.

PART IV

DISTRIBUTING
YOUR BOOK

You have a lot of choices when it comes to distribution. In this part of the guide you'll learn about all the different ways you can get your book to your readers, from self-distribution by uploading your book to each of the online retailers, to full-service distribution services who will do everything for you. Here's what you'll learn about in this section.

Book Distribution Basics
Distribution Terms and Definitions
Distribution's Place in the Publishing Flow
The Most Popular Distribution Solutions
Traditional Wholesale-Style Distribution
Hybrid Publishing and Distribution
Custom Book Publishing and Distribution
How to Avoid the Vanity Press Trap

Most authors who ask me about self-publishing are really trying to find out how to get their book distributed to all the online stores, bookstores, and libraries. As you've already learned, there are a lot of things to do before you start distributing your books.

The full-service distributors you'll learn about in this part of the guide can handle editing, formatting, production, and design. But before you hire these tasks out, I think it's useful to know at least a little bit about how to do it yourself. So I hope you'll familiarize yourself with the material the previous part (*Part III, Book Design and Production*), before you decide on a service.

19

BOOK DISTRIBUTION BASICS

WHEN MOST AUTHORS START THINKING ABOUT SELF-PUBLISHING what they're really thinking about is how to get their book distributed. But there is a lot to do before distribution, as you've already noticed by the number of chapters preceding this one.

You'll learn about POD distribution and traditional wholesale-style distribution (and why most authors choose POD).

Hybrid publishers can help you get traditional distribution and so can book packagers, custom book publishers, and small presses, if you make a hybrid deal with one. The word "hybrid" can mean a lot of different things in the world of publishing, as you'll see.

Finally, I'll show you how to avoid the vanity press trap and how to extricate yourself from one if you're already trapped.

As long as you own your ISBNs you can experiment with retailer and distribution solutions as much as you like. Many authors use the online retailer tools to upload their ebook directly, but others like using an ebook aggregator like Smashwords to do the work for them.

Lots of authors upload their print book using Amazon KDP Print to reach the Amazon store while reaching all the other print book markets with IngramSpark.

It's up to you, of course, because you're in charge. This is where the *Consumer's Guide* in Part VII is going to come in very handy. Make sure to sign up for the reader updates because these companies change the scope of their services all the time. At this writing IngramSpark is promising an easier-to-use interface and an EPUB creation tool in the cloud, and Draft2Digital's new POD distribution solution is in beta. So stay in touch.

www.selfpubbootcamp.com/readers

You'll get access to the *Consumer's Guide for Self-Publishers* ebook, which I obsessively update, as well as lots of tools like a metadata cheatsheet (which you're going to need before you start uploading your book) and book launch checklist.

In the Author Friendly podcast I interview the people behind these companies in about 30-minutes per episode. In the podcast they talk about features that may attract you to the service, so I hope you'll listen.

www.authorfriendly.com

20

DISTRIBUTION TERMS AND
DEFINITIONS

Before we begin, let's get familiar with the terminology and definitions used in the book distribution world. Some of these terms aren't intuitive. (Also, let me apologize in advance if you find some of this information repetitive. I want you to be able to find the information you need in one place, without being referred to other chapters. It's a difficult balance to strike.)

Ebook distribution

Ebook distributors like Smashwords and PublishDrive distribute and sell your ebook to a wide range of online retailers. Some companies provide both POD print book distribution as well as ebook distribution. Find reviews in *Chapter 39, Distribution Tools and Services.*

POD book DIY distribution

A Print On Demand (POD) distribution service sells your print book to the online booksellers and even makes your book visible to brick-and-mortar bookstores. Examples are IngramSpark and PublishDrive. You'll find reviews of these services in chapter 39. This is the most economical way to go.

Please note that Amazon's KDP Print is not a distribution tool and should only be used to reach the Amazon store directly (even though they offer a distribution program).

POD book full-service distribution

Full-service companies that help you create and distribute POD books include Bublish and BookBaby. You'll find reviews of these companies in chapter 42. These kinds of companies charge $1000 and up but do a lot for you.

Traditional-style or wholesale distribution

Traditional-style or wholesale distribution companies employ a sales force to sell your books to chain and independent bookstores, wholesalers, libraries, the gift and specialty markets, and the online booksellers. This is the most expensive way to go with the least profit margins but, as you'll see, there are reasons you may want to go this route.

Online retailer

An online ebook retailer is an online store that sells books. The major online book retailers include Amazon (which enjoys the majority of the market), Kobo (with its wide international reach, Walmart eBookstore (powered by Kobo), B&N, Apple, and Google Play. These are just the major outlets.

But rather than dealing directly with multiple retailers, many authors find that using an ebook aggregator is much more efficient, giving us more time to do what we love to do, which is to write.

Direct to retailer platforms

Direct to retailer platforms are the tools provided by the online retailers to help you publish books to their store: Amazon KDP, Apple iBooks Author, Kobo Writing Life, B&N Press, etc.)

Bookstore

It may seem kind of silly to include the definition of a bookstore in this list but the definition is changing. A bookstore is a store where books are sold, but often the definition includes the online retailers who sell books, such as the above-mentioned Amazon, B&N, Apple, Kobo, Walmart, and Google Play.

If you provide a curated list of books you like on your own website, that web page (or pages) is also a bookstore. (This can be a great way to make extra money via affiliate sales which is covered *Part V, Selling Direct*.) Tools you can use to do this include Smashwords, Ingram-Spark's Aerio product, and StreetLib. They work much like distribution companies that fulfill orders and deposit earnings automatically into your bank account. Find reviews in *Chapter 55, Direct Sales Tools*.

Pure-play retailers

A pure-play business is one that focuses on a particular product. For example, B&N only sells books in their physical and web-based stores and is therefore considered a pure-play retailer (even though they've added products like games and music). Amazon and Walmart, because they sell all kinds of products and not just books, are not pure-play retailers.

Sales channels

A sales channel is the pipeline to the stores that sell your book.

When you upload your ebook to an ebook distribution service like Smashwords, Draft2Digital, or PublishDrive, they're your sales channel to the online booksellers. You can exclude certain retailers, like Kobo, for example, if you've decided you want to go direct with Kobo because of their great marketing programs. (Except with IngramSpark, where you can only exclude Amazon.)

When you upload your ebook to the Kindle store using Amazon KDP, that's your sales channel to Amazon. There's no distributor in-between. Likewise, if you upload to B&N using B&N Press or to Kobo using Kobo Writing Life you're going direct to those stores.

Don't mix your channels. If you uploaded your print book to B&N using B&N Press and later decide to use IngramSpark for distribution, log into B&N Press and turn off sales first.

Title

In the book publishing world, you'll hear people say things like, "Once you've uploaded your title it will be visible to readers." Most of us would use the term "book," but in publishing, a book is called a "title" and is not the same the title of your book.

Metadata

Metadata is the information about your book that you need to upload before it is accepted with the retailer or distributor. Metadata includes your book title, subtitle, author name, keywords, book description, author bio, and testimonials.

Each retailer and distributor has their own rules on the number of keywords allowed and word and character count restrictions. So I created a metadata cheatsheet for you so you can figure it out before you start uploading. Get this and other worksheets by subscribing to reader updates:

www.selfpubbootcamp.com/readers

Publisher

My publisher name is Misadventures Media and I've set up a DBA, EIN, and bank account for that name. (See *Chapter 5, Create Your Publishing Business*.)

Imprint

An imprint is a brand identity or marketing tool associated with a publisher who wishes to attract different types of audiences. Publishers can form more than one imprint and you should if you publish books in completely separate genres.

I have created two imprints. Self-Pub Boot Camp is the imprint I use for books like this one for self-publishers. Motorcycle Misadventures is an imprint for readers of motorcycle adventure travel books.

These imprints are not businesses on their own but associated with

Misadventures Media. So I don't have or need DBAs or EINS or bank accounts for Self-Pub Boot Camp or Motorcycle Misadventures. They're both associated with Misadventures Media.

When you fill out your ISBN record for your book you'll be asked for your imprint name. If it's not already on record here's how you do it in the US: Login to your Bowker MyIdentifiers account and add an *Imprint* under your Publisher or Company Name by clicking on the *MyAccount > My Profile Data > My Company* menu. Scroll to the bottom and add the name of your new imprint.

You don't need any proof at all but do your due diligence make sure you're not using a name already in use or trademarked. Helen Sedwick has great advice on this in her *Legal Guide for Self-Publishers* (2nd edition), listed in the back of this book.

21

DISTRIBUTION'S PLACE IN THE PUBLISHING FLOW

DISTRIBUTION IS THE FINAL STEP IN ALL THE STEPS REQUIRED TO self-publish. Concurrent activities may include selling direct (which you may have started doing in the beta publishing phase) and will certainly include marketing (which happens before, during, and after every other publishing activity).

Here's an outline of what the publishing flow might look like for you, more or less.

1. Start writing and marketing and don't stop.
2. Do the research to make sure the market (your readers) wants your book.
3. Involve critique partners in developing your story.
4. Recruit early readers (beta publishing) and start cultivating your super-fans and street team.
5. Publish privately or publicly on a site like Leanpub or Wattpad.
6. Do all the business things like DBAs and ISBNs and LLCNs and CIP blocks and websites.
7. Get your book edited, designed, and produced.
8. Publish directly to one or more retailers, like Amazon KDP

or Kobo Writing Life to use their marketing tools. (Some authors only publish directly to the retailers and never use a distribution service. Or they use a print book distribution service and publish their ebooks directly.)

9. Sell your book directly from your website using a tool like Gumroad or PayPal.
10. Distribute your book using one or a combination of print and ebook distribution services. Or use traditional wholesale-style distribution.
11. Keep writing and marketing.

So by now, you've done a lot of work to make sure your book will be a success and launch to five-star reviews.

Have you decided to distribute? The next chapters will help you decide how you will distribute your book.

22

THE MOST POPULAR DISTRIBUTION SOLUTIONS

MOST AUTHORS I WORK WITH END UP WITH A COMBINATION OF services that look something like the following. (Find reviews of these and other services in *Chapter 39, Distribution Tools and Services.*)

1. **POD to the Amazon store:** Upload your PDFs to Amazon KDP Print to sell your print book directly to Amazon customers. (It's important to upload to Amazon first before you upload to any other distribution service like IngramSpark or Draft2Digital . If you do it the other way around Amazon will reject it citing that the ISBN is already being used. The ISBN should be the same for print, no matter where it's sold, and this is just an Amazon glitch.)
2. **POD everywhere else:** Upload your PDFs for wide distribution everywhere else. (Choices are IngramSpark, PublishDrive or StreetLib).
3. **Kindle ebook to the Amazon store:** Upload your interior file plus a cover image to Amazon KDP for ebook sales in the Amazon Kindle store.
4. **EPUB to the Kobo store**: Upload an EPUB and cover image

for ebook sales and marketing opportunities in Kobo Writing Life.

5. **EPUB for everywhere else:** Upload a Word doc file or EPUB to IngramSpark, PublishDrive, Smashwords, Draft2Digital, or StreetLib, along with a cover image for distribution everywhere else. Make sure to deselect the direct channels you're using (such as Amazon, Kobo).

6. **Full color POD print:** If you want to distribute a POD full-color book or hardcover book your best DIY choice is IngramSpark. If you need handholding and you don't want to manage your own project, Gatekeeper Press is a good option.

7. **Fixed-layout ebook:** Use Apple iBooks to sell your book in the iBookstore and Kindle Kids Book Creator to sell on Amazon. BookBaby, Blurb, and Gatekeeper Press are other options with wide distribution.

8. **Offset printing:** After you've tested your book with POD, you might want to order a large quantity of books to sell directly to your readers from your website and events. Be careful with this. You don't want a garage full of unsold books.

If you want to make it easy, use a one-stop shop and pay the 10 percent in distribution fees. If you want to maximize your profits, upload your book directly to each major retailer, and then use a distributor to get to the rest of the hundreds of outlets you can't reach directly.

Remember that as long as you own your ISBNs you can experiment and change and mix and match as much as you like.

23

TRADITIONAL WHOLESALE-STYLE DISTRIBUTION

SELF-PUBLISHERS CAN ENJOY THE PROFESSIONALISM OF traditional-style production, printing, and distribution with companies that have catalogs and sales forces that pitch your book.

Costs

Traditional-style distribution companies will take 65 percent or more of your book's profits and insist on exclusivity, which may mean you can't sell your own book. Not online, not even from your own website. If you have a speaking engagement, you can purchase books from your distributor at 50 percent of retail. This is not unfair as they put a lot of labor into selling your book.

You'll print your own books and order them shipped to their warehouse. They'll let you know when they need you to print more books.

Why use traditional distribution?

Some authors write books specifically to boost their business or enhance their careers. They don't expect to make money from the book but they expect the book to make money for their business. They look at the book as an investment.

For example, my friend Allan Karl, a successful business owner in San Diego, was burnt out, newly divorced and needed a break. So he sold everything and set off on a life-changing round-the-world solo motorcycle journey. During the years-long trip, he connected with lots of people, mostly over food. Allan is a great photographer and graphic artist and his book, *FORKS: A Quest for Culture, Cuisine, and Connection*, is a luscious full-color hardcover travelogue and cookbook that took much more time and money to produce than he ever hoped to make back in book sales. But he's a great marketer and the high quality of FORKS, paired with his natural enthusiasm, landed him on television around the US, including on big shows like Good Morning America. Consequently, his keynote-speaking career has soared.

Allan chose Small Press United (SPU) to distribute his book. SPU is a division of Independent Publishers Group created specifically to serve indie authors and start-up small presses. If you're one of the fewer than 20 percent of authors accepted into their program, they will present your book to resellers next to offerings from the mainstream press. They can also print your book on-demand and format your ebook.

24

HYBRID PUBLISHING AND DISTRIBUTION

HYBRID PUBLISHING IS AN UMBRELLA TERM FOR ALL KINDS OF services, such as author-assisted publishing, co-publishing, agent-assisted publishing, and partnership publishing.

As a self-publisher, you can make a hybrid "deal" with a small press who agrees to distribute your book and include your title in their catalog. For best results, find a small press who publishes books like yours. You might even make a hybrid deal with them to edit and design your book. You'll pay more but you get professional assistance with your book by an expert in your genre.

A hybrid author is an author who both self-publishes and publishes with a traditional book publishing company.

Hybrid publishers fill the gap traditional publishing left empty when they thinned out the mid-list. A hybrid publisher may hire out their expertise to a self-published author for a consulting fee. At the same time, they may publish another author under their own brand. A hybrid publisher may acquire your work, and publish you as a traditional press would, or they might split work and profits with you.

Hybrid publishers can help with the difficult job of traditional-style distribution—such as through Ingram Professional Services—which cannot be accessed by self-publishers. They may also deal with foreign rights, film rights, and licensing contracts for you.

It's important to note that hybrid publishers, unlike book packagers and vanity presses, vet their authors. They often curate books in a certain genre. A lot of vanity presses pose as hybrid or small presses and I know many authors who have been fooled by their so-called "application" process, being pleased to be "accepted." So do your research and scour their catalog. Find some of their books on Amazon to see if they're selling.

Some respected hybrid presses are She Writes Press, Inkshares (which is also a crowdfunding platform), Evolved Publishing (fiction), EverAfter (romance), Fuse Literary (fiction and nonfiction), and Hyperink (non-fiction blogs to books).

Brooke Warner of She Writes Press writes a lot about hybrid publishing and the publishing world in her excellent book *Green-Light Your Book*. Get a free PDF of the first chapter on her author website at this URL:

http://brookewarner.com/green-light-chapter-giveaway/

25

CUSTOM BOOK PUBLISHING AND DISTRIBUTION

TRAVEL WRITER LARRY JACOBSON CHOSE TO OUTSOURCE THE production and distribution of his book, *The Boy Behind the Gate*, to a book packager. His goal was to make a living as an inspirational speaker and business coach, so he felt the investment was worthwhile.

Custom book publishing is expensive and authors who use them are, for the most part, businesspeople who invest in a book to promote their business or speaking career.

Very few fiction book authors I know have used these companies but I know lots of nonfiction authors who have used them. I can whole-heartedly recommend two companies, Authority Publishing in Sacramento and Aloha Publishing in Idaho.

I think of custom publishers and book packagers as almost the same. They're completely professional, and you can hand your book off to them.

Book producers are more like hands-on coaches who create and manage your team. I know lots of fiction book authors who have used a book producer. When you're looking for book producers you might also compare them with author assistants.

Book packagers

Book packagers do everything except marketing and promotion. They print, format your ebook, fulfill, and distribute. This is expensive and the fees can pile up, but again, if you're using a book to enhance your speaking career, business, or promote professional services, it can be worth the investment to free yourself to concentrate on your revenue-generating business.

As with a distributor, your deal with a book packager may be exclusive and you must buy your books from them (at a discount) if you want to sell on your own website or at an event. Two well-known book packagers are Greenleaf Book Group and Baker and Taylor Publisher Services.

Book producers

Like a book packager, a book producer can manage your entire publishing project from beginning to end. They know how to do things like buy ISBNs, format books, manage metadata, and create Amazon Central author pages. They'll have access to a stable of editors and designers, web developers, and other pros, and can teach you how to use social media. They can help you with or completely take over all the production functions a literary agent or publishing house might traditionally do for you. In fact, many book production professionals used to work at traditional publishing houses. You can find them in all price ranges. Make sure to get recommendations and samples of their work, and also make sure you like each other. You'll pay thousands of dollars for this service and will work very closely together.

Author assistants

Author assistants, like book producers, come in varying levels of expertise, competence, and capabilities. I hired an author assistant to help me deal with my website and mailing list auto-responder, which is something a book producer wouldn't normally do. But my author assistant was also capable of formatting a book, helping to hire a cover designer, uploading the files to the retailers, enrolling it in promotions, creating sell sheets, and booking blog tours.

Every author assistant, like every book producer is going to be different and you should find someone you respect and get along with because you're going to be working very closely with them.

Literary agencies

Many of today's literary agents offer author-assistant services as an alternative solution for authors they don't believe they can sell. Before you sign a contract with an agent it's important to understand their role.

An agent is traditionally the individual or firm who represents your work and negotiates with publishers for the best possible advance and royalty. An agent's fee is about 15 percent of your net profit. An agent who has sold your book might offer to help you self-publish other materials to boost sales.

Beware of literary agents who say they will shop your book and if it doesn't sell to a publishing house, they will help you self-publish it. Because how much effort will they put into shopping it if they know they're going to get a fat fee from you for their assisted self-publishing service?

However, agents are often well connected with a network of very good editors, designers, ebook formatters, and publicity professionals, and have formed their own in-house publishing companies.

If the agent contacts you and says no, we **can't accept your book** in the agent role, but we have an author-assisted service, that's legit. But again, be wary of agents who **do accept your book** in the agent role and then offer the service.

26

HOW TO AVOID THE VANITY PRESS TRAP

WATCH OUT FOR VANITY AND SUBSIDY PRESSES WHO LURE YOU IN with fancy marketing and promises of literary success. I spend a lot of time helping authors extricate themselves from these companies, and sometimes we manage to do it without too much of a cash loss.

Promises, promises

These companies make a lot of promises offering basic to deluxe packages with some of them priced into the five-figures. They say they'll help you with all aspects of book development—editing, design, marketing, ebook conversion, copyright, returns programs, and distribution, and they will, maybe even competently, but for a much higher price than you need to pay.

Where's the money?

In general, vanity presses make money from selling services to you and not from selling your books. They also make a tidy profit by over-charging for printing. For example, I can get this guide, the one you're reading now, printed from Amazon for about $3 a copy, plus postage. With a vanity press, my cost per book will be over $6. In addition, they would charge me hundreds, if not thousands, for a publishing package.

The great majority of self-published authors sell fewer than 200 books, and most of those are to friends and family. The fact that these companies make a profit (Author Solutions, Inc., to the tune of about $100 million a year) speaks to the number of authors they attract and the amount of money they charge for their services.

Lots of hype

Here's how to identify vanity presses: They sell high-priced "packages." They have a large enough marketing budget that their name pops up again and again and again in ads and search engines. They use language like "your book deserves to be published," "tell the story that needs to be told," and "imagine your book on the shelf at your local bookstore." They offer add-ons that claim to get your book in front of literary agents and movie producers. This might be true, but I don't know who these agents and producers are or what they've produced.

ISBNs... again

Vanity presses often do not allow you to assign your own ISBN. This is okay if you have a partner publisher or hybrid deal with a company who is truly invested in your book's success. But a vanity press's business model is to sell you the highest-priced package they can, and they'll keep selling to you as long as they can.

When a company, and not you, owns the ISBN for your book, your book is effectively trapped with that company until they release you from their contract. Vanity presses will lock you in, but there's an out. You can retire your book and make sure the world knows it's available in a new edition by recording the previous or replaced ISBN in your ISBN record. More on that in a moment.

Naming names

Authors who do their due diligence almost always identify these companies and avoid them. But many authors are so anxious to publish that they buy the sales pitch—hook, line, and sinker. All the companies owned by Author Solutions, Inc., fall into this category (iUniverse, Author House, Trafford, Xlibris, Balboa for HayHouse, Archway for Simon and Schuster, Westbow for Thomas Nelson, and more), and many others. Do your research and avoid them. A look at the Writer Beware website will also identify predatory vanity presses (see the Writer Beware section below).

Extricating yourself

If you need to extricate yourself from a vanity press, here's what to do.

First, call them and ask them to email you all of your original files—the Adobe InDesign files for your interior and cover, the EPUB files, the PDFs, the Photoshop images, the fonts, the graphics… the whole package. Listen… you've paid for all of this, so insist upon it, okay?

Now, after you have all your files, call them to "retire" your book.

Purchase a set of ten ISBNs from Bowker. In the Bowker record for each new ISBN (print, EPUB, MOBI), indicate it replaces the old, vanity press ISBN.

In your original files (InDesign or on the PDF), replace the old ISBNs with your own and make any associated changes to the copyright page regarding the publisher, including name and logo. If there's a PCIP block for library sales, you'll need a new one or eliminate it. You should be able to outsource this, under your own management, for a few hundred dollars.

Go to your Amazon Author Central page and claim all of your books —the old editions and the new. In the first line of the description of the old book, let readers know that it has been replaced and to search for the new ISBN.

(I do this very same thing when I put out a new edition of this guide. If you look at my Amazon Author Central page you'll see that the 1st through 4th editions of this guide refer to this new 5th edition.)

It will take a while for the book systems to stop referring readers to your old book—which will show up as out of print—and direct customers to your new one. However, your old book will be available from resellers forever, which is frustrating, but there's nothing to be done about it. Be patient, do your marketing, and be happy you've reclaimed your book.

The Writer Beware watchdog site

The awesome Victoria Strauss keeps a running tab of predatory publishing companies on Writer Beware, sponsored by the Science Fiction and Fantasy Writers of America, with additional support from the Mystery Writers of America, the Horror Writers Association, and the American Society of Journalists and Authors. Thank you!

https://www.sfwa.org/other-resources/for-authors/writer-beware/

This website is beloved by all authors as it includes alerts on current scams, thumbs-down agencies and publishers lists, a list of vanity/subsidy publishers, and a lot of sensible advice for writers looking for services and freelancers.

Check these lists before you sign a contract with a self-publishing service, marketing and promotion service, literary agency, or small press. Scammy vanity presses know how to look like real publishers, and many authors are fooled to the cost of thousands of wasted dollars.

How will you distribute?

So how will you distribute your book? By uploading it to one retailer at a time, testing the market, and then expanding to a few others? Or will you launch with a bang to all the retailers at once? Have you read the reviews of the various distribution services in Part VII yet? I'm always interested in how authors choose distribution, so feel free to reach out to me to let me know. I'm easy to find online and if you're on my email list you can reply to any of my missives to let me know.

I think that *Part V, Selling Direct to Stores and Your Readers*, is going to be very interesting to you now that your book is in print, EUB, and MOBI formats. Check out how fun it can be to sell directly to retailers and your readers.

PART V

SELLING YOUR BOOK DIRECT

I have a lot of fun selling my books directly to people at events and to retailers in my area and I hope you get a chance to do this too. It's a great way to connect with your tribe online and in person. Here's what you'll learn in this part of the guide.

Selling Books from Your Website
Selling to Bookstores
Selling to Libraries
Selling at Events
Selling to Non-Bookstore Markets

27

SELLING BOOKS FROM YOUR WEBSITE

YOU CAN SELL YOUR BOOK FOR GREATER PROFIT BY SELLING books from your website using a simple e-commerce tool. Use widgets or services to do the selling for you whether you're selling a complete book, offering a beta book, selling a book by subscription, autographed books, or books bundled with products.

Easy e-commerce with WordPress Widgets

Easy e-commerce platforms like Gumroad let you directly sell your work from their store or your website using a widget. You upload your digital files (or order forms for physical objects), and the typical fee is 5 percent of sales and 25 cents per transaction for their basic service. This is a great alternative to PayPal and other complicated e-commerce systems.

Embed their sales widget on your own website to handle credit card processing and automatic digital delivery. You can choose an overlay (lightbox) that opens a payment window, or simply embed the product in your web page. Customize the colors to match your site.

Find reviews of the tools to help you sell direct in *Chapter 55, Direct Sales Tools.*

Sell digital and physical products

You can sell any kind of digital file, such as audiobooks, digital art, photography, screen savers, videos, games, music, software, presentations, courses, or e-zines.

Digital downloads are automatically fulfilled, so you can sell in your sleep. You also get the buyer's email address and can invite them to join your email newsletter for updates, bonuses, and freebies, and ask them to review your book.

You can also sell physical items like print books, coffee cups, pens, journals, T-shirts, or bundles of things. You'll get an order form when the order is placed, so make sure you're ready to send it promptly.

I've sold more autographed copies of my books than I ever thought I would, especially before the holidays.

You can use an e-commerce system like PayPal or Gumroad to sell directly like this. I prefer Gumroad. Find reviews of these and other tools in *Chapter 55, Direct Sales Tools.*

How to mail books to your customers

When you mail your books, use a Priority Mail envelope and deliver the book to your customer right away. (Charge the customer a shipping and handling charge.)

One December I made the mistake of using Media Mail to deliver autographed books purchased for holiday gifts. Exactly half of my customers did not receive their books until well after the New Year, and some didn't receive them at all. I sent out new books and received a few torn and battered original packages months later because the customers' addresses were no longer visible. I imagine that some of them ended up in the trash. I asked customers who eventually received a duplicate to gift it or donate it to their local library.

You can also send your book internationally, though obviously the shipping charges will be higher. Go ahead and offer autographed books or special editions to readers outside your country and charge them shipping. Most will buy your book from Amazon in their country, but I've sent autographed books, at the buyer's great expense, overseas to collectors and super fans.

How to send updates to your readers

If you find an error in your book, if your book needs updating often, or you're publishing a serial book, you can publish updates to the customers who bought it. This is one of the features that makes Gumroad and similar e-commerce platforms great beta-publishing tools.

How to sell your book by subscription

The subscriptions feature on Gumroad lets you set up recurring funding for your serial book or all of your latest writing, an e-zine, audio-video, training courses, private YouTube Hangouts—again, use your imagination—you can upload any kind of digital file and deliver physical goods after receiving payment and an order form. Choose to offer a monthly or annual subscription.

The idea of recurring funding is an attractive one. A company called Patreon takes it to the extreme with its platform created to provide artists a way to achieve sustainable income.

Gumroad allows you to do the same thing, but in a different format, so take a look at both. Patreon is a real commitment needing constant attention to posting blog posts and customer feedback, sales, sharing widgets, and videos.

How to use analytics

Today's online tools provide analytics so you can see how many people looked at your book versus how many bought it.

Analytics are an essential element of marketing. When you know what people look at versus what they buy, you can figure out if things are working okay or a change is needed. That change might be a new book cover, marketing copy, or pricing. When you sell direct, you can experiment endlessly. And because you own customer email addresses, you can ask them to give you some input. (Give them an incentive, like a new story or a tip sheet.) Use analytics as much as possible. Other tools I use are Google Analytics, Buffer, and Bitly. Do use Google Analytics on your website.

28

SELLING TO BOOKSTORES

JUST BECAUSE YOUR BOOK IS LISTED AS AVAILABLE DOES NOT mean bookstores and libraries will buy it. So you need to market to booksellers, specifically.

Start with your local independent bookseller. Get to know them, ask their advice, and make sure your book is up to their standards. Ditto for librarians. Your local librarian can help you get into the greater library market.

I think the best way for American authors to market to bookstores and libraries is by advertising in IBPA's catalog (at $215 and up). These mailings reach approximately 3,400 chain and independent booksellers across the US. Orders from bookstores will be made to your distributor. If you've used IngramSpark, that will be Ingram.

How to meet bookstore standards of quality

Bookstores and libraries look for a certain standard of quality in a self-published book, so make sure yours meets it. Here are some of the things they may look for.

- Professional cover and interior design
- Publishing house name and logo
- Library of Congress LCCN and PCIP block
- City and state on copyright page
- ISBN and price embedded in barcode
- No Amazon, Lulu, or other self-publishing company logos on book
- Advance praise and reviews on the cover or in the front of the book (or the back of your hardcover)

Search the web for IBPA's *Industry Standards Checklist for a Professionally Published Book* for a detailed list of content and production considerations that will make your book compete alongside those from the big publishing houses.

How to discount for bookstores

If you want brick-and-mortar bookstores to buy your book, you'll need to set the discount to 53 percent at the distribution channel and accept returns of unsold books. IngramSpark, Gatekeeper Press, and other distributors allow you to do this, but Amazon does not—they set their "expanded distribution" discount to 40 percent, which is not attractive to bookstores. So do not use Amazon to distribute to bookstores.

If you sell to your local bookstore on consignment, you can discount your book at 40 percent. Most bookstores do not buy direct from the author unless they have a close relationship with the author. Buying on consignment requires a lot of extra bookkeeping they dread. So start wooing your local bookstores now.

Most authors rightly concentrate on sales to online retailers because the great majority of books are sold online and you can set the discount to 30 percent and make a better profit. So be sure bookstore sales are a lucrative market for your book before you commit to a 53 percent discount and returns program. Don't worry. Bookstores can still special order your book if a customer requests it.

You may consider distributing your hardcover with the 53 percent discount and returns program attractive to bookstores—because who knows, maybe you'll get an Oprah endorsement—and assign the 30 percent discount to the paperback. Or, if you know you are going to get big media, you can set the discount temporarily to 53 percent and returns.

The what and why of bookstore returns

Unfortunately, your book isn't really sold until purchased by a consumer. You should think of bookstore sales as if the bookstore is borrowing your books, with money down, until they can sell it. When your unsold books are returned to the distributor, the distributor then returns them to you, at your cost.

Meanwhile, you may receive a report from your distributor that 1,000 books were sold. Don't celebrate yet. A few months later you may receive a report stating that 900 were returned. This is not an uncommon scenario, so don't make plans for all the money you see stated on the first report.

You can resell these returned books on your own site using a sales widget from Gumroad or another e-commerce provider, but many of these returned books will be damaged. You can sell "hurt" books on eBay, or as an Amazon reseller as used books in poor condition, or give them to libraries. (But only if you have an LCCN and PCIP block, and your libraries want them. Many libraries shelve donated books on their FOR SALE counter.)

What if you don't mark your book as returnable? Bookstores are very unlikely to stock it, so your title will be relegated to the special orders category. That means they will order it only upon customer request.

How can you prevent your books from being returned? By selling more of them. I know some authors who found their books were commonly stocked on the wrong shelf. This can be avoided by printing the BISAC categories, in order of relevance, on the back of your book near the barcode. Other books had covers that didn't compete or look like they belonged. There are a lot of reasons for returns, which is why it's important to consult your local bookseller before you go to print. Ask them where they'd stock your book, go to that shelf, and see if your cover fits in enough (yet stands out enough) in the genre. Ask the bookseller to evaluate the odds of book sales. Indie booksellers love selling books by local authors and are likely to help, so it can't hurt to ask.

29

SELLING TO LIBRARIES

ANALYZE THE IMPORTANCE OF THE LIBRARY MARKET FOR YOUR book by talking with your local librarian about it before you make the effort. Acquisitions librarians are understandably overwhelmed, with approximately 300,000 titles by traditional publishers released each year and independent publishers releasing at least 100,000 more than that. About 90 percent of authors I know come to realize the library isn't the best place to focus their sales efforts.

Your marketing materials to librarians should include a one-page sales sheet about the book and a one-page sheet about you. In addition, you should show them a marketing plan including how you will promote the book, and book reviews from sources they trust.

Get book reviews

A book review in *Kirkus*, *Library Journal* or *Publishers Weekly* will get the attention of librarians, which may be a reason to pay for a review. (Find more about this in *Chapter 37, How to Get Book Reviews* and in *Chapter 53, Book Review Services.*

Use IBPA's mailings service

The best way to get in front of librarians is to join the Independent Book Publishers Association (IBPA) and participate in their library-mailing program. The cost is $215 per title to reach 3,900 public libraries.

By the time you've paid for a book review and an IBPA mailing, you'll have spent over $500. Is it worth it? Only research will tell.

If you want to market to a particular library or libraries in a certain region, contact them directly. The Library of Congress website even advises working with your local librarian to get cataloging for your book. Your local librarian can help you get into the national library market.

Publish ebooks to libraries

I devour ebooks, and mostly I check them out for free on my local library website. How do self-publishers get into this market? Well, many distributors send your book to both OverDrive and bibliotecha so your book will reach the library market in both print and digital formats.

OverDrive

OverDrive is a digital distribution platform that supplies the industry's largest catalog of ebooks, audiobooks, streaming video and periodicals to 38,000 libraries, schools and retailers worldwide. OverDrive supports all major computers and devices, including iOS, Android, Chromebook and Kindle (US only). OverDrive delivers all digital media on a single platform, and offers innovations such as OverDrive Read, the breakthrough EPUB and HTML5 browser-based reading experience, and Read-Along eBooks. Founded in 1986, OverDrive is based in Cleveland, Ohio, and is owned by Tokyo-based Rakuten. (Rakuten also owns Kobo, which powers Walmart eBooks.)

bibliotheca

bibliotheca [with a lower-case "b"] distributes to 300,000 libraries in 70 countries. Their digital platform features content from over 1,000 publishers and is available through almost 3,000 libraries.

How libraries purchase ebooks

Libraries can purchase ebooks permanently, or via a limited period, or for a certain number of checkouts, also called "per use." An examination of these models may help you choose an ebook aggregator based on the availability of these options.

- One Copy, One User (OCOU)
- Cost Per Checkout (CPC)
- Per Use

One Copy, One User (OCOU)

Most public libraries lend ebooks the same way they lend physical books. Once the book is checked out, it is no longer available for others until it is returned. This checkout practice is referred to as "One Copy, One User" (OCOU). If a library wants to lend to more than one person at a time, they must purchase each book copy separately, just as they would for physical copies.

When selling to libraries with the OCOU model, you'll want to price your ebook high.

. . .

Cost Per Checkout (CPC)

Cost Per Checkout (CPC) allows libraries access to the same title for more than one user. Instead of a fixed price, libraries are granted access to a title and then pay per each loan of the ebook. For each checkout through CPC, the author is paid 1/10 the price of a full purchase, however, CPC allows an unlimited amount of people to check out a library's ebook at any given time. This allows librarians to take risks on which books to include in their system which may help expose authors to new readers.

When selling to libraries with the CPC model, you'll want to price your ebook low.

Per-Use

The per-use purchase option allows librarians to meet a short-term demand for a popular title without having to overburden their budgets or turn patrons away if the copies in their permanent collection are already borrowed.

The library may purchase your book for a certain number of days or for a certain number of checkouts.

If your book is sold to the library at 10 percent of the list price and your list price is $10 then you are paid $1.00.

Draft2Digital

When you choose Draft2Digital as your distribution service your book will automatically be available to libraries with the CPC model where available, though you can turn off this option.

Draft2Digital's Marketing Director Kevin Tumlinson says their company is finding that the CPC model has more value for authors in both sales and discoverability. You can listen to my discussion with Tumlinson on the Author Friendly Podcast at www.authorfriendly.com.

. . .

Smashwords

Smashwords offers Library Direct, a program that automatically distributes their top-selling books to libraries. Find out how to use Smashwords to market to libraries in Episode 6 of their Smart Author Podcast.

Listen to my discussion with Smashwords founder Mark Coker on the Author Friendly Podcast at www.authorfriendly.com.

Using the same distributor as for print

Librarians pay a lot of attention to book reviews, but ebooks don't get reviews unless you've used the same service to distribute your print version. That way, the review pertains to both formats. IngramSpark and Draft2Digital are good options for publishing in both formats. You may also want to look at StreetLib and PublishDrive as well as the other ebook aggregators listed in the *Consumer's Guide*.

Because services provided by book distribution companies change so often I've created a web book version of the *Consumer's Guide* found in Part VII. Subscribe to get access, updates, and other reader perks. Find them here:

www.selfpubbootcamp.com/readers

The SELF-e program

SELF-e is a collaboration between *Library Journal* and a company called BiblioBoard. If accepted, your book will be included in a "module" with other books made available to libraries from time to time.

There's no cost to participate, and you make no money. So think of SELF-e as a marketing investment. They state that "SELF-e is a marketing and discovery service aimed at helping authors build an audience of readers." So, if you've got a book with a message, and you want to get the word out, or if you want to get the word out about your book, this may help.

Don't use the Amazon ISBN to get into libraries

Many authors have told me they used Amazon ISBNs to make their book available to libraries. But the Amazon ISBN merely gets your book into the Baker and Taylor catalog. Amazon's important, but buy your own ISBNs. You cannot apply for an LCCN and a PCIP block unless you do.

About LCCNs and PCIP blocks

What are LCCNs and PCIPs and why do you need them? First, let's decode the alphabet soup:

- LoC = Library of Congress
- PCN=Preassigned Control Number
- LCCN=Library of Congress Control Number
- CIP=Cataloging in Publication data
- PCIP= Publisher's Cataloging in Publication data
- MARC=MAchine Readable Cataloging.

Why self-publishers need an LCCN and PCIP

In the US and some other countries an LCCN and CIP block indicates a measure of professional standards. This is one of the things libraries and bookstores look for when judging your book. Self-publishers are not eligible for a CIP, which is why the PCIP program started.

The PCIP data block is used by librarians to file your book on the right shelves. You need to have purchased a block of at least 10 ISBNs to get a PCIP data block. When you buy 10 or more ISBNs you'll get a publisher number, which will be embedded in all the ISBNs. If you think you're going to publish more than three books, or publish multiple editions (translations, hardcover, large print), you should buy 100 ISBNs.

Requirements in the US

Here are the requirements in the US.

- The PCN program is for print books in the US only.
- You must apply in advance of publication.
- You must list a US place of publication on the title or copyright page in the format: City, State.
- You must purchase a block of ten or more ISBNs from Bowker, assigned to your publishing house. (A book with a free Amazon ISBN is not eligible.) During the application process, you'll need to enter your publisher identifier number (the third part of your ISBN).

How to get them

In the US, apply for a free LCCN from the Library of Congress (LoC). There is no barrier to entry.

To get your PCIP data block you'll pay a cataloger who is certified by the LoC. But first you'll need an LCCN and the publisher number you were assigned when you bought your ISBNs. (Find out how to identify your publisher number in *Chapter 12: All About ISBNs*.) Getting an LCCN only takes hours or a couple of days.

Now choose a cataloger. In his excellent reference guide titled, *Register Your Book: The Essential Guide to ISBNs, Barcodes, Copyright, and LCCNs*, author David Wogahn recommends the following agencies, all which charge around $160: Cassidy Cataloguing, The Donahue Group, Five Rainbows, and Quality Books.

You'll receive your PCIP data block in a week or two. Paste it exactly as is on your copyright page. It may have strange capitalization and other characteristics that look like flaws, but you must not change anything about your PCIP data block.

Do you also need a MARC record?

If you really want to push your book to libraries then get a MARC record in addition to your PCIP block. Some of the catalogers listed above provide them as an add-on for as low as $20.

A MARC record is code read by machines, not humans, to make it easier for librarians to catalog your book. This may make your book more attractive to librarians and get your book into the library system, and to patrons, faster.

With a MARC record you'll get a listing in WorldCat, the world's largest online library catalog. Things like your buy links and Goodreads reviews will appear here. You might also get a listing in SkyRiver, a smaller database used by some libraries.

Authors outside of the US

Do a web search on *CIP Block yourcountry* to find out how to get a CIP block or equivalent. In the UK it's the Cataloguing-in-Publication (CIP) Programme. In Australia the Prepublication Data Service has been retired and now they use a cataloguing statement instead of a CIP block. In New Zealand CIP blocks are free as are ISBNs.

If you're confused about the necessity of cataloguing in your country, ask your local librarian or bookseller. Also look at the copyright page of books published in your country as a model for professional standards.

A good reference guide

Purchase David Wogahn's guide, *Register Your Book: The Essential Guide to ISBNs, Barcodes, Copyright, and LCCNs*, for a lot more information about the workings of the US Library system, along with details about ISBNs, barcodes, and copyright.

30

SELLING AT EVENTS

B<small>ACK-OF-ROOM SALES ARE DIRECT SALES TO A GROUP YOU ARE</small> speaking to. This can be a great way to make money. Here's my success story about back-of-room sales, as an example.

American Borders is the story of my solo journey around the US test-riding a cranky Russian motorcycle for the American specialty motorcycle market.

My book launch plan included a tour with the *Cycle World International Motorcycle Shows*. I spoke on the main stage four times a day for thirty minutes in exchange for a free booth where I could sell my books. That same booth cost other vendors a few thousand dollars each.

At the show, the motorcycle dealer who sold the brand of motorcycle featured in my story rolled one of their bikes onto the stage during my talks. They also sold my books from their booth.

The shows were in November and December, so Christmas was coming up. I priced it at $20, including tax, and people tossed $20 bills at me all day long. The end of the day was especially profitable, as their leftover money was burning holes in their pockets and they became ever more desperate to find holiday gifts.

These people came to the motorcycle show to look at new bikes and to buy, buy, buy. They bought boots and helmets, earplugs and key chains, sunglasses and scarves, jackets and vests and gloves and socks, and every little motorcycling-related gadget they could find. It was loud with announcements and demonstrations and people laughing and sloshing beer, and I autographed until my hand was cramped. I made about $4,000 a weekend. After the first event, I recruited my dad to help me handle the line and the cash box.

The big motorcycle show didn't pay me to speak, but you see that it was a high-value opportunity nonetheless. So don't be afraid to negotiate with event organizers. There is no standard rule. Organizers may agree to buy a certain number of books at a reduced rate or full cost. They might pay for travel expenses, or a speaker fee or stipend, depending on their budget, your credibility, even their level of desperation to fill speaking slots. I knew I had one group at the limit of their budget when they asked if I could stay in the organizer's guest room instead of a hotel.

In San Francisco I spoke at a women's motorcycling event held at a motorcycle-gear shop. I sold all the books I brought and took orders for more. I had also brought copies of several women-travel themed anthologies that included my stories (as a contributing author I was able to buy them at 50 percent of cover price) and I sold all of those too. This is only one reason contributing to anthologies is a great idea.

What I had was a niche book in front of the right audience at the right time.

Today I have saturated the lucrative motorcycle market, yet I still struggle to reach the general market. My plans are to change the cover and title to make it seem less motorcycle-centric and more the travel and adventure story it is, to attract readers who liked *Wild* or *Eat Pray Love*. Stay tuned for that.

Meanwhile, this self-publishing book sells very well at writing conferences and whenever I speak to authors. But I haven't experienced anything like the frenzy of that first *American Borders* launch. I will work to recreate it with my next adventure book. Fingers crossed.

What is your niche? Who is going to go crazy for your book? Can you make yourself useful to a group, an organization, or a club? Can you put yourself in a place that whips people into a frenzy for products and experiences?

31

SELLING TO NON-BOOKSTORE MARKETS

SALES OUTSIDE OF THE BOOKSTORE AND LIBRARY MARKET, SUCH as in catalogs and stores that are not bookstores, are called "special sales."

Retail stores

Around October I start to ask motorcycle dealers and gear shops if they'd like to carry my book on consignment for 40 percent of the sales price. (That's 60 percent for me.) I let them know that I'll take any unsold books back. Even if they say no I leave them with an autographed book and a card with my phone number and email address. Many call back to order a dozen or more. In more than one case, after realizing I have a large social media following, they have asked me to speak at the store. Retailers sell a lot more than books when people gather in their shop for events.

I know many authors who are very successful selling on consignment to non-bookstore retailers. One with a New Age title, another with an alternative medicine book, a cookbook author, and one with a gardening book make a significant amount of money with these kinds of sales.

Remote events

It's also possible to sell at shows, conferences, and events you are not able to attend. For example, I have motorcycle travel author friends in Europe and they've sold my books for me at motorcycle shows there. Since I use IngramSpark, I can print the books in the country where the event is being held, paying local postage.

At almost every kind of conference or trade show, someone is in charge of selling books. You might be surprised to know how open they are to carrying yours. (These are the kinds of contacts you'll find on LinkedIn and Twitter rather than Facebook.)

Catalogs

There's a catalog for everything. Whether you write about trolls and fairies, gardening, nature, women's issues, health and beauty, or fill-in-the-blank, you can find one. I sell my motorcycle travel book in several motorcycle-gear catalogs.

Big store sales

Wouldn't it be great if you could sell thousands of books to a big company like Walmart or Costco? It's possible! If you aspire to this, make sure to prepare a very professional proposal for them and offer a whopping discount for buying thousands of books. Look at offset printing instead of POD to lower costs.

For example, Sonia Marsh sold her travel anthology *My Gutsy Story* to Costco. Read her story about how she made it happen at http://bit.ly/sonia-costco.

Special sales is a big job and not for everyone. If you're interested, you'll need Brian Judd's 387-page book titled *How to Make Real Money Selling Books*. It's the best resource for those of you who think you may be able to sell lots of books to special markets.

How will you sell?

By now you might be as excited to sell direct as I am. I love developing one-on-one relationships with my readers and with store owners in my area.

Don't forget to revisit your business plan and incorporate all your thoughts and strategies around selling direct. You may want to create a spreadsheet with the names of stores that might carry your book, their contact information, and ideas for pitching them.

That's it for this part of the guide. Next is *Part VI, Book Marketing and Promotion*. You started your book marketing activities in the very first part of this guide with foundational activities like connecting with your readers and creating a beta team of superfans.

PART VI

BOOK MARKETING AND PROMOTION

So your book is ready to be published. Or is it? Most authors start this process too late, but if you started the book marketing process way back in *Chapter 2, The Importance of Beta Publishing*, you *are* ready. It's time to kick your beta team into gear, because you don't want to do this alone. Here's what you'll learn:

Marketing and Promotion Basics
Advertising and Giveaways
Your Website and Blog
Social Media Marketing
Metadata and Discovery
How to Get Book Reviews
Your Book Launch

32

MARKETING AND PROMOTION BASICS

THESE DAYS MARKETING AND PROMOTION IS LARGELY WEB-BASED, and traditional marketing tools like press releases are simply no longer as effective as they used to be. That's not to say traditional media is dead. Your readers watch news, listen to the radio, and read daily and weekly newsletters. In this chapter, I hope to help you understand how marketing and promotion works for book authors today.

Can you hire it out?

For the indie author, affordable and effective professional marketing and publicity are nearly impossible to find for a reasonable price.

Nobody can guarantee which publication, blog, radio, or TV show will review your book or interview you. Still, a dedicated publicist can customize the PR (public relations) campaign and improve the odds of you getting picked up by media.

Traditional PR pros charge $1,500–$5,000 and up per month for a three-month minimum. That's because they practically have to become "you." They have to read your book, research the market, know you and your history and reason for writing the book. They use relationships they've cultivated for years to get you in a publication or the media. They work hard, and still, results are not guaranteed. So, unless you've got a lot of money to throw at this, you'll need to do a lot of this yourself.

The different kinds of PR professionals

There are many kinds of PR professionals. Many are good. Many will, to put it bluntly, rip you off. That kind of PR pro will take anybody's money to send out cookie-cutter emails and press releases. They don't even read the book.

The kind you want to hire will have a vetting process. They don't take just anybody because they know they can't do a good job if the client doesn't have the skills, product, or motivation to work with them. However, they can be very expensive.

There are also PR coaches. These people can coach you through your social media activities, your email newsletter, and help you polish the media page on your website. Most authors are better off with marketing and PR coaching.

Make sure they're expert in your genre

If you write in a particular genre, you should know what publications and prominent blogs are likely to be interested in your book and your story. So use your existing relationships or start cultivating them now. Once you have a few books in the market, you might be able to justify the expense of hiring a PR pro.

If you do spend money on marketing tools and professionals to help you set up systems, you will still have to do plenty of follow-up on your own. In other words, you cannot expect to hire this process out and not participate.

For example, you can hire people to set up your social media sites—banners and the first few posts for three or four of the sites—for about $500. But then you'll need to take the ball and run with it.

You can hire someone to set up your website and blog. But then you need to write regular blog posts, keep your calendar current, and update your media page regularly.

You can buy templates for media pages, book launch activities, and blog post ideas, but you still have to write and update these pages.

Nobody can be you but you

The bottom line is that nobody can be you but you, and no matter how much money you throw at a marketing service, you're still going to have to get involved. Readers want to connect with you, and not someone you've hired.

Hire an author assistant?

An experienced virtual or author assistant can help you monitor and maintain your social media presence, draft blog posts, and organize blog tours. They can help book webinars and podcasts, update your Amazon Author Central page, and complete your Bowker ISBN records. They can make calls on your behalf, draft emails, mail books, book speeches, monitor book launches, and do research and fact-finding.

Author assistants are awesome. Before you hire an assistant, request a detailed plan that includes the specific projects that they consider part of the job, the timeline for delivering on these projects, what you as the author are expected to provide, and the process by which your helper will keep you updated on their progress. Don't forget to ask for references.

Your email marketing newsletter

Your email list is your most important marketing asset and your newsletter is your most important marketing tool. With it, you get direct access to readers who are interested in you, whether they randomly found your website, were recommended by a friend, met you at a conference, or read about you in a magazine. Make sure to put an email signup form on your web pages as well as a pop-up. You may find them irritating but studies show they work.

Note: Don't just add people to your list. It's illegal. They must "opt in" to getting your missives.

Find reviews of email marketing tools in *Chapter 58, Email Marketing Tools and Services*. Some, like MailChimp, offer a free version with a limited number of subscribers and limited functionality. Others, like ConvertKit, offer a few weeks for free so you can play with it. No matter what tool you use, it's easy to place a sign-up form on your website and blog.

List vs visual flow

I switched from MailChimp to ConvertKit because of its visual flow and the ease of creating autoresponders and emails for various interest groups. The visual flow makes it particularly attractive to creators who think visually. ConvertKit is priced a bit higher than MailChimp but I think their system of tags, broadcasts, sequences, and autoresponders does a much better job of helping me communicate with my readers.

Landing pages

Many newsletter tools also create landing pages for you, so you can entice readers to sign up without using expensive landing page software like LeadPages. So if you don't have a WordPress site with a premium theme that provides landing pages (like Thrive Themes, which I use), you can use the newsletter tool to create a landing page for each of your books and any special offers you may have.

How often?

You may hear advice that you should send an email update to your readers at least once a month, but you'll have to test this out and see what works for you. One author I know says his readers get over-whelmed with once-a-month emails and start to unsubscribe. So he sends very long emails with lots of photos once every two months, and that seems to make them happy.

Another author tells me that once a week doesn't seem like enough for her readers. So she writes very short posts and tips with both original content and updates on her talks, social media posts, and YouTube-channel uploads.

The ethical bribe

To encourage readers to sign up for your email list, promise them something they need or want. This "ethical bribe" can be a story, a how-to, a tip sheet, a video, videos of kittens… Only you know what will tempt your audience.

Authors who write series often make their first book permanently free (permafree) and sell the rest of their series.

Writing your newsletter

What do you say in an email newsletter? Send them exactly what they signed up for, to start, along with a welcome message. Ask them a question. My most successful email blasts have been interactive. I've asked them to tell me about their current writing project, or what's their most burning question about self-publishing or, for my motorcy-cle-adventure-travel newsletter, to tell me about their dream trip and dream motorcycle. I get the most awesome answers.

If you're a fiction author, you might ask your readers what they're reading now, what they've reviewed on Amazon, or who's their favorite author in a certain genre or of all time. This will give you some great clues about what to write in your next newsletter.

You can also invite them to join you on social media to discuss a certain topic, or to join a reading group on a site like Goodreads or LibraryThing.

Imagine being in a room with all of the writers in your genre and the readers who love you. What are you all excited about? What will you talk about? Simply start a conversation.

Above all, be yourself, and be generous and genuine. It's as simple as that.

Your online press kit

Make sure your website includes a press or media page. This is where reporters, podcast interviewers, bloggers, and other media can find the materials they need when writing about you.

Provide them with high-resolution author photos and your book cover suitable for print media as well as lower-resolution photos for the web.

Also provide links to all the media that have interviewed you or published your articles and stories. This is social proof and it also helps the media ask new questions.

Elements of a media kit can include the following:

- Press release
- Contact information
- Overview and summary (synopsis)
- Fact sheet
- Sell sheet

- Speaker information
- Cover art in various resolutions for digital delivery and print
- Sample pages or excerpt
- Book reviews
- Author photos in various resolutions for digital delivery and print
- Video book trailer
- Interview questions
- Links to interviews
- Links to stories and articles you've penned
- Download link to the full media kit

Check out the media kit for a book my friend Allan Karl wrote, *FORKS: A Quest for Culture, Cuisine, and Connection.* I think he's got it nailed. Here's the link:

www.forksthebook.com

Press releases

Many press release distribution services promise distribution to national and international media outlets but who are you reaching, really? Press releases have to be incredibly well written, titillating, topical (automotive, gardening, politics, etc.) or timely (tied to a major news event) to get noticed. Journalists are busy, newsrooms are virtual, and mailboxes are full of spam, so there's no guarantee your story will be picked up. As a former producer at CBS and NBC explains:

"Newsrooms around the world work the same, every reporter typically has access to various newswires that are syndicated by the news organizations, like AP, Reuters, CNN, TV affiliate feeds, local newswires, etc. These different newswires inside the newsroom are all vetted sources for news. Reporters know when they review these different AP or Reuters stories that they are written by journalists. It's different with commercial newswires. Reporters know these press releases are written by publicists–not journalists. It's another reason why many newsrooms don't even provide access to these PR newswires. In a world where information needs to curated, newsroom leaders frequently choose the option to eliminate this PR feed."

If you decide to put out a press release, and I think you should as it helps raise your online profile (your SEO), make sure it's well-crafted, try to make it newsworthy (even if you simply link your book with a holiday or other calendar event).

Think creatively. You might hire a magazine editor or well-known personality in the field you're writing about to send emails to their contacts. The email can have all the information a press release has in it but crafted as a personal note. For example, I hired a retired motor-cycle magazine editor to send out an email to her peers about my new book on motorcycle travel. You can bet those editors clicked on her email and I know they would have completely ignored an email from me, an unknown, and certainly, they would have ignored a PR service. As a result, news of my book was included in every major motorcycle magazine in the country, and it also reached a lot of the international motorcycle publications.

Professional organizations

Many writers work in isolation, so joining a professional organization can provide you with an energizing boost. You'll also find sponsoring organizations and recommendations from others in the community, which will help you avoid spending too much money on services that don't work.

Consider joining a national or international organization and a local one that offers face-to-face meetings and marketing opportunities. You may not need to be a member to attend their events. Search for "independent publishers associations" in your area.

Meetup offers lots of writing, reading, and social groups for authors, not to mention groups in business or social niches. I run a Meetup group for self-publishers in my city. If there's not a group in your area, consider starting one.

Find reviews of organizations in *Chapter 62, Professional Organizations.*

Trade organizations

You may benefit from participating in trade organizations related to your topic. Funded by dues, they have money to spend on speakers to appear at their events and conferences.

Fiction authors: Does your main character belong to an organization or have a related special interest?

Some examples of trade organizations are The Fragrance Foundation, Organic Trade Association, International Housewares Association, Motorcycle Industry Council, Adventure Travel Trade Association, and The United States Association of Professional Investigators. These are a very few of the thousands of trade organizations you might mine for publicity opportunities.

Amazon's promotional tools

Amazon is more popular than Google as the search engine of choice for product search. Make no mistake, your book is a product, and when people are ready to buy, most flock to Amazon.

Marketing to Amazon customers requires that you think of it as a search engine and not a bookstore. To Amazon, the customer is king, and their biggest goal is to make it as easy as possible for customers to buy what they are looking for with the least possible friction. Amazon provides lots of how-to pages to make it easy for their vendors—that's you!—to succeed in sales.

Start with good metadata so your book can be discovered on Amazon (and everywhere else). Metadata is very, very important as the building block to your marketing success. Find out more about it in *Chapter 36, Metadata and Discovery.*

Amazon Author Central

The first thing to do as soon as your book is published is to claim your Author Central page. Author Central is your author homepage in the world's biggest bookstore. Along with your bio, you can add multimedia, blog feeds, a Twitter feed, and events. You'll claim your book and edit or correct Amazon's list of your books. A sales tab lets you track your book sales over time, you can check your current Amazon ranking, and all your reviews are collected on one page.

Populate your Author Central pages in as many countries as you can. I created a page for the US, Canada, the UK, India, Australia, and a bunch of European countries, for those residents who can read in English. I know which ones are important because I look at Google Analytics on my web pages and can see I have a lot of fans in Sweden, Norway, Germany, and Spain. (See more about Google Analytics in *Chapter 34, Your Website and Blog.*)

Behind the scenes, you can look at sales data, make corrections to book data, link multiple editions, remove books, and even report copyright infringement, to name a few functions.

Amazon KDP Select

Your participation in the exclusive KDP Select program gives you access to Amazon Kindle marketing programs, but at a price—you give up the ability to sell anywhere else, even your website.

KDP requires you sell your ebook exclusively in the Amazon Kindle store for ninety days. It will keep automatically renewing unless you opt out through the KDP website beforehand. Many authors make the mistake of letting this go on and on forever.

There are pros and cons to going exclusive, such as the inability to give away books or distribute to the other major retailers. So don't click the "Enter KDP Select" button seems to appear on every screen. If you're going to use KDP Select, use it consciously, and make it part of your book launch plan. Study the marketing tools and figure out if it seems worthwhile to you.

Amazon customer reviews

Ask beta readers (and other fans) to post reviews on publication date. And don't forget to ask the people who have downloaded your book for free to post a review. Put this in the back matter of your book as well as emailing them gentle reminders.

Goodreads

Goodreads, which is owned by Amazon, is the largest social network for readers to discuss and recommend books.

An alternative to Goodreads is LibraryThing, which many authors prefer because it's noncommercial, and they offer a Member Giveaways program to find early readers and reviewers. Other social networks for readers include Bookstr, Book Glutton, Bookish, Readernaut, and weRead. You can be active on these sites and even buy ads for your book, budget allowing.

Amazon Associates

Earn a commission on each sale of books or products by registering to become an Amazon Associate. When someone clicks your link, it will credit you a few pennies for their purchase. This can add up. All the

Amazon links in this guide use my affiliate link. Smashwords and other vendors also offer affiliate programs.

So You'd Like to. . . guides

Write a "So You'd Like to…" how-to article in your niche topic. These are a lot like newspaper articles, but are longer lived and consulted much more frequently. Consider an excerpt from your non-fiction book.

Look Inside!

As soon as your book is published on Amazon, sign it up for the *Look Inside!* feature. It has a lot of advantages.

When customers search for books on Amazon, the search engine processes the actual words from inside your book, not just the metadata (author, title, and keywords supplied by the publisher). For matches inside the book, they also display a short excerpt and links to the page where the query matched.

When you enroll in the program you'll get a lot more exposure when the words inside your book match keywords readers are searching for, even if you haven't listed them in your book description.

Look Inside! also allows Amazon customers to browse your book much as they would if they found it in a brick-and-mortar bookstore.

Pages from the main body of the book, beginning with chapter 1 and ending with the final chapter, count towards the percent viewable limits. Front matter and back matter are not included in this percentage. You can increase the percentage by sending an email to insidethe-book-submission@amazon.com with this information:

- Publisher Name and the percentage desired, or
- ISBN and the desired percentage for that particular ISBN.

The sample is selected automatically and you can decrease or increase the percentage of pages revealed from between 10 percent and 80 percent for paperbacks. For ebooks, it's between 5 percent and 45 percent.

Sign in to your Amazon author account and visit the <u>Look Inside the Book program</u> for details.

33

ADVERTISING AND GIVEAWAYS

MANY AUTHORS USE FACEBOOK AND AMAZON ADS TO SELL books. A Facebook ad can send customers to your book sales page or it can tempt readers to sign up for your email list with a free ebook or giveaway. Amazon ads send readers directly to the Amazon buy page for your book.

You can also reach book buyers in bookstores, libraries, and non-book retail stores with ads in cooperative mailings.

Finally, you can grow your readership by using a giveaway site like BookBub or Prolific Works.

———

Advertising

You can advertise using Facebook Ads, Amazon Ads, and ads in catalog mailings to bookstores and libraries. Let's take a look at these different kinds of ads.

. . .

Facebook Ads

I think Facebook Ads are a great way to grow your email list, do market research for your book, and sell ebooks.

Facebook also owns Instagram, and if that's your platform of choice you may want to advertise using Instagram Ads using photos, videos, carousels, and Instagram Stories ads.

You've probably seen a lot of expensive marketing trainings around using these ads and wondered if they are worth it. I don't know. Their documentation is pretty thorough and it is cheap, easy, and fun to experiment with creating ads that target a very narrow audience. Take a look at their inspiration page and try them out before investing in training.

You can run ads across all four of Facebook's platforms: Facebook, Instagram, Audience Network and Messenger by creating a single campaign, reaching people on their favorite apps and websites.

One thing I like about Facebook ads is the "Lookalike" audiences. You'll find out a lot about your audience when you experiment with Facebook ads and use their analytics to see who's clicking.

Amazon Advertising

Use Amazon Ads to feature your titles next to similar books and authors, feature new releases to drive sales as soon as they publish, and target readers by keyword, product, or interest, including related genres, titles, and authors.

Login to your KDP account and click 'Promote and Advertise' next to the KDP title you want to promote. From here you can enroll in KDP Select and run a price promotion. (Be careful, here This makes your book exclusive to Amazon for 90 days.)

Set the budget, targeting, and timing of your campaign, and you pay only when customers click your ads. Choose from two campaign types:

1. **Sponsored Products Ads** deliver relevant ads in search results based on customer keyword searches. When clicked, ads send shoppers to your book's detail page. Ads appear below search results and below the fold on product detail pages.
2. **Product Display Ads** deliver interest or product-targeted ads to customers on detail pages and Kindle readers where eligible. When clicked, the ad redirects shoppers directly to your book's detail page. Ads appear on related product detail pages and on Kindle reader screensaver and home screens.

Amazon Advertising offers free webinars, case studies, and a learning console to get you started. You can also subscribe to their blog.

Catalog mailings

There are a couple of well-respected organizations that can get your book included in cooperative catalogs that advertise to book buyers.

If you're a member of the Independent Book Publishers Association (IBPA) you can advertise in their *Books for Review* catalog mailed quarterly to about 3000 reviewers, journalists, and bloggers across the United States.

Other IBPA bookstore and library mailings ($200-$500 est) will get your book in front of booksellers, libraries, and university bookstores. See their page for details.

Read more about the IBPA in *Chapter 62, Professional Organizations.*

Amy Collins of New Shelves also organizes catalog mailings to bookstores, libraries, and retail markets like gift shops and boutiques, big-box stores, and airport stores.

If you need help with ads and campaigns, New Shelves can help you with a customized store database and sales materials, sales outreach email and cover letter, follow-up coaching and one hour of training to help get your book sold into the marketplace. Most campaigns cost between $500–$1000.

Giveaways

Use BookBub and Prolific Works to advertise your discounted book to an eager audience these companies reach with their targeted mailings.

BookBub

BookBub is a free service for readers that helps them discover books the editorial staff thinks they'll love through unbeatable deals, hand-picked recommendations, and updates from their favorite authors.

Many self-published authors are rejected for reasons ranging from poorly produced books with inappropriate covers and unprofessional interior layout to not enough reviews. So make sure your book is produced to professional standards (see IBPA's checklist) and get those reviews.

Your book will need to be available on Amazon Kindle, B&N, Apple iBooks, and others. Readers choose the types they'd like to get notified about—with categories ranging from mysteries to romance to cookbooks—and BookBub sends them great deals in those genres so you are sure to hit your target market.

Featured Deals cost from a bit under $100 to above $500 depending on genre and the deal ($0-$3+) you're offering. See their chart.

Prolific Works

Prolific Works (formerly InstaFreebie) doesn't have a gatekeeper like BookBub, and is therefore more accessible to self-published authors. Connect with new readers and fans through your sneak peeks, advance previews, special giveaways, and/or group giveaways of your free ebook to readers.

Their free service offers unlimited giveaways and distribution at no cost for completed books or ARCs for review. You can set limits and expiration dates for giveaways, add DRM if you want (though I advise against it), and your books are eligible for additional promotions to readers.

For $20/mo you can add MailChimp integration, custom giveaways, and tracking. For $50/mo you'll get personalized branding.

Group giveaways is a great way to partner with other authors in your genre and expand your audience.

Your readers get your books on their reader app instantly with easy sideloading via email or the Prolific Works app.

Prolific Works includes a double opt-in process for your readers.

34

YOUR WEBSITE AND BLOG

YOUR WEBSITE IS A STOREFRONT AND A SCRAPBOOK, A PLACE TO attract, inform, connect, collect, and communicate. Your website is "You-Central." But the most important function of your website is to win a personal connection with readers by getting them to hand over their email address. When they give you their email address, they have given you permission to contact them directly. So whatever you put on your website, make sure to place your email newsletter signup form in a prominent place on each page. Website visitors are tired of being sold to, so entice them with an "ethical bribe." This could be a free story, tip sheet, or anything you can think of that has informational or entertainment value to your audience. Make it good and make it irresistible!

Now, here's all the technical stuff you need to know to take the mystery out of creating a website and blog.

Websites: Easy or geeky?

When you're first deciding on creating or redesigning your website, you may become overwhelmed with choices. Most authors use Word-

Press. Others use SquareSpace (great if you're selling stuff, more than books), or Wix, or Weebly, which are two popular freemium choices I see authors using badly. But I'd like to recommend just three platforms: WordPress, SquareSpace, or PubSite.

WordPress

WordPress is easy, open source, and the world's most popular website builder. There are thousands of themes and plugins for it and thousands and thousands of web pros to help you with it. WordPress "plug-ins" extend the platform to create communities, stores, and anything you want to do on the web.

SquareSpace

Though it's easy to sell things (physical and digital) using WordPress, SquareSpace was especially built for selling things, so take a look at that, too.

PubSite

But if you're a total newbie and intimidated by the web, or you only need a simple author page and no other web presence, then PubSite may be your answer. It costs $19.99/mo and is plug-and-play.

If you are an author and only an author, PubSite makes it very simple. And don't worry, you can migrate to WordPress or SquareSpace later.

Is this confusing? Yes! Do you want to learn more about it, including how to do it yourself, integrating your email marketing newsletter and BUY buttons for your books? I have a course for that! Take a look.

www.selfpubbootcampcourses.com

Premium Themes

I particularly recommend using WordPress with GoDaddy hosting and adding the themes and tools available as you get to know WordPress better. I especially recommend the Thrive Themes membership. Thrive Themes is specifically designed to convert website visitors into subscribers. And their page builder, lead pages, email signup forms, everything, is awesome. The difference is they focus on conversion. That is, turning website visitors into subscribers.

You don't need to start with a premium theme at first, though. Get acquainted with WordPress using one of the free themes (templates) that comes with your hosting package (such as the GoDaddy hosting I recommended). Keep it simple and get familiar with WordPress as you advance in your publishing journey. Then, when you're comfortable, consider the premium themes like the Thrive Themes membership.

WARNING: You'll see a lot of people recommending BlueHost. Why? Because they offer a BIG commission to affiliates. The company used to have a good reputation, but it was purchased and absorbed by the Endurance International Group and is no longer the brand many admired.

Find website building tool reviews in *Chapter 57, Website and Blog Tools.*

Choosing a domain name

The first order of business when you're setting up your website is to buy a domain name. I recommend using the domain name and hosting package by GoDaddy. GoDaddy's Basic WordPress Hosting is often on sale for only $1/month when you purchase several years of hosting, and you should.

Your domain name is a part of your brand, so consider it carefully. You should not only buy your name (and your pen name and nicknames), but the name of your book and the name of your publishing house. You can "redirect" or "forward" all those domain names to your main website, which is, ideally, your author name.

If your name is difficult to spell, try to buy the common misspellings as well, and forward those domains to your main site.

If you have a common name, it is likely to be taken. If not, grab it now and choose .com—don't bother with .net and .org or .biz or .tv or any of the other tags if you can get a .com tag. If you cannot get a .com tag for your author name, consider adding your middle initial (carlasking.com) or even append the word "author" or "writer" to your name (such as carlakingauthor.com). If you write for a niche market, you might use a descriptive word in your name (carlakingmotorcycles.com) and if you have a great nickname, use it (missadventuring.com).

Here are tips for selecting and managing domain names:

- Make a list of all the domain names you might need and see if they're available. I like to use GoDaddy.
- Buy them. GoDaddy sells domain names cheaply and offers bulk discounts. They also offer cheap WordPress hosting and an email service. It's great to handle everything in one place. TIP: When you purchase WordPress hosting you get a free domain name, so purchase the hosting first.
- Set your main website to renew automatically so you don't lose your domain name when it expires.
- Purchase your most important domain names for the maximum number of years possible instead of one or two years. The price goes down and search engines give more weight to domains that have committed to a longer term.
- Redirect, or forward, all the names you buy to your main website.

Landing pages

If you don't have a website yet, consider using a single landing page for your site so you can collect email addresses.

Sometimes it makes sense to add a landing page for your book as well as a website for your author presence. A landing page contains no distractions. It offers no menu items and no links other than sales links to your book. It's a single-purpose, one-page site whose only job is to sell the book.

You can create a landing page inside your WordPress site or purchase a landing page plugin, but I recommend Thrive Themes for building websites and landing pages. See their Beginner's Guide to Landing Pages.

Landing pages are also awesome for presenting your "ethical bribe" or giveaway, distraction free, so it compels visitors to give you their email addresses.

The structure of an author website

Just like a house, a website should start with a solid and proven foundation and architecture. Web professionals who structure large sites for corporations are called information architects. But your site needn't be complex. You can build a basic site and add to it later. Start with these standard foundational pages.

HOME | ABOUT | BOOKS | BLOG | MEDIA | CONTACT

Many authors nest the MEDIA in a subheading under ABOUT, and a REVIEWS page under BOOKS. Do use the word "books" instead of "book." It may even help to motivate you!

Too many authors, tiring of these standard headings, get creative with their page titles. As much as we love being creative writers, please resist the urge to get cute with headings. Visitors, especially reviewers and journalists, become impatient and will click away if they can't find the page they want. These headings may seem boring to you but, as standards, they are effective.

Here is a checklist for creating content for your website:

Home: You need to really hook your readers on this page. Use great copywriting and a giveaway to make it irresistible to sign up for your free email newsletter. Once you've got their email address, you can woo them into buying your books without a hard sell. Read more on email newsletters in *Chapter 34, Your Website and Blog.*

About: Include a generous bio with an author headshot. The ABOUT page is the most visited page on any site. Don't be shy. You're wrong if you believe people shouldn't be interested in you. They are. Remember, no matter how great your book is, people connect with people. So be a human.

Media: Include a media page that journalists, bloggers, and interviewers can use. Provide a collection of bios in various word counts along with high-quality versions of your author headshot, book covers, and other photos appropriate for interviews and articles. (Make sure they're 300 dpi CMYK for print and 70 dpi RGB for web.) Also include details about your book—those boring bits like ISBNs and publication dates, along with the standard book description and any other information you think media may be interested in using.

Store: Make sure your readers can easily purchase your book on your Books page. Books2Read is a free tool from Draft2Digital anyone can use to create a Universal Book Link (UBL). You enter the URLs (including affiliate links) of all the places your book is sold and Books2Read creates one link for you to embed in your site. When customers click on the link they'll be able to choose their preferred retailer.

You can also set up direct sales so people can purchase print and ebooks directly from you. (Especially those super-cool personalized autographed print editions.) For this, you'll need to use a product like

Gumroad, reviewed in *Chapter 55, Direct Sales Tools*. Also see *Part V: Selling Your Book Direct*.

Social Sharing: Make sure readers have the ability to share your content on social media by providing shareable content they can post on Facebook, Scribd, Twitter, Pinterest, and the other socials.

Reviews: Add reviews you get from trade reviews, bloggers, influencers, and a select number of readers. Refer to *Chapter 37, Book Reviews*, for ideas on where to look, how to prepare your book, and how to ask for reviews.

Contact: Make it easy for readers to contact you using a form on your site, so you don't have to publish your email address. Your email address should be your domain name, not Gmail, Yahoo, Comcast or any other brand. Mine, for example, are carla@carlaking.com and hello@selfpubbootcamp.com. This is easy to set up in GoDaddy and other web hosting companies. Email services like Gmail will also let you do this, for a small fee.

35

SOCIAL MEDIA MARKETING

IF YOU USE SOCIAL MEDIA, YOU HAVE LIKELY RECOMMENDED OR discussed a book, film, or work of art with these friends and connections, so you already know how valuable these sites are as marketing tools. Ideally, you'll start marketing and promoting yourself via your website and social media long before you publish your book.

But which ones?

Twitter and Facebook are popular with many authors because they're easy to use, enjoy large audiences and provide one-click connectivity to and from many other social media sites. LinkedIn, another popular social site, can help you to reach large groups of professionals in particular industries, and Pinterest and Instagram are great image-oriented social tools. Google owns Google+ and YouTube, so when you post there you enjoy better visibility in the Google search engine. You can also reach readers by becoming active in forums and groups focused on narrow topics.

See *Chapter 52, Social Media Marketing Tools*, for a list of platforms and tools like Hootsuite that can help you manage and batch posts.

First, grab your name

Your author name is your strongest brand, so try to register yours on all possible sites. Just to have them. You don't have to start using them yet (maybe you won't use many of them at all), but at the very least create a keyword-rich profile that links to your website.

Twitter

Twitter is a news commentary and sharing platform that provides up-to-the-second information on anything from a concert to a conference, a war, or a sports event. Or to post fun facts, links to books and articles, or anything at all as long as it fits into 280 characters or fewer. Lots of journalists are on Twitter, so you can stand out as an expert or a person of interest to readers and reporters. Connect with and follow other Twitter users and sort tweets by topic or interest using hashtags.

Hashtags

Learn about hashtags (the # symbol) so you can communicate with interest groups on Twitter. When you start to "get" hashtags, you'll find it an incredible publicity tool. Use hashtags to categorize tweets by keyword. That way you can converse or gather information organized by topic. Clicking on a hash-tagged word shows you all the tweets marked with that keyword. Sometimes they can become what's called a trending topic. To start your Twitterverse training, find a topic you know about or want to learn about and contribute to the conversation. Sometimes the conversation is random and disorganized, other times an organizer sets a theme and a date and time for a group chat so everyone can converse in real time. You can start a hashtag and make it happen. Though Twitter users can also search for keywords without hashtags.

One popular Twitter hashtag is #FF—Follow Friday—where you can recommend friends to follow. It's important to mention people and organizations with the @ sign. Here's one of my #FF tweets:

@missadventuring: #FF My adventurous motorcycle gal pals @adv-goddess @fuzzygalore @overlandexpo @trilliumliz @madsocial @ruggedrider @daiquiric

This kind of tweet can start a frenzy of FFs that help you identify others you'll want to follow.

Facebook

Facebook separates personal pages from groups, business and author pages, virtual events, book pages, and other kinds of pages. If you're starting from scratch, create a personal page first, then an author page. (These pages are linked so Facebook knows who owns what pages.) You can set up a business page without creating a personal account first, but then you'll miss out on a ton of features and tools you'll want.

Use your Facebook pages to post updates on your writing, alert followers to sales, freebies, interviews, and articles, solicit beta readers, and run contests. Facebook Notes is a great place to share stories.

Facebook also makes it easy to embed a button to place on your website to encourage readers to "Like" your page, so they're more likely to see your posts in their Facebook newsfeed.

Use Facebook Live to broadcast live video in your followers' news feeds. Live broadcasts go right to the top of your followers' feeds so, if they're looking at Facebook, or get notified when friends are posting, they'll see your broadcast right away, which will get you more engagement.

Should you create a separate author page or use your personal page as a marketing tool? This is totally up to you. The limit for Facebook friends on the personal page is 5,000. People can't "Friend" you on an author page, but they can "Follow" you. The argument for using your personal page is economy—it'll save you time. The argument against is separation of the personal from the professional.

Facebook, like the other social media sites and free services, change things all the time. Listen... people get mad at Facebook for making changes to their platform but remember they're a free service and you can never, ever count on a free service to stay constant, or even free. If you want to keep what you post, duplicate it on your own blog or website.

Goodreads

Goodreads is not really a social media site, but you might think of it as a Facebook for book lovers. You can use Goodreads to find book reviewers.

Google+

Google+ used to be popular but experienced a privacy glitch that triggered a decision to shut down their free service. Their enterprise product (where co-workers can engage in discussion behind a corporate firewall) will remain. So they say. Social media platforms come and go. This is normal. Still, you should upload and maintain a current profile on Google+ because it will help people searching for your or the kind of books your write to find you more easily.

Images in social media

Visual content gets great results with readers. Studies show you'll get 80 percent more engagement on a post that includes an image on Facebook, and over 50 percent more clicks on Twitter. So use images to create interest in your posts. Also consider incorporating visual elements like infographics or even inspirational quotes.

Pinterest is a virtual bulletin board that lets you share links by "pinning" an image to one of your boards. Tumblr is a hosted blog tool for visual content. Instagram is a mobile app that lets you post on various social media sites. Flickr is a place to share your photos. There are many more.

Instagram is popular these days, but six months from now another app may rise to the top. Instagram lets you cross-post to Facebook and, though it's image-based, it allows you to write long posts.

Your mobile device with a built-in camera is your best friend for keeping in real-time contact with your friends, family, and readers using images. Add images and infographics on your web pages so people can share them using one of the Pinterest browser extensions.

Canva is a free tool that makes it easy to create professional-looking social media banners, buttons, and even ebook covers.

LinkedIn

LinkedIn is a good platform for reaching influencers, so your profile should be as well written as a resume. Professional groups in LinkedIn can be very profitable places for you to spend your time. Every group has a discussions tab where you can start or contribute to a conversation. Use the promotions tab to post information about your seminars, book press releases, awards, and information about articles you have written.

YouTube

Many people use YouTube to search for video content much like they use retail sites to search for products. Videos, especially a short, concise, entertaining, and well-made video, is a really good marketing tool. You can also use YouTube Live for conversations, meetings, and courses.

YouTube is an important channel. I publish a self-publishing channel and an adventure travel channel on YouTube, and my Author Friendly podcast is also published there.

Forums and groups

Forums and groups are amazing places to get attention because they're so focused and interactive. People who want to learn or to be inspired flock to them. You can become a star by sharing what you know, especially if you're an expert, as long as you don't step on the group leader's authority. Use forums to test ideas for blog entries, articles, publicity, and invite people to friend you on Facebook and follow you on Twitter. I belong to forums about living in Baja California, Mexico, motorcycle adventure travel, sidecar motorcycles, overlanding, writing and publishing (on the IBPA site), and yoga.

LinkedIn is the best place to reach members of professional groups. Yahoo and Google both host groups, though since Yahoo was purchased by Verizon, nobody knows what will happen to the platform. (Verizon also purchased AOL.)

Reddit is a very active forum with too many groups to list, both serious and quirky. You are sure to find places to beta publish your writing, exchange ideas with other writers, and discover readers.

Meetup is focused on in-person meetings. You might even create your own group, as I did in San Diego, for self-publishers.

Cake is the latest social media space to emerge. It was founded by Chris MacAskill, the founder of SmugMug and ADVR der. It's based not only on conversations but invite-only panels. Much more depth than the other platforms. MacAskill has lot of experience with forums so I think this may get traction. Follow me there.

The social media rule of thirds

The social media rule of thirds is simply this: One-third of the time it's okay to promote your book or business, another third goes to supporting or curating like-minded authors or businesses, and another third of the time you want to be yourself, posting things unrelated to your business, but related to you as an individual.

1/3 be yourself, 1/3 curate and questions, 1/3 your book

For example, I'm an expert in a very narrow niche—women's adventure motorcycling. I give lots of advice and encouragement to other women who want to motorcycle (and to the men who love us). But I also share my interests in publishing, gardening, yoga, travel, and my family.

It turns out a lot of people who share those interests also like travel and motorcycling or know someone who does. They have helped me sell books, connected me with editors who pay me to write articles, and they've even helped me secure highly paid speaking engagements at conferences, which is one of the most profitable places I've found to sell books. Best yet is the number of people I've met who live around the world and have become my friends.

Productivity tools

Streamline your social media tasks by using tools like HootSuite, Buffer, and Feedly. I use Feedly to collect items of interest when I find them on the web. Buffer lets me choose which social media platform to post on. I don't post the same thing to Twitter that I do to Facebook, LinkedIn, or Pinterest, but quickly craft different words (and word counts) for each. This is not as time-consuming as it sounds.

You can choose to send your posts out immediately or "buffer" them to send later, at a time you choose or at a time Buffer figures is best. Usually, I trust Buffer. Buffer and the other tools also provide analytics to show you how popular your posts are.

Buffer shortens links and tracks them, and so does Bitly, which I use most often if I want to tweet something. It also lets me customize links to acronyms or something that resembles English. I keep a list of affiliate links and sites I refer to often in Bitly and refer to them again and again.

I like Feedly to aggregate all the bloggers I follow. I use it like a magazine or newspaper.

Widgets encourage sharing

Most of us are familiar with Facebook "Like" and "Share" widgets, and Twitter feed and "Retweet" widgets on web pages. WattPad's widget shows off your stories and readers there. Scribd has an awesome document-sharing widget that you and your fans can plug into your websites and blog posts. E-commerce tools like Gumroad let you sell digital and physical products right inside your WordPress website.

However exciting all this widget action may be, you'll need to decide if widgets enhance or detract from your marketing efforts at the time. If you have a new book out, maybe you don't want people clicking off to your social media sites. In that case, it would be smarter to remove the widgets to funnel readers to the book sales pages. If you want to attract people to join your social networks, then widgets can help a lot.

36

METADATA AND DISCOVERY

METADATA IS USED BY SEARCH ENGINES TO AUTOMATE A formerly labor-intensive task by connecting readers, curators, and distributors to sell books more efficiently than ever before. The self-publisher who understands metadata levels the playing field to compete alongside big publishing—but only if you use it.

What is metadata?

Metadata is simply words that describe your book and it is your best marketing partner. Metadata is searchable information about your book like its title, author, genre, book description, ISBN, price, and keywords. Creating metadata tags is a marketing challenge that requires both editing skill and narrative common sense, two qualities that most writers possess. People make entire careers out of SEO and metadata, but you really can do this yourself.

Metadata is everywhere. On your website, in the book systems like the Bowker record, on retailer sites, social media, and in PDFs, images, videos, and audio files.

You need to supply complete metadata to the resellers when you upload your book. You should also pay close attention to the metadata for everything you put on the web. Every web page, every document, image, video, and audio file that you upload needs metadata if you want people to find it. This chapter focuses on book metadata. Find out more about metadata for your website in *Chapter 34, Your Website and Blog.*

Keywords and phrases

When people search for books, they often use a string of words, such as "19th century western romance," "paranormal thriller with strong female lead," or "how to self-publish." These are key phrases, and they're very effective for describing your book. When people refer to keywords, they mean both keywords and key phrases. When you list them, you'll set them off by commas so the system knows the words belong together. For example, "self-publishing, author marketing, social media rule of thirds."

How to create good keywords

Learn the difference between categories and keywords. Categories are where the book is shelved (romance, historical fiction, cookbooks) and keywords get much more specific. So when creating keywords for the online retailers, you can leave out the category names in your keywords.

Start by creating a worksheet to help you narrow down your keywords. Many people work best by jotting ideas down on paper rather than on the computer. Get messy and cast a wide net. Then start narrowing the list.

Record words and short phrases you think your readers might use to enter into a search engine to find you and your book. Then eliminate the more generic words and phrases from your list.

Aim for a final list of between ten to twenty keywords (or phrases) with a 900-character maximum, and keep the number of repeated keywords to a maximum of three.

There are several tools that can help you with this task. Among them are Google Adwords Keyword Planner, KDP Rocket, and Kindle Spy. You'll find reviews of these and more in *Chapter 50, Market Research and Competitive Analysis Tools.*

Where to put your metadata

As you see, your author and book metadata is disseminated everywhere —your website, on other people's websites (when you guest blog or are interviewed), on the online retailer sites, on the ISBN records for print and ebook versions, on social media sites, and wherever else you are active on the web. Don't leave any profile empty. Use my metadata cheatsheet to keep track of book metadata. Get it by signing up for reader updates.

www.selfpubbootcamp.com/readers

Book description

Your book needs a punchy tagline with a few words to create excitement followed by a paragraph with emotional impact to entice your reader to buy.

What is "high-stakes" about the book? Don't plod on about plot, treat it as a movie trailer and leave the reader wanting more. If it's a nonfiction book, the description should explain how to solve a problem for the reader.

You may not be the best person to write your own book description. Copywriting help can be had for your description and bio. Find resources in *Chapter 60, Copywriting Services.*

Author bio

Your author bio should make it clear that you are the best person to write your book. Nonfiction authors can list degrees, business successes, special interests, and expertise. Fiction authors might describe themselves as having been immersed in or fascinated by a particular genre topic since childhood.

Metadata and your website

Use keywords and phrases, plus your keyword-rich book descriptions and bios, on your website so readers can find you. WordPress makes it easy to insert this information without having learn any coding.

Metatags are snippets of text that search engines read that describe a page's content. These tags, or words, do not appear on the page itself, but only in the page's code.

Take a look at the websites of successful authors in your genre by right-clicking on their web page. Choose "view source" from the menu to see the metatags they use to describe their site to the search engines.

Don't be intimidated by the HTML code that appears. Just search "keywords" to find the description, keywords, and website title they use. It'll be near the top of the page and will look something like this.

<meta name="description" content="Carla King is a motorcycle adventure travel writer." />
<meta name="keywords" content="adventure travel, motorcycles, women, solo, books, Baja, China, Africa, America, Europe, India" />

<title>Carla King – A travel writer's writings, readings, gear, and recommendations.</title>

Make sure to edit your website to include your unique metadata.

Title and description tags

Most major search engines (like Google) no longer read keyword metatags in search results, so you must create relevant TITLE and DESCRIPTION tags.

Similarly, your file names should be descriptive. So if you upload a Word document to the web, make sure to edit the *Properties*, entering the correct title, author name, and other fields.

Many website-creation software programs and blog services provide you with simple forms where you can enter these various metatags. (Yoast is a premium tool and considered the best.) These tools help you automatically insert metadata into the page's HTML source code.

Here are some tips to help you create metadata for your web pages.

- Draft a TITLE metatag for each separate page on your website that describes that particular page in a nutshell.
- Use your top keywords and make it informative first to users, and second to search engines.
- Set a maximum of sixty characters, including spaces.
- Finally, considering both your keywords and your TITLE, draft a succinct but keyword-rich DESCRIPTION of your book. Make this one informative to search engines first and users second.
- Keep it to a maximum of 150 characters, including spaces. (If you make it fewer than 240 characters it's tweetable.)
- Try to use your keywords in the first sentences of each page so the search engines can compare those words to your metadata description and keywords.

- Craft keyword-rich headings using heading tags (H1 and H2) to split up your narrative. Search engines look at these first.
- Begin each page of your website with words and not images.

The Yoast plugin will rate your metadata and give you suggestions on how to improve it. The Yoast plugin costs much less than an SEO consultant.

Alt tags for images

Metadata also includes ALT tags, which is text that describes your images. You should include ALT tags for accessibility (so speech-to-text tools used by the visually impaired can tell the user what the photo is about) and also for search engines. ALT tags, like other metadata, are collected by search engines to identify and rank your pages.

Here's what you need to tag:

- Tag the image of your book cover with ALT =["target term, what you think people will enter in a search engine to find it"]
- Tag your author photo with ALT =["Your name: short, keyword-rich description of the author."]
- Tag any photo on your web pages with a thorough description of the person, object, place, or other descriptive words.

Website builders make it easy to tag your images as you insert them into your site.

Document and media properties

Search engines look inside all of the documents and applications you publish on the web for clues about their content.

Almost all applications let you edit the metadata associated with the content, though they might not call it metadata. For example, metadata resides in every Microsoft Word document you create and, if it's posted on the web, search engines will collect the author and company name (yours, or the owner of your bootlegged copy) to describe it.

To edit the metadata in a Word document, simply open the document and click FILE > PROPERTIES to change or add the data. Here's an example of what this looks like.

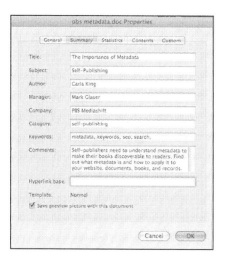

Metadata lives in Word .doc and .docx files. Make sure yours has the right keywords!

If you're publishing audio, video, or any other media, make sure you also edit the metadata inside that application. For example, Audacity, a free program handy for recording music, podcasts, and audiobooks, uses ID3 tags. These tags identify the file as an audio recording to search engines and services like iTunes and Windows Media Player.

Metadata in an audio file.

Metadata on reseller sites

Every reseller wants you to succeed so they make it easy for publishers to insert metadata. No matter what you publish or how you publish it, you'll be asked to enter keywords, descriptions, and other metadata.

You'll be asked to insert descriptions and keywords and categories and other data by IngramSpark, Smashwords, Draft2Digital, Amazon KDP, Kobo, B&N, Apple, and all the other distributors and retailers. Each of these services specifies what metadata you need. Please sign up for my reader's news to get a metadata cheat sheet so you know how many words and characters each reseller allows.

www.selfpubbootcamp.com/readers

Metadata on social media sites

Never leave a social media profile field empty. Use all available information spaces on Twitter, Facebook, Pinterest, LinkedIn, About.me, Instagram, YouTube, Google+ and every other social site you find, to create incoming links to your website. (Your website is "you" central, and should motivate readers to sign up for your email list and find out where to buy your book.)

Get a gravatar

Gravatar means "globally recognized avatar," and automatically connects your profile with your comments and activities on the web. When you register, your comments on weblogs and websites display your photo and links to your website. Register an account based on your email address, and upload an avatar to be associated with the account. This should be your author profile photo.

You may want to sign up for more than one Gravatar—one for professional and one for personal use. If you're writing under a pseudonym, get a different email address to associate with that alias so you can register a separate Gravatar.

You can add multiple emails to one Gravatar.

Many news and blog sites use Gravatar plugins. When someone posts a comment, it checks the associated email address and displays that person's Gravatar next to the comment. Your image is linked to your biographical data, which should mention your book, of course.

Gravatar also allows you to list your websites and social media activities. If you contribute to a group blog, it may also use your Gravatar to identify you as the author of each post you publish.

Gravatars are critical in book-promotion activities such as guest blogging and commenting on blog posts. Every incoming link to your website counts.

By the way, even though Google+ is pretty much dead as a social platform, add your profile to it anyway. Your profile image on Google follows you around the web and helps people find you.

37

HOW TO GET BOOK REVIEWS

BECAUSE NO ONE LIKES TO BE THE FIRST TO ARRIVE AT A PARTY, it's helpful to have a few reviews right out of the gate. This is why you should include legitimate trade reviews in addition to influencer and reader reviews as part of your book-launch strategy.

Plan ahead because though bloggers and other casual reviewers might review your book immediately, the best of them have a backlog. Trade review channels require a four- to six-month lead-time.

The practice of paying for book reviews used to be widely criticized, but has now become accepted as a necessary step in the publishing flow along with editing, formatting, and design.

Trade reviews

The "trade" is the term for the professional book industry. Book reviews by the publications that booksellers and librarians read are called trade publications. These are Publishers Weekly (PW) and its associate, BookLife (where PW Select now lives), plus Kirkus Reviews,

Foreword Reviews (with their paid counterpart, Clarion), Indie Reader, and The Midwest Book Review.

These companies offer both free and paid review services, plus advertising opportunities. Paid reviews are not guaranteed to be good reviews, and you will have the option to publish the review or not. So before you spend the money to pay for a review, you might benefit from a manuscript review by an editor who knows your market. (See *Chapter 4, The Importance of Editing*, for more about manuscript reviews.)

Paying for fake reviews violates Amazon's policies. However, paying reputable publishing industry sources for *editorial* reviews is fine.

Find a list of trade review services in *Chapter 53, Book Review Services.*

Consumer and Blogger Book Reviewer

Consumer and blogger book reviews are considered reader reviews, even if those reviewers are professional authors or pro-bloggers. But don't worry. Many consumers give more weight to reader reviews than they do trade reviews. These include NetGalley, San Francisco Book Review, LibraryThing's Member Giveaways Program, The Indie View, The Book Blogger List, and Goodreads Giveaways.

Get a complete list of consumer and blogger book review services in *Chapter 53, Book Review Services.*

Tech Tools to Find Reviewers

Google search: It may sound obvious, but most authors don't think of using Google search for book reviewers and book bloggers in your genre. Search for "book bloggers" along with your genre to see what pops up.

Amazon Advanced Search: This is where you do your competitive research to see what books are like yours and who has reviewed them. You'll have to sort through the reviewers to see which ones have provided contact information. Not all of them do.

Writers' Blog Finder: Check out this free search engine for finding the top blogs in your genre.

Don't forget Twitter, Facebook, Pinterest, Instagram, LinkedIn, Goodreads, and other social media platforms. You probably know where your readers hang out. As always, use the social media rule of thirds and engage with the community before asking for favors.

You'll find more tech tools for finding reviewers in *Chapter 53, Book Review Services.*

Wooing Reviewers

A couple of years ago I was approached by an author on my Adventure Travel Books group on Goodreads. She had penned a book about a solo-bicycling adventure in Italy that was similar in topic and spirit to one of my books, which she had clearly read. Her message to me was well written, funny, and not at all pushy. Yes, I read her book and reviewed it favorably.

I encouraged the author of a fictional book featuring Shakespeare to cultivate relationships with famous actors and directors of current Shakespeare plays. She already knows a few, as she teaches and directs students about the Bard and his works, so she can test the waters by approaching them first. I advised her not to ask for reviews, but offer the book (digital or print edition), as a gift after a conversation or an email exchange or two.

Don't burden a potential reviewer with an obligation to read the book, especially if you've never met the person or interacted with them on social media. They might even not like to read. But who knows? They may be very pleased and honored. Still, a too-quick request might also alienate them and can kill the relationship before it starts.

Asking for blurbs

Book blurbs are short reviews—a sentence or maybe even a word—from a fellow writer or a celebrity or a known media outlet. You've seen blurbs like this: "Compelling!"—USA Today.

You may have solicited the blurb or taken it as a pull quote from a more extensive review. You've probably seen blurbs on the front cover of a book, on the inside pages of a paperback, and on the back covers of hardcover books. Blurbs are also used on websites and promotional materials.

A good blurb will compel the potential reader to pay attention to your book, but only if they have heard of and respect the person (or media outlet) who blurbed your book. So, get a blurber, or reviewer, whose name is known, and who knows what a blurb is. These people are very busy, but 1) if they like you, and, 2) when they glance through your book it doesn't have any obvious shaming qualities, they are 3) more likely to do you this favor.

I've found that asking someone to blurb my book is more successful than asking for a book review. After all, a review is a writing project that takes time and hard work.

So do you ask for a blurb or a review? It depends. If it's a blogger who needs content, I ask for a review, and then excerpt the blurb from that. If it's somebody famous who has no time, I ask for a review or a quick blurb. If it's a media outlet, I ask the editor for a review, and look for a blurbable phrase.

Remember that this is not the first time they should have heard from you. Start building your relationship and extending your professional network far in advance of publication.

How to Create and Deliver Advanced Reader Copies (ARCs)

It's important to create an ARC several months in advance of publication. Create ARCs in print, EPUB, and Amazon Kindle formats. Not everyone likes to read in print. In fact, my clients are often surprised that the most requested version is for Kindle. You need ARCs for several reasons, not all of them for book reviewers.

- To send to early readers and influencers
- To send to book reviewers (see *Chapter 53, Book Review Services*)
- To obtain a CIP block

Don't worry if your book hasn't been designed yet. An ARC doesn't necessarily need to look like your finished book. In fact, in some cases, I don't think it should look like it at all. I have a difficult time convincing some of my clients of this as they believe that the more professional their book looks, the better. Actually, a not-perfectly-formatted uncorrected proof sent early to readers, influencers, and book review services quickly and early will give you more time to gather feedback and reviews, more time to organize book marketing activities like blog and podcast tours, and more time to build your email list and other promotional tasks.

Your ARC does, however, does need all the things the final book needs, especially these two:

- Half title and title page
- Copyright page with LCCN

An LCCN (as covered in *Chapter 29, Selling to Libraries*), "position[s] your book for success should you wish to market to libraries, and the only time you can request one is before the book is published," as pointed out by David Wogahn in his helpful guide, *Register Your Book: The Essential Guide to ISBNs, Barcodes, Copyright, and LCCNs*.

You also need an LCCN to obtain a CIP Block (a topic also covered in Chapter 29), and to obtain a CIP Block you'll need to submit your title page and copyright page to the agency you use to create that CIP Block.

Ask your cover designer to create art for your title pages. They should provide it for free along with your cover files. If you haven't hired a cover designer yet, you can create half title and titles pages in Microsoft Word. (See *Chapter 15, Interior Book Design*, for details.)

Once you have created your ARC, I recommend using BookFunnel to deliver it. You'll upload all three formats (PDF, Kindle, EPUB) to BookFunnel so that your reader can choose which format they want to read in. BookFunnel is also a great delivery system for delivering the content you promise to readers who sign up for your mailing list, Facebook ads, and ongoing distribution to reviewers and influencers. See more about BookFunnel in *Chapter 51, Marketing Ads and Apps*.

How to Create an ARC

I think the best way to create an ARC is in Microsoft Word or whatever program you're using to write your book (Pages, OpenOffice, Scrivener, Leanpub, or whatever book creation and publishing tool you like to use).

Make sure it looks as much like a book as possible, with headers and footers in the print edition, a table of contents, and make sure the front and back of the book is prominently marked with the disclaimer Advanced Reader Copy and "Publisher's uncorrected proof—not for sale." If you don't have cover art, you can create a separate, plain cover for the ARC or use a tool like Canva to create a temporary cover.

On the back cover or one-sheet marketing copy you send along with the book (in print or electronically), list the following so reviewers can reference this information in their book reviews:

- Release date
- Number of pages

- Book size
- Formats available (print, MOBI, EPUB)
- Sales channels (for example, "all the usual online retailers")
- Price (for each format)
- ISBNs (for print, Kindle, and EPUB)
- Author photo
- Book cover (if you have one)
- A link to your website or specific link the media kit on your website if you have one

Include a notice on the back of the book that reads something like the following:

PLEASE NOTE: This is an uncorrected proof. Any quotes for publication must be checked against the finished book. Price and publication date are subject to change without notice. Inquiries should be directed to <your name> at <your email address>.

Again, the "one-sheet" description of your book should contain all of the above information plus marketing copy. This needs to include metadata such as the book categories, description, and author bio. Find instructions on how to create good descriptions and how find your categories in *Chapter 36, Metadata and Discovery*.

How to Print ARCs

You can print your ARCs using a POD service like IngramSpark, Draft2Digital, or Amazon, or print a short run with a local or online printing service like 48 Hour Books. I find that Amazon is the least complicated, the least expensive and fastest. To use them, upload your book for print but—IMPORTANT!—do not fill in the publication date field. If using IngramSpark, do not check the box to release the book for distribution.

Amazon only allows you to order five proofs at a time but Ingram-Spark allows you to order an unlimited number of pre-publication proofs. They will refund their $49 setup fee with your order of fifty copies if you order them within ninety days of creating your book. Sign up for their email newsletter to be notified when they have specials like free setup, or search the web for coupons. If you're a member of IBPA you'll get further discounts and freebies.

Delivering Digital ARCs

Digital ARC options include PDFs, Kindle, and EPUB versions. Personally, I dislike getting PDFs because I don't like to read on my computer. If I'm very motivated to review the book I convert it to Kindle format using Calibre and send it to my Kindle device. If I'm not motivated, I just don't get to it.

So make it easy on your reviewers and send them the version they want. You can create your own Kindle and EPUBs for download, but it's much more convenient for everybody to use BookFunnel, because they make it so easy to download the exact format they want.

Read about BookFunnel and other ARC delivery systems in *Chapter 53, Book Review Services*. Don't forget to subscribe to the readers list to get updates to products, tools, and services like this, because they change frequently.

38

YOUR BOOK LAUNCH

You've finished writing and polishing your book after multiple edits. You've got production underway: the PCIP has been ordered, you have your ISBNs, you've gotten production and distribution set up.

Advanced Reader Copies (ARCs) have been printed and sent out to superfans and influencers with whom you've established a relationship. You've been building and nurturing a support group and increasing your visibility with contributions to local papers, magazines, blogs, etc.

Your street team is standing by and they're ready to help launch your book. It's time to start.

Book launch checklist

Subscribe to reader updates to get access to a handy book launch checklist you can edit and make your own.

www.selfpubbootcamp.com/readers

Four to six months in advance

- Set your goals for the launch.
- Complete your metadata book descriptions and bios and all the messaging you have about your book.
- Perform a competitive analysis for your book.
- Identify influencers, including book bloggers, podcasters, and media and build relationships with them.
- Build your community and your email list to build relationships with readers.
- Participate in online groups.
- Complete your brand identity and apply it across media (website, social media, printed materials).
- Contact your local libraries and bookstores about talks and signings and launch parties.
- Prepare a timeline document that details what content you will release and when.
- Submit stories and articles to publications.

Two to four months in advance

- Submit your book to paid review services.
- Solicit book reviews and blurbs from influencers.
- Set your release date and announce it.
- Prep your website and book landing page, including media reviews and blurbs as they come in.

Thirty days in advance

- Create social media banners, images, ads, and buy buttons. Craft posts and tweets.
- Create pre-orders and encourage people to order via your list and social media.
- Claim and build your Amazon Author Central page.
- Send free ebooks to loyal readers and ask them to prepare to give an Amazon review on the day the book comes out. Send

them two or three emails on this.

Week of book launch

- Create excitement about your book in social media, blog posts, podcasts, and interviews.
- Create a special offer and price low to boost sales.
- Launch your book.

Upon publication

- Ask your lists and influencers to add book reviews to Amazon and other online sites, if they haven't already.
- Incorporate book reviews and blurbs on your website.
- Keep up with your blog tours and other publicity activities.

Again, get the handy book launch checklist to edit and make your own by subscribing to reader updates.

www.selfpubbootcamp.com/readers

Congratulations!

If you've read this guide all the way through, you're done… sort of. I'm sure you have a lot of to-do lists and that you'll be diving into the various chapters as you need a refresh during your publishing journey.

The next part of the guide is *Part VII, Consumer's Guide* with reviews of the products, tools, and services you can use to publish. You've already learned about a lot of them in the course of reading the guide.

But right now I hope you feel a huge sense of accomplishment and also relief that, broken down into steps, the job of publishing your book is achievable.

Please email me

I'd love to know your thoughts at this point, so if you're willing, shoot me an email and let me know how you're feeling, how this guide helped, how it might be improved, and please don't be shy about asking questions. Readers of the 1st, 2nd, and 3rd editions asked me questions that helped me improve it for this 5th edition. Help me make the 5th edition even better. Ask away!

You can email me at hello@selfpubbootcamp.com. I try to answer every email. Thank you!

PART VII

CONSUMERS GUIDE

Because the companies who offer products, tools, and services reviewed here are always evolving, I'd like to offer you access to my obsessively updated ebook version of the Consumer's Guide.

Get free access to the *Consumer's Guide for Self-Publishers* and other perks like a metadata cheatsheet and book launch checklist.

www.selfpubbootcamp.com/readers

The products, tools, and services in this part of the guide are divided into these segments.

Distribution Tools & Services
Direct to Retailer Tools
Design and Formatting tools
Full Service Companies
Audiobook and Podcasting Tools
Online Marketplaces

Book Sales Tracking Tools
Writing and Editing Tools
Social Publishing Tools
Beta and Critique Tools
Business and Productivity Tools
Market Research and Competitive Analysis Tools
Marketing Ads and Apps
Social Media Marketing Tools
Book Review Services
Crowdfunding Sites
Direct Sales Tools
Affiliate Programs
Website and Blog Tools
Email Marketing Tools
Publishing by Subscription
Copywriting Services
E-Commerce Solutions
Professional Organizations
Your Publishers Bookshelf

39

DISTRIBUTION TOOLS AND SERVICES

YOUR DECISION ON SERVICES TO USE FOR PRINT-BOOK distribution is one of the most important you'll make in your self-publishing journey. But don't let it stop you from moving forward. As long as you have purchased your own ISBNs you are free to change course at any time.

This chapter reviews distribution tools, but please see *Part IV, Distributing Your Book*, for an explanation of how to combine them to sell to readers.

Subscribe for access to updates in the *Consumer's Guide for Self-Publishers* web book:
www.selfpubbootcamp.com/readers

Amazon's Tools

See *Direct to Retailer* for details on:

- Amazon Advantage

- Amazon Kindle Comic Creator
- Amazon Kindle Direct Publishing (KDP) for ebooks
- Amazon KDP Print
- Amazon KDP Select
- Amazon Kindle Kids' Book Creator

Apple iBooks Author

See *Direct to Retailer Tools.*

B&N Press

See *Direct to Retailer.*

BAM!Publish

bampublish.com

See FastPencil, below, and *Full Service Companies.*

Blurb

blurb.com

See *Design and Formatting Tools.*

BookBaby

bit.ly/bookbabyforauthors

See *Full-Service Companies.*

Bublish

bublish.com

Bublish has my vote for one of the most interesting and innovative independent author services companies of the year. They're experiencing high growth and a constantly evolving suite of hybrid solutions for developing your author platform and getting your book quality distribution.

Bublish describes itself as a "publishing technology company that offers cloud-based tools, metrics and resources to equip today's business-savvy authors for success. An innovative, award-winning platform, Bublish empowers *authorpreneurs* by providing a complete social marketing and digital publishing solution."

Here's how it works. Join (for free). Create a bio and upload your photo. Upload your ebook in EPUB format and add a synopsis, a link to your website, and at least one link to an online retailer where readers can purchase the book.

Now you create a Book Bubble, or excerpt of your book, along with an "author insight" to personalize what you shared. You can share the Book Bubble on social media and track how many people looked at it.

Bublish can help you build your platform, create Amazon and Facebook ads, and promote your book on their newsletter and by hand-selling at national (USA) book and library shows. You can bring your completed book to them or use their editing, design, and formatting services.

The Bublish premium service is $9/mo or $99/year and they take a 15% commission on sales. Look for additional services for select authors coming soon.

Draft2Digital

draft2digital.com

Draft2Digital is a popular ebook and POD (in beta) creation and distribution service admired for its ease of use and customer support (email and telephone). Upload your manuscript, your cover, and basic sales information, and they do the rest.

Your book gets distributed to iBooks, B&N, Kobo, Inktera, Scribd, 24Symbols, and Tolino. You can choose to opt out of any of them.

They give you the EPUB to distribute in other places if you like but they hope you'll use their service. You also get a PDF they can distribute or you can choose another service.

D2D sends pre-orders to almost all partners from ninety days to a year in advance. They are famous for their 24/7 customer support. You pay a 15 percent commission on net royalties (approximately 10 percent of list price) upon sale.

FastPencil

fastpencil.com

FastPencil offers an online ebook and print book creation tool with templates and a cover creator in the cloud with version control, writing, editing, and collaboration tools. Despite its impressive suite of tools and services, I can only recommend it for professional independent publishers if you are willing to pay $599 for a *Small Publisher Custom Imprint Setup* in addition to the other costs. Why? Because otherwise, you do not get to apply your own ISBN. Therefore your publisher is FastPencil.

It's free to create and print your book privately. It costs $249 to distribute your book to Amazon, BAM!, Ingram, Kobo and more. They charge $999 to add project setup, review, and cover design, and $1999 for a premium version of the same. This is very expensive.

If you are a prolific blogger who wants to turn your blog posts into books, you may want to consider FastPencil, but I recommend you try Pressbooks first.

They also provide book marketing services, which I don't recommend because you need to personalize your book marketing. See *Part VI, Market Your Book*, to learn more.

The bottom line: If you are a multi-book author or small press looking for a cloud-based book creation tool and distribution service, and you are selling enough books to recoup the fees, this could be a solution for you. However, their print markup is so steep that you may want to use another printing and distribution service, such as IngramSpark.

FastPencil is the technology behind BAM!Publish, which guarantees your printed book in their stores across the US. (See *Full Service Companies.*)

Gatekeeper Press

See *Full Service Companies.*

Google Play

See *Direct to Retailer Tools.*

Kobo Writing Life

See *Direct to Retailer Tools.*

Kbuuk

kbuuk.com

Kbuuk is an ebook publishing subscription service with great analytics tools. You'll pay $0 (2 books) or $5 (unlimited books) per month. Upload a .docx or EPUB file. Their services include EPUB conversion, sales in their store, wide distribution, and 80 percent royalty, even at the $0 per month level.

Premium and professional plans include marketing tools and a dashboard analytics tool called PubHub which helps you build your platform by showing you how customers read your book and how many sales you made.

IngramSpark

ingramspark.com

Ingram is the giant in the traditional book distribution world and IngramSpark is their simplified tool for self-publishers and small presses. (Lightning Source is Ingram's publisher tool and the system that runs the IngramSpark platform.)

IngramSpark lets you set the higher discounts and returns programs that brick-and-mortar bookstores require. So if you're sure your book has been produced to professional standards and are convinced that bookstores is a big market for you, *and* you're willing to do the promotion work to reach them, IngramSpark can be a great choice.

If you aim to sell your books via the online retailers, you only need to set your discount to 30 percent. If you're marketing to brick-and-mortar bookstores, you'll need to set the discount to 55 percent and opt-into the Returns program.

IngramSpark can print your books on-demand to any of their many locations around the world and have them sent to your destination using local postage rates. They also offer offset printing.

When you print with IngramSpark your $49 print (POD) setup fee is deducted and refunded after you order 50 books. (This is a reasonable number of books to order for gifts and publicity.)

Get free title setup with an IBPA membership or sign-up for Ingram-Spark's mailing list and watch for occasional free title setup offers.

You can set your print book and ebook to pre-order status up to twelve months in advance of publication. This is currently the only way to get your print book in pre-order status at Amazon without using the unwieldy Amazon Advantage program. You can make changes to your book up to fifteen days before publication, as Ingram will start printing the book ten days before publication to supply the retailers in preparation for their orders.

IngramSpark pays 40 percent of *list price* (rather than *sales price*). Sales price is calculated on the price the retailer sells your book for on their site, so the profit you make will depend on the discounted price on any given day. When you're paid based on the list price, you consistently get the same profit on each sale.

IngramSpark offers customer support by phone and email.

If your self-published author business grows into a successful small press, IngramSpark can move you into Ingram Publisher Services (IPS), which provides full distribution services including warehousing and sales into major and independent booksellers.

Listen to my conversations with Robin Cutler, Director of IngramSpark on the Author Friendly Podcast at www.authorfriendly.com.

Lightning Source

See IngramSpark.

Lulu

lulu.com

Lulu is a popular self-publishing service because they do a great job of printing and they offer trade paperback, hardback, photo books, and even calendars. The platform is very easy to use.

PublishDrive

publishdrive.com

PublishDrive will distribute your ebook, paperback book, and audiobook to all the major retailers (Apple iBooks, Google Play Books, Kindle, Scribd, Barnes & Noble), and many others, plus 240k digital libraries (schools, universities, public libraries including OverDrive and Ciando for 10% after net sales. Use them to reach the Spanish subscription service 24Symbols, Tookbook, Casa De Libro, RedShelf, eSentral in SE Asia, and India's Rockstand. Their partnership with

DangDang in China gives your English-language book great exposure in the largest emerging ebook marketplace for ESL speakers in the world.

PublishDrive uses a subscription plan instead of a royalty share. You can distribute one ebook for free to 8 distributors, up to 6 titles in ebook/audio/pod format to all their retailers for $19.99, up to 24 titles for $49.99/mo, and so on.

Upload your Word doc to convert it to EPUB format for free. You can use their converter to format your book even if you don't use their service to distribute.

PublishDrive offer you a better royalty rate from Amazon than going direct to Amazon. They also offer some great marketing programs and are growing exponentially. You'll find perks such as co-royalties, shared costs, analytics, an Amazon Ads interface, and other time-saving gadgets. Listen to my interview with founder Kinga Jentetics on the Author Friendly Podcast at www.authorfriendly.com.

Scribl

scribl.com

Scribl distributes your ebook to Apple iBooks, Amazon Kindle, B&N, Kobo, and hundreds of others, and it also offers your ebook and audiobook (and podcasts) in their store to customers who are hungry for free and low-cost books, using a CrowdPricing system.

Scribl claims CrowdPricing encourages readers to take a chance on new, undiscovered authors by pricing them at free or almost-free. When books are first posted, they're free for a brief promotional period, so readers keep checking in to see what's new. Books that have proven popular cost more. If a book gets lower ratings at the higher prices, and fewer people download it, the price comes back down. The most popular books among readers cost about as much as you would pay for a typical popular ebook at your favorite online bookstore. Books that have not yet sold as well cost less.

They also estimate that CrowdPricing produces thirty times more total revenue for content than with conventional, author-priced systems because customers trust the prices, so they're more willing to pay. They also report that most downloads are paid downloads—unlike conventional systems, where most of the downloads are free.

Use CrowdPricing Everywhere to earn 70 percent royalty (often more than if you posted directly) along with a listing in their CrowdPricing site with price-based ratings. You earn 75–85 percent of gross revenue (not net), minus PayPal fees. They keep 15–25 percent. If you only provide your ebook you get 75 percent. If you supply your ebook and audiobook, you get 85 percent and other benefits. You are paid every forty-eight hours.

Due to the nature of the CrowdPricing system, Scribl requires a long-term exclusivity contract.

Slicebooks

slicebooks.com

Slicebooks is the manifestation of the imagined future of digital publishing with the reader's ability to create custom ebooks and print books.

I listed this company because authors can use their service to slice existing books into ready-to-sell packaged chunks at $1 per file.

They also have a "create a store app" service that lets you deliver books by author, publisher, category, keywords, or even ISBNs (for your own books) for sale in an app.

With subscription pricing in tiers from $9–$999 per month, it's really a system for medium-to-large publishers who have enough books to slice to make it worthwhile.

Here's how it works. Publishers upload their books into Slicebooks (for a fee of $10 per book) to slice and dice them into chapters and sections. You can remix your book(s) into completely new titles with new covers and sell them along with the individual slices in the Slicebooks iTunes-style retail platform. You get your EPUB and PDF files to do with as you wish (such as to sell them in your own store).

Consumers can mix and match slices from the books with any other slice sold in the Slicebooks store. Embed your own store to offer your content sliced and remixable. You're paid by the slice. Travel books? Anthologies? Cookbooks? Imagine the possibilities.

So your travel essay on Rome might be mixed with the Rome chapter of the Lonely Planet guide to Italy and some recipes from an Italian cookbook. Pretty awesome.

Smashwords

smashwords.com

If you've written an ebook, the fastest and cheapest way to get it distributed quickly everywhere is to pair Smashwords with Amazon Kindle Direct Publishing (KDP). As a distributor, Smashwords will distribute your ebook to the most important major retailers and library platforms, except Amazon Kindle. After you upload to Smashwords, also upload your ebook to Amazon KDP.

Smashwords also operates their own small ebook store where authors earn royalties up to 80 percent of list price.

You can upload either a Word file or an EPUB file. Smashwords will automatically convert your Word file into multiple ebook file formats (including EPUB and MOBI, the most important) so your book is readable to customers of the Smashwords Store on any reading device. Then they distribute the EPUB version to its retailer and library partners.

Use a Book Design Template or create a Word document that adheres to *The Smashwords Style Guide* (available as a free download at Smash-words). This guide provides step-by-step instructions for how to professionally design and format your manuscript prior to upload. I think it's easier to use Book Design Templates instead of starting from scratch.

Format your book first for Smashwords, and then use that same formatted Microsoft Word file to upload to Amazon. (Hint: For best results with Amazon, save your Word file as "filtered HTML" before you upload it to Amazon).

Download the free *Smashwords Style Guide* as it includes useful tips on paragraph styling to help your book render better on Kindle reading devices. If you don't have the time or patience to learn how to format with Microsoft Word, or you haven't used a template, another option is to hire a low-cost freelancer from *Mark's List*. Formatting for novels starts as low as $35 and goes up from there depending on complexity.

Another option is to upload an EPUB file directly to Smashwords. If you've already hired a professional ebook designer to create an EPUB file for you, or you've already created your own professionally designed EPUB file, this is a great option, especially if your book requires charts and graphs. Smashwords lets you upload both a Word file and an EPUB file. The EPUB will replace the Smashwords-generated EPUB with your own custom EPUB.

For sales of your ebook through Smashwords distribution to iBooks and all other major retailers, you'll get 60 percent of the list price (the retailer takes a commission of 30 percent list and Smashwords takes a commission of 10 percent list). Smashwords pays monthly.

Once your book is successfully converted, Smashwords offers it for sale immediately in their Smashwords store, and then sends it to a very large number of ebook sellers—except the Amazon Kindle store. So, remember to upload a separate file (with a different ISBN) to the Kindle store using Amazon KDP.

Smashwords has one of the widest ebook distribution services in the market and is always expanding.

Smashwords offers several unique (and free) ebook marketing tools, the most prominent of which is Smashwords coupons which allows you to run custom book promotions. They also offer a merchandising feature called Special Deals. Create a public coupon for your book, and Smashwords gives your book extra promotion within their store.

Smashwords founder Mark Coker provides lots of informational and how-to videos on their Smashwords YouTube channel and his Smart Author podcast is a great educational program with each podcast a lesson that builds on the previous lessons.

Find out more about Smashwords in my interview with Mark on the Author Friendly Podcast at www.authorfriendly.com.

StreetLib

streetlib.com

StreetLib is a digital ebook creation and distribution service with wide reach into international markets, especially online stores in Germany, Austria and Switzerland, Turkey, and Latin America.

You can compose or paste your book into their free cloud-based book creation tool, which is capable of formatting comics, cookbooks, and poetry. Export to EPUB, MOBI, fixed-layout, and PDF for print. They distribute to the Big Five ebook retailers and they take 7–10 percent of the cover price to US authors.

StreetLib also has a partnership with Perlego, a subscription service that gives readers access to over 90,000 professional and academic books. You get paid depending on the number of pages read, based on 45 percent of the membership revenues. (StreetLib keeps 65 percent.)

If you sell from the StreetLib book page you earn 15 percent of sales revenues. Add other books from their large catalog to your store and earn a 15 percent commission. This is a great way to offer a curated bookstore for additional income. (It's similar to Aerio, which is described in *Chapter 56, Affiliate Programs*.)

A sales widget (similar to Gumroad) is also included to embed in your website, so you can ask your website visitors to buy from StreetLib so you make more money than with Amazon.

They offer a la carte formatting, editing, cover design, and EPUB correction and validation.

StreetLib offers book translation services via a partnership with Babelcube, which takes a percentage of your translated book's sales revenue.

Listen to my interview with StreetLib's AC de Fombelle on the Author Friendly Podcast at www.authorfriendly.com.

Tablo

tablo.io

Creating a book and building a profile on Australian-based Tablo is free. Global distribution costs from $99 to $299 per year. Every distribution plan includes all required ISBNs, but I strongly recommend you purchase your own as explained in *Chapter 12, All About ISBNs.*

Authors keep 100 percent of their sale proceeds after retailers' margins. Authors can also order paperback copies from Tablo directly using their print-on-demand service.

All of this can be accessed through Tablo's online writing and publishing platform that allows anybody to upload or write a book for free that's then automatically typeset for all formats.

Type and Tell

typeandtell.com

British authors may be interested in Type and Tell. It's the UK-based, English-language version of a Swedish self-publishing service created by Bonnier Books Ventures, which is a branch of Bonnier Books. (Swedish authors, go to https://www.typeandtell.com/sv/.)

Authors can use their cloud-based writing and editing (book creation) tool or upload their own document, and get cover design, professional interior design, and worldwide print and ebook distribution. Their publishing packages range from £199 to £3399. You can also choose a la carte services like cover design (£285) and editing (£789 for 50,000–75,000 words). Distribution is handled by Ingram Content Group.

Walmart Books by Rakuten Kobo

See *Direct to Retailer.*

XinXii

xinxii.com

XinXii sounds Chinese but it's a German ebook aggregator that give you 85 percent royalties. It reaches all the usual ebook retailers and some foreign markets you may not be able to reach with other ebook aggregators.

They offer an author page where you earn 70 percent of net sales when your book is priced over $2.49, and 40 percent if less than that.

40

DIRECT TO RETAILER TOOLS

THE TOOLS LISTED HERE ARE PROVIDED BY THE ONLINE retailers so you can upload your book for sale in their stores. Plenty of authors "distribute" by uploading their book to each retailer separately. This will give you a larger royalty but it's time-consuming to upload, track, and keep accounts.

It can be smart to go direct to one retailer before "going big" with a distribution service for the simple reason that when you go directly to a retailer you can take advantage of their marketing programs. Amazon Kindle Direct Publishing (KDP) "Select" is Amazon's program and Kobo Writing Life also has really great marketing programs.

Worth noting is that you can use Amazon Advantage, Amazon KDP, KDP Print, and Kids Book Creator to enjoy a direct relationship with Amazon while distributing elsewhere using IngramSpark, Smashwords, StreetLib, or another service. See my blog post on print book distribution on how to use both Amazon Kindle Print and IngramSpark for your print distribution.

The considerations and nuances of all of these decision-making processes are explained in my blog post on how your book gets to readers and in a more detailed manner in earlier parts of this guide.

Subscribe for access to updates in the *Consumer's Guide for Self-Publishers* web book:
www.selfpubbootcamp.com/readers

The Big Five

To clarify, when people talk about "the Big Five online retailers" or bookstores they mean: Amazon, B&N, Apple, Kobo, and GooglePlay. When people talk about the Big 5 publishing houses they mean Hachette Book Group (HBG), HarperCollins Publishers, Macmillan Publishers, Penguin Random House, and Simon and Schuster.

Amazon Advantage

amazon.com/advantage

If you've printed hundreds or thousands of books using an offset printing company to keep costs down, you can use the Amazon Advantage fulfillment service to get your book into the Amazon store. The $99 annual fee is deducted from your sales. If you don't generate enough sales, they waive the unpaid difference.

In this scenario you have printed your book elsewhere (probably with an offset print company). You ship your books to them (at your cost) at their request. They'll ask for them when they need more. They will pay you 45 percent of your book's list price. You do risk returns of unsold books.

Authors have used Amazon Advantage as a workaround to get print book pre-orders in the Amazon store (since Amazon Kindle Print does not have pre-order capability), but you can distribute pre-orders to Amazon using IngramSpark. (See below.)

Why would you do this instead of using Amazon to get your print books into the Amazon store? If you have a great platform and you know you can sell thousands of books on Amazon, you might use an offset printer to maximize profits and cut your printing costs in half (or more). Use IngramSpark's POD service to distribute everywhere else.

I advise most authors to distribute their books POD first to get the bugs out (there's always something) before printing a large quantity. It's heartbreaking to have paid for 1000 copies of a book with errors.

Amazon Kindle Direct Publishing (KDP)

kdp.amazon.com

Amazon Kindle Direct Publishing (KDP) distributes your ebook in Kindle (MOBI) format to the Amazon store only. You can upload your manuscript in the following formats: Word doc or docx, HTML (ZIP, HTM), MOBI, EPUB, RTF, TXT, PDF, or KPF. Most authors use Word but saving the doc to HTML first is preferred. You'll find clear instructions on how to do this when you're ready for it. Amazon is very good at hand-holding.

TIP: If you have already formatted your book for the Smashwords edition (using their style guide or a book design template), give it a new ISBN and make adjustments as spelled out in the KDP formatting guidelines. (Or vice-versa, you can copy your KDP file and modify it for Smashwords.

Price your book between $2.99 – $9.99 USD and you earn 70 percent minus 15¢ per megabyte. (Other countries have similar pricing but for authors in Brazil, India, Mexico, and Japan it defaults to 35 percent flat royalty.)

Amazon KDP provides email customer support with knowledgeable staff and good response times.

You can also get your book in the Amazon store by distributing with IngramSpark, Draft2Digital, StreetLib, PublishDrive, and the full-service self-publishing companies listed in chapter 42.

Ebook royalty rates are 35 percent of list price in all territories or 70 percent of list price minus delivery costs in set territories (and 35 percent of list outside those territories). To get 70 percent your ebooks must be priced between $2.99 and $9.99.

Amazon KDP Select

When you publish an ebook using Amazon KDP you will be invited to use KDP Select. Don't do this unless you educate yourself on the exclusive program and you're using it for your book launch. You can always do this later.

Amazon makes you think that you haven't finished uploading your ebook if you don't click Enroll in KDP Select but you don't have to so ignore them.

Amazon Kindle Kids' Book Creator

See *Design and Formatting.*

Amazon KDP Print

kdp.amazon.com/en_US/help/topic/G202059560

Amazon KDP is the tool Amazon wants you to use to get your ebooks and print books into the Amazon store. They produce paperbacks "on-demand" for sale in the Amazon store, but not hardcover books. (For hardcover books I suggest IngramSpark.)

Create your files (I recommend using Book Design Templates or Vellum, or a professional book designer, for the interior files and not the Amazon templates) and upload a PDF of the interior and the cover.

IngramSpark will distribute your POD to Amazon. Instead, I suggest going directly Amazon KDP to upload and distribute your books to the Amazon store. That way, you'll never get those pesky "Out of Stock" messages on Amazon. In addition, you can experiment with keywords and categories without incurring a change fee.

Don't use Amazon ISBNs, okay? Because when you distribute your paperback with IngramSpark or elsewhere you will need a second ISBN and things get weird. Remember, one ISBN = one book format. Paperback is a book format. So use the same ISBN for your paperback no matter where it's published, as explained in detail in chapter 12.

Royalty rates are 60 percent in the Amazon store worldwide with some exceptions.

Do not use Amazon's Expanded Distribution, either. Yes, it will make your book available to other online retailers and bookstores but there's a problem. The discount is set at 40 percent discount, which is all wrong in several ways:

1. You only need to set a 30 percent discount to sell to online retailers.
2. For bookstores, you'll need to set at least a 53 percent discount plus opt-into a returns program, which Amazon does not offer.
3. And finally, bookstores don't like Amazon and are hesitant (to say the least) to order books from them.

So, upload your paperback direct to Amazon using KDP Print but use a distribution service (or go direct-to-retailer) to sell everywhere else.

Apple iBooks Author

See *Design and Formatting.*

Barnes and Noble Press

press.barnesandnoble.com

Use BN Press to get your book into the BN store. Royalty rates are 65 percent for ebooks priced $10 and above on all copies sold, and the ability for authors to set ebook pre-orders 12 months in advance. On the print side, you'll find a variety of trim sizes, glossy cover options (in addition to matte), and color printing.

Your book will appear in ebook and print formats in their store. Best-selling authors are eligible to pitch their book to BN store buyers and host store events and book signings.

They have teamed up with 99 Designs to give you a special price on book cover design, interior book formatting, and ebook conversion.

Google Play

play.google.com/books/publish

With Google Play your ebook has the potential to reach one billion Android users in over 50 countries on multiple platforms. Your books can be discovered and previewed on the world's most popular search engine through Google Books.

To upload books directly to Google Play, sign in using an existing Google Account, or create a new account. Use the Play Books Partner Center to upload content, set prices, and choose the countries where you want to sell your books.

You will receive 52 percent of the list price (before taxes). In the US, if your book is priced at $14.95 you'll get $7.77. If the book is sold in another country, the earnings are calculated at 52 percent of the book's price at the exchange rate at time of sale.

Kobo Writing Life

kobo.com/us/en/p/writinglife

Kobo Writing Life is a do-it-yourself publishing portal that gets your book sold into the Kobo store and the Walmart eBookstore. In my opinion, Kobo has the best marketing programs of all the stores. If you apply to participate in a marketing program and don't get accepted they tell you why: an inappropriate cover, incomplete metadata, or weirdly formatted book interior.

Simply upload your document and they automatically convert it to

EPUB format. (As long as it's formatted correctly with styles.) As with other direct-to-retailer ebook services, you don't need an ISBN; they'll assign a number for you though I always think you should purchase and assign your own ISBN to each format of your book.

Kobo is a Canadian-based company with retail partners around the globe and an arrangement with the American Booksellers Association to sell ebooks in bookstores. Their parent company is Japanese e-commerce giant Rakuten and in August 2018 they partnered with Walmart.

Your book will be available to over 12 million readers in 190 countries with Kobo and now, with Rakuten's deal with Walmart becoming the exclusive mass retailer of Kobo devices, the service extends Kobo's reach into the United States. Co-branded Walmart and Kobo apps are now available for ebook and audiobook content, and Walmart stores will sell digital book cards.

Kobo offers authors 70 percent of the list price on books priced $2.99 and higher, 45 percent for books priced between 99¢ and $2.98, and you can also offer your ebooks for free.

Listen to my interview with Chrissy Munroe, Director of Kobo Writing Life, on the Author Friendly Podcast at www.authorfriendly.com.

41

DESIGN AND FORMATTING TOOLS

I've used most of these design, formatting, and conversion tools and services at one time or another and I like them for different reasons. Browse through them to find the ones that attract you.

See *Chapter 44, Online Marketplaces* for places to find professionals to do this for you (including Bublish, Fiverr, PubLaunch, and Reedsy).

You'll find interviews of the people behind these companies in the Author Friendly podcast.

Subscribe for access to updates in the *Consumer's Guide for Self-Publishers* web book:
www.selfpubbootcamp.com/readers

Adazing

www.adazing.com/free-tools-templates-graphics/
Find free book cover mockups, editable media kit, business card templates, sell sheet templates, etc. They upsell you constantly but this is good stuff for design and marketing.

Adobe Acrobat Pro / Document Cloud

acrobat.adobe.com/us/en/acrobat/acrobat-pro.html

Acrobat Pro and the new Acrobat Cloud are Adobe's software for viewing, creating, combining, and controlling Adobe PDF documents. If you're doing your own book formatting and conversion to PDF, you need these and you need to keep them updated. Most authors, however, hire this out.

You can create PDF files from any application that prints, combine files into a single PDF document, protect documents with password protection, annotate and collaborate, sign documents, create fillable forms, and export to Office apps retaining layout, fonts, formatting, and tables. Acrobat Pro can be purchased for about $50 if you search around the web and Document Cloud is a $14/mo subscription alone but it's included with a Creative Cloud subscription. The cloud version comes with many extras but most self-publishers won't need them.

Adobe InDesign

adobe.com/products/indesign.html

InDesign, unlike Word, was designed as a professional book and magazine production program. It is the de-facto standard used by professional book designers. It's expensive and a challenge to learn.

InDesign's paragraph styles are more accurate. It allows you to fine-tune line and letter spacing, images stay put and export to CMYK for print (instead of RGB), and it produces a more professional, polished book.

A subscription to InDesign costs about $10 per month. Whether you are using it yourself or hiring a professional, make absolutely sure they are using the latest version.

The easiest way to learn and format your own book in InDesign is to buy a template. If you get stuck, you can always pay a professional to finish it.

You'll spend about $70 for the template and $10 a month for the software subscription from Adobe, and it's a good idea to spend $25 a month for a subscription to Lynda.com for video instruction. (Try it free for a month.)

If you hate formatting, you won't do a good job, so spend the money to hire a pro if you want your book to look good. You can find adequate help for low cost using a service like Fiverr, Guru, or Gigbucks but most really good designers charge $500-$2000.

Get book design templates for InDesign at http://bit.ly/interiorbdt.

Amazon Kindle Create

kdp.amazon.com/en_US/help/topic/GHU4YEWXQGNLU94T

Kindle Create is Amazon's tool for creating Kindle ebooks. You can create text-heavy books like novels and memoirs, fixed-layout ebooks (they call them *Print Replica* ebooks), and comic or graphic novels with Kindle Create.

This tool is Amazon's answer to book design templates and I think it may eventually replace Amazon's other book creation and formatting tools like Kindle Comic Creator and Kindle Kid's Book Creator.

Remember that this tool only creates ebooks for the Amazon Kindle devices and apps.

Start by downloading Kindle create to your PC or Mac and importing your document (doc, docx, pdf).

Import your doc or docx file to create a text-heavy book like a novel, memoir, or business book. This will create a Kindle for MOBI document that reflows in the Kindle devices and apps. Choose from various styles and themes to design your book interior. Readers can read your books on all the various ebook reading devices and apps.

Upload a PDF to start building a fixed-layout book with lots of images like textbooks, travel books, and cookbooks using your print PDF file. This PDF is converted into a *Print Replica* ebook that maintains the look of their print editions but does not allow the reader to resize the pages. These kinds of books can only be read in Kindle Fire and tablet devices.

If you have a comic or graphic novel you can use Kindle Create to create a comic ebook. A *Guided View* feature animates panel-to-panel movement with each swipe to move the story forward across each page.

Amazon Kindle Comic Creator

amazon.com/gp/feature.html?docId=1001103761

Kindle Comic Creator is Amazon's older (than Kindle Create) tool for Windows or Mac. It turns comics, graphic novels, and manga into Kindle books. You can import artwork, create guided navigation, set double-page spreads or facing pages, and preview how your book will look on Kindle Fire tablets and Kindle eInk readers. Don't be surprised if it gets retired and replaced with Kindle Create.

Amazon Kindle Kids' Book Creator

kdp.amazon.com/kids

Use Amazon Kindle Kids' Book Creator to create and sell children's ebooks to owners of Kindle Fire tablets. The authors I know who have used it say that it's still pretty basic, but expect improvements and enhancements over time. This is the only way to create a children's book for the Kindle Fire other than doing it yourself or hiring a professional designer and, I think, a great way to break into publishing books for kids. I think this tool may be replaced with Amazon Kindle Create.

Apple iBooks Author

apple.com/ibooks-author

Available free on the Mac App Store, iBooks Author enables you to create ebooks for the iPad and the Mac. You can use an Apple-designed template or use your own imagination. If you have a full-color ebook or interactive book idea, know that you can create swipe-friendly photo galleries, animations, scrolling sidebars, pop-over widgets, and 3D objects. Widgets can be set to play automatically, offering your readers a fun surprise when they turn the page. Then export your book in iBooks format to publish and sell on iTunes. You can also upload your book to Gumroad or another direct sales tool. Royalties are 70 percent of list price.

If you have a simpler book and don't need all the bells and whistles of iBooks Author, or a plain text book, a good alternative for creating EPUBs to upload to Apple (and other stores) is Vellum.

Author Marketplaces

See *Online Marketplaces*.

Author Solutions

WARNING: iUniverse, Author House, Trafford, Xlibris, BookTango, Balboa for HayHouse, LifeRich for Reader's Digest, Archway for Simon and Schuster, and Westbow for Thomas Nelson.

See *Full-Service Companies* to understand why a professional self-publisher should not use these companies.

Barnes and Noble Press

See *Direct to Retailer*.

Blurb

blurb.com

Blurb's self-publishing creation and distribution service is free and they take a fee when you make a sale. They specialize in glossy, full-color books but can also help you produce trade paperbacks and hardcovers with their DIY tools

I often recommend Blurb as a design concept tool. It's easy to use and you can create a draft book to test your concept and even sell your book if you like. But printing costs are astronomical.

Recently I was at a boat show and one of the yacht rental companies had created a Blurb book as a glossy, expensive brochure for potential clients who pay the equivalent of my annual income on a ten-day vacation. Wedding photographers use Blurb to print and sell albums. I've also recommended using Blurb as a marketing tool—an easy way to create small color books that advertise your other work.

Use their BookWright tool if you want to test ideas for a full color book. But I hope you'll eventually hire a pro.

BookWright, however, is proprietary software, so you can't export it for import into InDesign. You can purchase a PDF of your own book and conceivably print it elsewhere.

BookBaby

See *Full-Service Companies*.

Bookbuilder's Almanac

amzn.to/2psP6Yj

I love this book. The Bookbuilder's Almanac is an idea book of typefaces you can use to choose fonts for your book. It includes articles on how to accurately estimate length, on page density, and photos. The section on grayscale conversion illustrates how the various profiles change tints and photos. Samples of tints and lines settle concerns about detail and screened areas. With it, you can predict how your design will perform before you print the book.

Book Design Templates

bit.ly/interiorbdt

These are my favorite templates. The easiest and cheapest way to format your book in Word is by using a template. Simply choose a design you like, paste your Word document into it and apply the appropriate styles that are predesigned for each element of your books such as your chapter headings and body text.

It's easy to customize the template to make it your own. Simply change the fonts, leading, headers, and footers. The Book Design Templates company provides easy instructions to guide you through the entire process to make your book look beautiful and professional.

The Book Design Templates company also offers a media kit for your website, press release template, book proposal template, and lots of other products. These tools offload much of the hard work of design and rote work by providing do-it-for-you products and services for reasonable prices.

All the major book POD and distribution companies accept these templates, including Amazon, IngramSpark, Draft2Digital, Kobo, and Smashwords.

Bublish

bublish.com

Bublish is a hybrid publisher for independent authors that offers a la carte book creation services and packages that include design and formatting, marketing, and distribution. Premium services include Amazon and Facebook ads, email marketing, hand-selling at events, professional distribution, and even more perks for select authors. All this for $99/yr and a 15% commission on sales. Get details on Bublish in *Chapter 39, Distribution Tools and Services.*

Calibre

calibre.com

Use the free, open-source Calibre desktop app to convert your book files into MOBI and EPUB format.

When you're creating Advanced Reader Copies (ARCs) for reviewers, I always recommend providing a choice of print, PDF, MOBI, or EPUB. Personally, I like reviewing books on my Kindle. I travel too much to haul books around with me. If they're not in MOBI format, I'll never get to it.

Once you download the Calibre application you simply add your book —it can be in Word format—complete the book metadata (title, author name, description and all that), create a simple cover or upload your professionally designed cover, click the CONVERT button, and download it to your computer. Then upload it to a private folder on DropBox (or similar, see Business and Productivity Tools), and invite your reviewers to grab a copy.

Canva

canva.com/create/book-covers

Use Canva's free book cover maker to create temporary covers and as ideas to give to your designer.

Canva offers premade templates in various genres to choose from with images and typography that work well together. I also like Canva's social media banner and blog post templates.

Canva's Book Cover Maker is free if you upload your own images, but their images cost only $1 or $2. Cost is $0, $9, and $18/mo which includes over a million royalty free images and about 600 templates.

Here are a few Canva competitors: Design Wizard and Stencil are two, and Depositphotos, a site for stock photos, has a similar tool called Crello.

DesignWizard licenses your design for as many uses as you need while Canva makes you license every single use.

Convert Town's Change DPI of Image

convert.town/image-dpi

See Conversion tools.

Font Squirrel

fontsquirrel.com

Use Font Squirrel to find free fonts for commercial use. It also offers a font identifier so you can upload an image of a font you like and it will tell you what it is.

FastPencil

See *Full-Service Companies.*

Gatekeeper Press

See *Full-Service Companies.*

Kobo Writing Life

See *Chapter 39, Distribution Tools and Services.*

Kotobee

kotobee.com

Kotobee helps you create EPUB-based interactive ebooks that run across all devices and platforms. It's a desktop app for Windows and Mac an affordable $150 or $300 lifetime subscription. You can also create mobile apps at $30, $150, or $500 levels.

Microsoft Word

bit.ly/interiorbdt

Microsoft Word is the most popular program for writing, designing and formatting a book interior. Over the years it has evolved from a simple word processing application to a sophisticated page layout program.

To format a book interior, you'll need to learn about Word Styles. Styles automate character, section, and paragraph formatting. This is how Word "programs" your document to display your book correctly in all the ebook reading devices.

When you work in Word to format your book, it's essential that you use Styles instead of line and paragraph breaks, spaces and tabs.

I wrote a how-to guide about this. Download it free at Smashwords with code EC55D. (One of the reasons I like Smashwords is that they have the ability to discount and offer freebies with coupon codes.) See more about them in *Chapter 39, Distribution Tools and Services*.

Pandoc

pandoc.org

GEEK ALERT! If you need to convert files from one markup format into another, Pandoc is your Swiss-army knife.

Pandoc can convert documents in (several dialects of) Markdown, reStructuredText, textile, HTML, DocBook, LaTeX, MediaWiki markup, TWiki markup, TikiWiki markup, Creole 1.0, Vimwiki markup, OPML, Emacs Org-Mode, Emacs Muse, txt2tags, Microsoft Word docx, LibreOffice ODT, EPUB, or Haddock markup to HTML, word processor formats, ebooks, documentation formats, archival formats, page layout formats, outline formats, TeX formats, PDF, lightweight markup formats, and custom formats written in lua.

Pressbooks

pressbooks.com

If you like WordPress you'll like Pressbooks, an online publishing tool that produces beautifully-designed PDFs for print and print-on-demand. Use it to create print books that you sell using vendors like Amazon and IngramSpark, along with ebooks you publish on Kindle for Amazon and EPUB for Apple iBooks, B&N, and Kobo.

It's built on the open source WordPress blogging platform so, if you're blogging on WordPress, you already know how to use it. I've created several books and booklets with Pressbooks, including an earlier edition of this guide.

I like the Pressbooks blog-to-book import feature. It's really the best tool for creating a first draft of a book from a series of blog posts.

Simply log into Pressbooks, paste in your text, add front and back matter, and choose one of their beautifully designed interior book themes. When you're ready, export your book to PDF, EPUB, and MOBI.

If you're intimidated by Pressbooks, start small by using it to create a short book to give away to your email newsletter subscribers. Or pay Pressbooks to do it all for you.

You can create and format a book for free and pay $19.99 to remove the watermark from your ebook and $99 to remove it from both the ebook and print book.

Listen to my interview with Elizabeth Mays of Pressbooks on the Author Friendly Podcast at www.authorfriendly.com.

Publish Xpress

convert.town/image-dpi

Very handy. You need images of at least 200 dpi for your print books, but what if your images (and screenshots) are only 72 dpi for digital publishing? If you don't have Photoshop or GIMP image-editing programs, or you want a fast way to increase the DPI of an image, use this tool. Drag your low-resolution to their site to make it either 200 DPI (for simple graphics) or 300 dpi (for photos).

Related is Zamzar, a file conversion service described below.

Scrivener

Windows or Mac

Scrivener is one of my favorite book creation tools. It's a desktop writing and organization app that costs around $40. It offers an amazing feature set that can help you develop stories and books, blog posts, articles, and any kind of writing. I learned about it from a screenwriter friend. It's got a visual view feature that shows you your scenes as notes on a cork board, which can be very helpful when organizing your work and can show you story and content gaps.

I use it to organize and write my blog posts, articles, and books. There's a 30-day free trial.

Vellum lets you import your Scrivener doc for final formatting. You can also sync your work amongst computers using DropBox.

Look for discounts on Scrivener during NaNoWriMo.

Text Mechanic

textmechanic.com

Use Text Mechanic's handy browser-based text manipulation tools to clean up your manuscript before formatting. Add or remove line breaks, remove duplicate or empty lines, and extra spaces. Combine lines, find and replace text, count characters, words, and lines, and even extract a single column of text. These are the basics. They also offer obfuscation tools, randomization, combination/permutation, and enumeration tools. Free.

Vellum

vellum.pub

Vellum is becoming the go-to app for Mac users to easily create beautiful ebooks. Book styles incorporate classic touches like custom drop caps and ornamental flourishes. A live preview instantly shows how your book will appear to readers and refreshes when you make changes.

In June 2018 they added auto-import from Scrivener.

Vellum Ebooks is $199.99 and Vellum Press for print (and digital) is $249.99.

I used Vellum to design and format this updated 5th edition of my book.

Zamzar

zamzar.com

Zamzar is a browser-based conversion tool for over 1200 kinds of document, audio, and video formats. I use this app all the time.

Use it to convert Word documents created on the Mac, which do not retain hyperlinks when converted to PDF. You can also convert your documents into MOBI and EPUB formats, which is great when you want to offer a freebie to your email subscribers. And you can also use Zamzar to convert image files.

I use the free version but if you convert lots and lots of files they offer basic, pro, and business versions for $9, $16, and $25 per month.

42

FULL SERVICE COMPANIES

THESE SERVICES DO THE DESIGN AND FORMATTING FOR YOU. Some may also provide e-book and print book distribution.

Subscribe for access to updates in the *Consumer's Guide for Self-Publishers* web book:
www.selfpubbootcamp.com/readers

Author Solutions Companies

BEWARE: iUniverse, Author House, Trafford, Xlibris, BookTango, Balboa for HayHouse, LifeRich for Reader's Digest, Archway for Simon and Schuster, and Westbow for Thomas Nelson.

All of the above companies are run by Author Solutions, Inc. and are overpriced vanity presses that do not let you assign your own ISBN, charge too much for printing, set unrealistic expectations, and upsell you at every opportunity. Do your research before you choose vanity or subsidy publishing. Victoria Strauss maintains the Writer Beware site, where she lists predatory vanity presses, unethical agents, contest and award fakes, and other alerts for writers. Check it before you publish.

BAM!Publish

bampublish.com

BAM!Publish is a "complete authoring and publishing solution" powered by FastPencil (see below) for the Books A Million bookstores across the United States. Their "packages" are $699, $1799, and $2799. I can't recommend this service for professional independent authors and publishers. However, if you have one book and dream of seeing it in a bookstore, and you have the money, who am I to deny you this personal but probably unprofitable satisfaction?

BookBaby

bit.ly/bookbabyforauthors

BookBaby offers full-service book creation and distribution as well as à la carte services like editing and cover design. Instead of taking a percentage of sales, they charge a flat fee and you keep 100 percent of net sales (after the sales channels have taken their percentage).

Disc Makers, the company that owns BookBaby, also serves indie musicians and filmmakers with CDBaby. Their HostBaby website builder is an easy-to-use content management system for building your author or musician website. You also get a BookShop page, where you can earn more royalty by selling direct, which is a handy link for your website.

Their paperback book printing service is very good with prices to match. They also produce color books, complex books, and hardback books.

At this time, BookBaby will be listed as the publisher of your book, even if you've supplied an ISBN under your publisher name. If branding with your publisher name is important to you, use a service like Gatekeeper Press and pay the extra fee to use your own publisher name.

Booklocker

booklocker.com

Booklocker offers self-publishing packages for any budget. Their DIY option costs a $25 setup fee with a $35 proof. The first year POD file-hosting fee is $18. Their most popular program is a basic service where you send your Word doc and cover and they do the rest. They can help with fiction and non-fiction as well as children's and other full-color interior books. Booklocker distributes with Ingram, library, and school partners. The company also owns WritersWeekly.com.

Bookstores Near You

Does a bookstore near you offer self-publishing help? Bookshop Santa Cruz's publishing service is a good example. I used to live in Santa Cruz and I know this independent bookshop is well loved by locals and tourists. There is a large writing community there and I expect they started the service at the suggestion of more than one author-customer. So check with your independent bookstores to see if they offer a service like this.

FastPencil

fastpencil.com

FastPencil offers an online ebook and print book creation tool with templates and a cover creator in the cloud with version control, writing, editing, and collaboration tools. Despite its impressive suite of tools and services, I can only recommend it for professional independent authors if you pay $599 for a Small Publisher Custom Imprint Setup, in addition to the other costs. Why? Because otherwise, you do not get to apply your own ISBN and therefore your publisher is FastPencil.

It's free to create and print your book privately. It costs $249 to distribute your book to Amazon, BAM!, Ingram, Kobo and more. They charge $999 to add project setup, review, and cover design, and $1999 for a premium version of the same.

If you are a prolific blogger who wants to turn your blog posts into books, you might consider FastPencil, but Pressbooks offers an easy alternative for $99.

FastPencil also provide book marketing services, which I don't recommend because you should do your own. Outsourcing book marketing (in my opinion) is the number one worst investment a self-published author can make. (See *Part VI, Book Marketing and Promotion.*)

The bottom line: If you are a multi-book author looking for a cloud-based book creation tool that allows multiple people to contribute to the book, along with a distribution service, and you are selling enough to recoup the fees, you may be tempted FastPencil's features. But print your book elsewhere because their inflated printing costs make your books more than twice as expensive as other services.

FastPencil is the technology behind BAM!Publish, which guarantees your printed book in their stores across the US.

Gatekeeper Press

gatekeeperpress.com

Gatekeeper Press is a full-service company that offers design, formatting, and distribution to the major online retailers. You can also use them for a la carte services like editing and cover design.

They offer great customer service (email and telephone), they have great prices on services and among the lowest prices I've seen on print books. (Find a price comparison in *Chapter 17, Creating Your Print PDF.*)

They'll handle your ebook and print book creation and distribution, editing, and cover design for about $600.00 plus 99¢/page beyond

200 pages. They distribute to all the major ebook and print book retailers. Gatekeeper makes its money by charging you up-front for services. You keep 100 percent of your royalties.

If you want to use your own imprint name they charge an extra $100 but they've offered my readers free imprint setup with code "carlaking."

You'll also get 10 percent off with an IBPA membership. (See more about IBPA in *Professional Organizations*.)

43

AUDIOBOOK AND PODCASTING TOOLS

PEOPLE LOVE AUDIOBOOKS AND THERE IS MORE DEMAND THAN supply. So it makes sense to consider creating one for your book. Don't worry, you don't necessarily have to be the voice actor.

You can also offer your book as a podcast. Browse these tools and services for a solution that matches your skillset and budget level.

Subscribe for access to updates in the *Consumer's Guide for Self-Publishers* web book:
www.selfpubbootcamp.com/readers

Amazon ACX

acx.com

You can narrate your own book, share royalties with a narrator, or pay a narrator up-front with ACX. Every audiobook you make on ACX will be available on Audible.com, Amazon.com, and iTunes. If you grant Audible exclusive distribution rights to your ebook you'll earn royalties of 40 percent.

Audacity

audacity.org

I use Audacity a lot to record interviews or audio lessons. It is a free, open-source recording software you can use to record your own audiobook. To record your own audiobook you'll also need the following:

- A computer with a USB port
- A high-quality microphone with a stand and a pop filter
- A quiet place with no background noise or echo
- Audiobook creation software (like Audiobook Builder for Mac) to create a MP3 file at CBR recorded in mono format, with opening credits, closing credits, and each chapter a "track."

You can sell your audiobook on your own website using an e-commerce system like Gumroad, or distribute it using Kbuuk or Amazon ACX.

Author's Republic

authorsrepublic.com

Author's Republic is an "aggregate distributor" that claims to be the world's widest audiobook distribution network with over 30 major retailers, library providers and distributors, with new channels added monthly. (Though Findaway, below, seems to have more.) Upload your audiobook (made by you or with a service) for distribution. If it meets their minimum standards they send it to their distributors who have the right to accept or reject it (takes 5-60 days), and receive 70 percent of earnings.

Book2Pod

book2pod.com

Book2Pod transforms your book into audio files using text-to-speech technology, and publishes each book chapter as podcast episodes on iTunes, Stitcher, Google Play, and Spotify. You get your own podcast channel and landing page. The robotic voices are not perfect but at $147 for a conversion it's a fraction of the cost of a professional narrator. (This could serve as a tool to catch copyediting errors.)

Findaway Voices

findawayvoices.com

Findaway Voices provides narration, production, quality-checking, and distribution services for audio books. They distribute to retail, library, and K–12 consumers in more than 170 countries. Royalty rates vary by retailer but works out to about 80 percent.

Narration cost is calculated on a per-finished-hour basis and varies based on book length, narrator selected, and complexity. There's a calculator on their site so you can estimate costs.

Their $49 administration fee is waived when signing up as part of Draft2Digital's distribution service.

ListenUp Audiobooks

listenupindie.pub

Listen up is an award-winning, spoken-word audio production company and audiobook publisher based in Atlanta, Georgia with studios and talent country-wide. They can distribute your audiobook at no extra cost at 80 percent net.

Podiobooks

scribl.com/info/podiobooks

Podiobooks merged with Scribl to supply readers with companion audiobooks and podcasts. Create an audiobook, upload the files, and upload your e-book files (EPUB and MOBI).

In a few days (or hours, sometimes), you'll see your audiobook in all of the audiobook outlets to which Scribl distributes. In addition, a free, serialized version will appear on iTunes and Stitcher, plus others, like Google. You'll earn 70 percent royalty.

You earn 85 royalty when your book sells on Scribl. If you opt into Scribl's CrowdPricing Everywhere system you'll get 90 percent royalty. This royalty is higher than going direct to some retailers, including Amazon.

SoundCloud

soundcloud.com

SoundCloud has been called "the YouTube of audio." It's a social sound platform that lets you create audio and share it everywhere on the web, privately and publicly, and to all your social networks. They also provide an embed widget for your site and blog. With the free account, you get 120 minutes of uploaded audio. It's easy to use and a great way to offer free audio previews of your work (excerpts, story readings, interviews) though there is no way for visitors to pay you for the content. I really like this app but the company may be in trouble, so hold off.

VoiceBunny

voicebunny.com

Get high-quality, professional audiobooks produced without paying royalty fees, keep all the rights to your audio, and distribute it however you choose. Crowdsourcing technology lets you choose from over 28,000 voice actors in many languages, accents, and age groups.

VoiceBunny partnered with Kbuuk, the audio book distributor, to get your book into Amazon, B&N, and Kobo.

When you're ready to create an audiobook, check out the new Voice-Bunny App available in the Kbuuk Publishing App Store. From there, a member of the VoiceBunny client services team will personally assist you.

On the VoiceBunny site you can either 1) browse for actors and book one, or 2) run a contest, or 3) get a "speedy" (do it for you, fast).

For the speedy option, a 60,000-word book would cost $1,197.

44

ONLINE MARKETPLACES

WHERE DO YOU GO IF YOU DON'T HAVE A RECOMMENDATION FOR book designers, formatters, editors, and marketers? These online marketplaces have sprung up to list vetted professionals to choose from.

Subscribe for access to updates in the *Consumer's Guide for Self-Publishers* web book:
www.selfpubbootcamp.com/readers

Bublish

bublish.leadpages.co/author-services/

Bublish offers a la carte design, formatting, editorial, and coaching services along with marketing and distribution. Choose a service or a package, and definitely use their free Book Bubbles book promo service. See *Chapter 39, Distribution Tools and Services* for details on Bublish.

Bibliocrunch

bibliocrunch.com

Bibliocrunch is a community of authors, curated publishing professionals and readers. Post a project, receive proposals and view profiles of rated and reviewed professionals. They have a concierge service to guide you through the self-publishing process for only $25/mo, which I think is a great price. Also fabulous is their new suite of promotional tools for authors to help you host contests and book giveaways. Start for free.

Fiverr

fiverr.com

Fiverr is useful for finding people to do simple jobs or fixes. I've found people to correct my website PHP, to remove backgrounds and touch-up photos, to create bookmarks in a very large Word file, help me produce audio files for my podcast, and other tedious jobs.

Unfortunately, I've found many problems with manuscripts formatted by people on Fiverr. I'm going to generalize here and say that they do not realize that headers and footers do not belong on the first pages of chapters, or that chapters open on odd pages, and they don't take into account half-title and title pages and other standard front and back matter.

In short, Fiverr people are likely to do exactly what you tell them to do, and no more. I've experienced exceptions to this rule, of course, but that's the general impression I've had from using it for a few years now.

Fiverr alternatives include FiverUp, GigBucks, and Guru. A more sophisticated Fiverr alternative is UpWork where you'll find more experienced (and higher-priced) professionals who are vetted by the company.

PubLaunch

publaunch.com

PubLaunch is a Canadian company that offers an online marketplace that's connected with a centralized book production platform as well as a crowdfunding platform. PubLaunch was founded by a longtime editor and they are especially careful about the editors they allow on their platform. Listen to my interview with PubLaunch founder Greg Ioannou on the Author Friendly Podcast at www.authorfriendly.com.

Reedsy

reedsy.com

Reedsy offers two things: a free online marketplace where you can find pros like editors and designers and a free, simple online formatting tool that exports ebook and print files so you can upload them to the various retailers. They don't have many styling options right now, but it's good enough for ebooks, and worth keeping an eye on this free tool.

Reedsy takes a 10 percent commission on each side of the collaborations that take place on the platform. For example, if the author accepts a quote for $1,000 from an editor, the editor will receive $900.

In exchange, they provide a smart collaboration interface with messaging, file sharing, integration to Dropbox and GoogleDrive, automated payments, and project protection, which offers mediation and refunds in case of dispute.

StreetLib

streetlib.com

StreetLib is an ebook and print book creation and distribution service that also offers a marketplace but it's pretty narrow at present, mostly for services in Italian. The company has expanded to the US so expect these services to grow. See more about StreetLib in *Chapter 39, Distribution Tools and Services.*

UpWork

upwork.com

Find a qualified freelancer to do your interior book design, formatting, or book cover design. Find an editor, proofreader, indexer, copywriter, ghostwriter, email marketing pro, illustrator, videographer, voice talent, translator, administrative support, and so on.

The UpWork interface forces time tracking and takes random screenshots to check that the worker is actually working on your job.

I found an interior book designer on UpWork who was extremely professional and did great work. I interviewed him by submitting a brief. (I only submitted briefs to qualified pros with 95 percent and higher customer ratings). He wasn't the least expensive but I think I got a deal because he did it fast. Quality counts.

Writers Boon

writersboon.com

Writer's Boon is a nonprofit organization with book promotion tools, discount marketplace, expert answers, and sales to libraries. $89/year.

45

BOOK SALES TRACKING TOOLS

When you use tracking you can monitor the effectiveness of your advertising, social media campaigns, and personal appearances. You can also use tracking to see if changes in metadata (keywords, book descriptions, book covers) are working to get it in front of the right audience.

Subscribe for access to updates in the *Consumer's Guide for Self-Publishers* web book:
www.selfpubbootcamp.com/readers

Amazon Kindle

Only shows 90 days of book sales. Free. Reach it through your Amazon Author Central page.

Amazon Author Central

authorcentral.amazon.com

Shows Nielsen BookScan, sales rank, and author rank for each of your books. Free. Reach this data through your Amazon Author Central page.

BookCore

bookcore.net

BookCore connects to your Amazon KDP, Apple iBooks, Google Play Books, and Smashwords, and collects your book's sales data, tracks reviews and stars, rankings, and revenue. It's in beta, so it's not perfect, but this is probably the best and most complete solution of all the tracking tools. Free for now.

Book Report for Kindle

getbookreport.com

Book Report is a free browser extension or "bookmarklet" to track your earnings in the Kindle store. It's free unless you earn more than $1000 from your Kindle books, then you'll pay $10/mo.

eBookTracker for Kindle

tracker.kindlenationdaily.com

See the impact of marketing efforts and price changes on your books' sales ranks and pricing, know right away when sales start to slow on one of your titles and see how your books' rank and pricing data compare to those of your competitors. Free.

TrackerBox for Windows

storyboxsoftware.com/tdownload.htm

Unfortunately for me, a Mac user, TrackerBox is only available for Windows users. It tracks your book sales across all the major retailers and generates reports that will help you with your sales strategy. Users report that it's well worth the one-time fee of $59.99.

46

WRITING AND EDITING SOFTWARE

Manuscript editing software programs do much more than the built-in spelling and grammar checkers in your word processor. Some offer "first-pass" or "last-pass" editing to clean up mistakes in spelling, grammar, and punctuation; others help you improve your writing with detailed reports.

These programs can alert you to overuse of adverbs, clichés, redundancies, overlong sentences, sticky sentences, glue words, vague and abstract words, diction, and the misuse of dialog tags, to name just a few. Some will even connect you with a human editor with a click of a button. In alphabetical order, here are some of my favorites (this is by no means an exhaustive list)

Subscribe for access to updates in the *Consumer's Guide for Self-Publishers* web book:
www.selfpubbootcamp.com/readers

AutoCrit

autocrit.com

AutoCrit is well organized and offers a lot of information in a clean interface. In my writing, it revealed an excess of generic descriptions, passive voice, and too many initial pronouns, names, and "ing" words. I also use too many "ly" adverbs. On the plus side, I'm great at showing and not telling, and I don't repeat words and phrases or use a lot of filler words or clichés.

All these were easy fixes once I was made aware of them. But hey, if you're feeling depressed about your errors, just click the "compare to fiction" tab to show how your writing stacks up against published works, including mass-market paperbacks and bestsellers. It might make you feel better.

The manuscript analysis provides a lot of constructive criticism in a clean, easy-to-read layout. I like the visual charts representing sentence length and paragraph pace.

AutoCrit is $29.97/month.

Consistency Checker

intelligentediting.com/products-pricing/consistency-checker

This free software will find the mistakes your spelling and grammar checkers don't see, such as inconsistent hyphenation (part time vs. part-time) and spelling (color vs. colour). It also finds things like numerals in the middle of sentences, compound words, and abbreviations that appear in different forms.

It does not check spelling and grammar, just consistency. Note: this is the freemium version of the $99 PerfectIt app for Microsoft Office 2013 and Google Docs.

It targets long nonfiction documents like proposals, grants, and how-to manuals. I wish this kind of tool had existed back when I was a Silicon Valley technical writer.

Install Consistency Checker in Word by visiting the Microsoft Office 2013 store. To install it in Google Docs, go to the store listing, log in and click "Free."

Now, when you run Google Docs, Consistency Checker will appear in the "Add-ons" menu.

Draft

draftin.com

Draft is a writing, editing, collaboration, and publishing tool you access online using your browser. Each contributor's changes show up in different colors, with "accept" and "reject" options. You can mark major revisions, find and revert to previous versions, import docs from Dropbox, Evernote, and Google Drive, and publish directly to places like WordPress, Tumblr, LinkedIn, and even MailChimp. They've provided a handy Chrome extension that lets you turn any text area on the web into something you can write and edit with Draft. You can even hire a human editor via the program.

Draft makes it clear what changes have been made and lets you collaborate with many others in the cloud.

You can email a document to your Draft account and create a simple presentation, then select segments of writing. The "simplify" robot catches common words and duplicate words and attempts to detect and delete unimportant sentences.

Other features include an audio-video transcription tool, analytics, and a website builder tool. "Hemingway Mode" provides distraction-free writing.

Draft is free, but donations unlock more benefits.

Fictionary

fictionary.co

Fictionary is a browser-based tool that identifies plot holes and time-line issues, pacing, scenes with no purpose, confusing points of view, or empty stages. It provides you with a word count per scene, rewriting tips, and a visual narrative arc with character evaluation (entry and exit), and more.

This could be a good tool to use before you send your manuscript to an expensive content editor.

Fictionary integrates with both Grammarly and ProWritingAid via the Chrome browser extension.

$20/mo with a free 14-day trial.

Grammarly

bit.ly/grammarlyforauthors

Grammarly delivers information both line-by-line and summary form. I like the way it follows me around the web to check my WordPress blog posts, my Google Docs, Gmail, and comment and feedback forms on others' blog posts and articles. Because I am a professional writer, it is embarrassing when I make basic spelling and grammatical errors in quick, social media posts and emails, so I appreciate this feature.

Grammarly costs $139.95 annually. There's a 7-day money-back guarantee so you can try it out. If you need a human editor, quick, you can reach one through their site for a reasonable price.

Like most robust editing tools, Grammarly offers settings for various kinds of writing: business documents, novels, creative nonfiction, medical, technical, and casual. I set mine to creative nonfiction. And it looks like I have some work to do.

Hemingway Editor

hemingwayapp.com

Hemingway is a distraction-free writing tool that displays a row of formatting elements across the top for bold, italics, bulleting, numbering, headings, and links. Slide it from WRITE mode into EDIT and you'll get a clean, visual take on what might be wrong with your writing. The word and character counters are also very handy.

With the $10 desktop app for Mac and Windows you can import and export your text to Word, and export as HTML or Markdown language for your blogging platform, WordPress, or CMS files.

Some people like to write and edit in Hemingway and then import into a tool called StackEdit, a browser-based Markdown editor, though you could easily use any of the other tools I've already mentioned.

The browser-based version is free. The desktop app for Mac and Windows costs $10.

MasterWriter

masterwriter.com

MasterWriter is a valuable addition to any of the editors described in this chapter. It's a thesaurus on steroids in the cloud that will improve your vocabulary and your prose. Enrich your writing with its synonym finder, rhyming dictionary, alliterations, word families, phrases, dictionary, and even a set of 11,000 icons of world culture to add imagery to your writing.

Instead of your story's sun being simply hot you'll find ideas like blazing, sizzling, fiery, torrid, punishing, merciless, or raging. Just put a word in the left side and click the dictionary you want to use and get results on the right side.

Check out the video tour and I think you'll be impressed. An audio page enables you to collect your thoughts or music. Free trial and then $99.95/annually or $149.95 for two years.

ProWritingAid

prowritingaid.com

Of all the tools I've used and reviewed, ProWritingAid probably offers the most value, especially with their clean, updated interface and detailed reports with the click of a link. I was so impressed I bought the annual subscription even though I also subscribe to Grammarly. I love their free Google Docs and Chrome browser extension. I still use Grammarly because it follows me everywhere on the web, but with its thorough critique, I think ProWritingAid makes me a better writer. As an editor and publisher, the reports also help me communicate better with my authors.

A scaled-down version of ProWritingAid is free online, with Premium editions offered at $40 annually, $60 for a two-year license, $80 for a three-year license, and $140 for lifetime use.

ProWritingAid also offers a couple of advanced features you may be interested in using. As a publisher, I can create my own rules and house style that detects patterns, wildcards, overused words, dialog, repeats, and lets me create customized advice messages for my authors. Their developer API allows software developers to add writing analysis to applications they are developing.

SmartEdit

smart-edit.com

SmartEdit is a first-pass-editing tool for creative writers and novelists working on Windows. Since I'm Mac-based, I couldn't review it but gleaned a lot of information from the screenshots and user reviews on their site. It costs $57-$67 for a desktop download, and there's a free 10-day trial period.

Like AutoCrit and Grammarly, SmartEdit runs a series of checks on your work and highlights areas of concern. You can open your manuscript directly in SmartEdit, or copy and paste from your word processor into the SmartEdit Editor.

Unique features include a sentence length graph and detection of curly/straight quotes, hyphen and em-dash counts. A sentence-start list displays your sentences and counts the number of times you begin them with a particular word, which can be shockingly instructive.

SmartEdit, like ProWritingAid, should be attractive to professional editors and publishers as it allows you to export lists of copyediting issues. Export to Excel, PDF, HTML, CSV, or text format to use when communicating with writers and editors.

WriteMonkey

writemonkey.com

The WriteMonkey folks describe their Windows desktop app as "zen-ware" for writers. Like Hemingway and Draft, WriteMonkey offers a stripped-down, distraction-free writing environment. You can customize your background, font, and what you see in the toolbar, such as word count, with a progress bar and the current time.

More advanced features are available as well, such as the ability to manage separate chapter files in a book-length work using a "Jumps" feature.

You write in simple text, formatting using Markdown language or the Textile markup language if you like. You can export to HTML and upload it to the web as a page or a blog post.

Like some of the other tools, WriteMonkey is supported by donations. Your donation gives you access to many plugins that are available separately.

SOCIAL PUBLISHING TOOLS & SITES

SOCIAL PUBLISHING CAN EXPOSE YOUR UNFINISHED AND finished books and stories to readers, allowing them to comment, like, and share.

Subscribe for access to updates in the *Consumer's Guide for Self-Publishers* web book:
www.selfpubbootcamp.com/readers

Booksie

booksie.com

Booksie is a free social publishing site that provides a place where writers and readers can connect from across the globe. Over the past seven years, tens of thousands of writers have posted hundreds of thousands of short stories, novels, poems, articles and more. Booksie is for writers 13+ (no adult content, use Booksiesilk for erotica).

Booksie organizes your portfolio and gives you tools (including a micro-blog) to connect with your audience. You can feature certain work in your portfolio, embed images and video, tell your readers about the latest news (micro-blogging), and keep tabs on your fans.

Booksiesilk

booksiesilk.com

A Booksie spin-off, Booksiesilk, is for erotica and adult content. "BooksieSilk is an adult place to explore those fantasies, share them, and read what thoughts and guilty pleasures others are thinking up. Whether your fantasy is imagined or really happened, you have found the place to let others enjoy the pleasures of your mind."

Bublish

bublish.com

Bublish is a hybrid publisher for independent author. Their free Book Bubbles feature is a great tool for social media marketing. Sign up for free to offer readers excerpts of your book presented professionally with your author photo, bio, book cover, and links to online retailers. Embed Book Bubbles in your website and share them on social media. They'll promote them in their newsletter, too. Realtime metrics show you which bubbles drive traffic to your website and social channels. Find out more about Bublish in *Chapter 39, Distribution Tools and Services.*

Facebook Notes

facebook.com/help/115983655152193

Facebook Notes is a great little publishing tool. You might commit to publishing your book so your fans, even if it's just your family and friends on Facebook, can hold you to a deadline.

Figment

figment.com

Figment is an online community and self-publishing platform for young writers. Created by Jacob Lewis and Dana Goodyear, who both worked at The New Yorker, the site officially launched on December 6, 2010. Figment currently has over 300,000 registered users and over 370,000 'books', or pieces of writing. Other features include frequent writing contests, a blog, forums, and The Figment Review. Figment is a Random House company. Make sure you read their terms of service before you sign up.

Scribd

scribd.com

You can upload your stories and books to Scribd publicly or privately and share them with your early readers. You can also sell there. See *Chapter 55, Direct Sales Tools* for details.

Wattpad

wattpad.com

Wattpad is worth more than a glance. It's the world's largest community for readers and writers. They have 60 million monthly users across the world who read the 400+ million uploads by 2.4 million writers in 244 different countries and 55 different languages.

The site's *raison d'être* is for sharing and commenting on stories. Genre writers and authors with a young adult audience get the most traction, but they are working to attract more mature readers. I have stories on Wattpad but they don't get much traction. However, I like the way they're presented and point my readers to my free stories there.

Here's how it works. Post your story on Wattpad, enter the metadata (keywords) and categories, and start being social. This is the key—

being social. Find other authors like you and comment on their story and, hopefully, they'll comment on yours.

Your story can be upvoted and readers can make comments on paragraphs. Readers can add your stories to their reading lists and mark it as a favorite. Wattpad curates a list of the best stories, called the Watties, which can also help float your stories to the top.

Wattpad blocks the copy/paste function, so you can post unpublished works on the site without worrying too much about copyright infringement.

Wattpad Premium for readers allows readers to get ad-free stories pushed to their mobile devices for $59.99 per year and there is no cost to authors.

WEBook

webook.com

Webook is geared towards discovering new writers and helping them on their path to publication by connecting writers, readers, and literary agents. WEbook was launched in 2008, with corporate offices based in New York City.

In addition to providing a venue for writers to reach an audience, WEbook actively helps writers find agents through their AgentInBox service. This service pre-screens query letters, guaranteeing that queries will meet industry standards, and allows writers to choose agents from the list of those interested in specific genres. Writers can also easily tailor manuscript samples to make sure every agent gets what they're looking for.

AgentInbox will automatically match each agent with the right sample version.

Writing.com

writing.com

Writing.com is geared to amateur writers and is one of the largest online writing communities o the web. The site offers writing portfolios, email, a newsfeed, groups, contests, survey forms, madlibs, submission tracking, and tutorials.

48

BETA AND CRITIQUE TOOLS

CRITIQUE PARTNERS AND BETA READERS SHOULD BE A KEY strategy in your marketing plan as described in *Chapter 3, The Importance of Beta Publishing*. Here are some tools that will help you connect with them. Subscribe for access to updates in the *Consumer's Guide for Self-Publishers* web book:

www.selfpubbootcamp.com/readers

BetaBooks

betabooks.co

BetaBooks is my favorite beta reading tool. It's a browser-based beta platform for sharing your manuscript and collecting feedback from your early readers. I used BetaBooks to share this guide with my beta team.

Your readers will love how easy and professional it feels to read and comment from any device and you will love the way it centralizes all the feedback.

The founders developed the platform to solve their own problem collecting reader feedback, and it shows.

No more converting between formats or dealing with you-know-who who can never manage to open your files. Invite your readers by email, and you're done.

Receive comments and track your readers' comments chapter by chapter and version by version. It saves so much time, you'll never wonder who's read what again. Filter your comments by reader, chapter, or character. Mark it as done when you've made the changes you want to make.

This is also a great tool for writing groups to share and comment on stories and books.

There are three ways to get readers to BetaBooks:

1. Bring your own beta readers to the platform.
2. Apply to share your book with The Beta Reader Pool.
3. Join The Beta Exchange and exchange manuscripts with other authors for critique.

Start with their free membership for one book and a max of three readers. The next tier is $149.99 for unlimited books and a max of 20 readers. The premium tier is $349.99/year with unlimited books and readers. They provide an embeddable signup form to place on your website, the ability to import your list from MailChimp, and other features they are adding all the time.

I'm use the premium plan and consider it an awesome value and investment in my author-publisher business. After all, beta readers are also book reviewers and you will need those (estimated) 50 Amazon reviews on launch day to cause the Amazon recommendation engine to kick in and also to be able to qualify for BookBub promotions.

BetaReader.io

betareader.io

BetaReader.io is a cross-device reader and feedback management platform for authors to share their work with their beta readers. Like Beta-Books, it's a web-based reader that centralizes feedback. It's in private beta now so you need to request an invite.

Scribophile

scribophile.com

Scribophile is one of the **largest and most active writing groups online**. Post your writing for feedback. Network, chat and discuss with other writers. Enter free writing contests. Educate yourself with their writing academy and writing blog. For all levels of writers. Subscription costs $64/year.

BUSINESS AND PRODUCTIVITY TOOLS

HERE ARE MY PICKS FOR ESSENTIAL BUSINESS AND PRODUCTIVITY tools you need for doing business as a professional author-publisher.

Subscribe for access to updates in the *Consumer's Guide for Self-Publishers* web book:
www.selfpubbootcamp.com/readers

Barcodes

Here are two ways to create free barcodes:

Derek Murphy at CreativIndieCovers provides a free online barcode generator here:

https://www.creativindiecovers.com/free-online-isbn-barcode-generator/

Create a free book cover template with IngramSpark to get a cover template with a barcode you can use anywhere:

https://myaccount.ingramspark.com/Portal/Tools/CoverTemplateGenerator

Be sure to always include the ISBN and the price of your print book in the barcode to meet professional standards for books.

Blasty

blasty.co

Blasty is an online tool that monitors Google for illegal copies of your content. With just one click you can remove references to these sites from Google search engine results. Blasty's system will alert you by email when it finds a Google search engine entry for your book. They may monitize by charging publishing houses for their service but it's free for authors at this time.

Blasty has an arrangement with Google to take down your listing when you click the orange BLAST button next to an infringing site. The listing will disappear, often in a few hours. Removing search results from Google means that people will not see them offered for free.

This is convenient because otherwise, you'd need to contact Google directly to remove each site from their search engine results.

In a checkbox next to each suspected entry you'll be able to click Forbidden (trusted by Google site), Whitelisted, or Blast.

Sites trusted by Google are retailers like Amazon, who may indeed be offering your ebook for free, with your permission. Whitelist the entries you recognize as blogs, excerpts, and interviews for which you've given permission by clicking the white flag. For infringing sites, click Blast and it'll be taken care of. (Sounds ominous, huh?)

BookLinker

booklinker.net/myaccount.php

Universal link creator for your book so your customer is automatically directed to the Amazon country website they live in. Allows Amazon Affiliate links.

Copyright Services

bit.ly/author-copyright

In the US you can register your copyright for $35 in about 35 steps and, coincidentally, it took me about 35 minutes. (It's $55 for credit card purchases.) I wrote a lengthy blog post about this detailing the step-by-step process with screenshots.

https://selfpubbootcamp.com/a-step-by-step-guide-to-copyright-registration-for-self-published-authors/

Other countries have similar copyright registration procedures. Read the post before you start so you can prepare all your materials and gather your information. There's a lot of it.

Learn about copyright infringement vs fair use. Get the Authors Alliance free guide to Fair Use for Nonfiction Authors, available in PDF format.

DropBox

bit.ly/af-dropbox

You're going to need to share your manuscript, your book cover, and images back and forth with beta readers, editors, artists, and all kinds of people. But lots of email hosting services block emails with large attachments, so your email may never arrive. Also, attachments can carry viruses.

You're better off using a free online sharing service like Google Drive, DropBox, Hightail (or SendOwl, SendThis, WeTransfer, and many others).

Most of these services will notify you when your invitee joins the site and downloads the document, so you'll never have to wonder if your document reached its destination.

Google Drive

drive.google.com

Don't use email attachments, use Google Drive, a free office suite in the cloud that allows you to share documents with others and even work on the same document, concurrently. Google Drive gives you 15MG of storage free, but for an additional $1.99 a month you get 100GB more (or 1TB for $9.99/mo) to store, sync, and share documents, images, videos, and other data, with the ability to access them via any web browser from any of your devices. This is a really good deal, and it's great for backups and for sharing your work. You can download your doc from Google Drive to Word and use a template to create your ebooks and PDF for print.

ISBN Agencies

myidentifiers.com

Maintain your independence and purchase your own ISBNs. Bowker is the official ISBN agency in the US. You should buy your own set of 10 or more ISBNs with their MyIdentifiers service as described in chapter 12.

Other countries have similar agencies. In the UK it's the Nielsen UK ISBN Agency and Canada it's Library and Archives Canada. Do a web search for your country's official ISBN agency.

Bowker has a partnership with StreetLib in the US to provide Word-to-EPUB formatting services bundled with 10 ISBNs and two barcodes for $395. This is an okay deal, but you're wasting money on barcodes because you can easily get them for free.

Rev Transcription Service

rev.com

A team of transcriptionists takes your audio or video recordings and transcribes them to 99 percent accuracy. Simply upload your files or use their iPhone Transcription App and get a complete transcript in as soon as 12 hours. $1.00 per minute. Done by people and not speech recognition software.

The Self-Publisher's Ultimate Resource Guide

amzn.to/2nNIUdy

The Self-Publisher's Ultimate Resource Guide is a book available in print and ebook formats that lists curated and verified resources for independent authors who plan to publish their own books. Produced by a team with long experience in both traditional and independent publishing, the over 850 resources are listed in an easy-to-use format that includes live links, phone numbers, email addresses, and brief descriptive copy. The Guide makes vendors and other resources easy to find by separating them into 33 distinct categories within the three main tasks the self-publisher must deal with: Prepare, Publish, and Promote.

50

MARKET RESEARCH AND COMPETITIVE ANALYSIS TOOLS

MANY AUTHORS SKIP DOING COMPETITIVE RESEARCH ON THEIR books but that's a mistake. Doing your research helps you figure out in what categories readers will look for your book and whether your book cover, title, and keywords are right for your audience. Here are the tools that can help.

Subscribe for access to updates in the *Consumer's Guide for Self-Publishers* web book:
www.selfpubbootcamp.com/readers

Amazon Advanced Search

bit.ly/amazonadvancedsearch

Amazon Advanced Search is where you do your competitive research. Find books like yours that have been published recently, figure out what your cover needs to look like, narrow down the best categories for your book, find keywords that work, and see how bestselling book descriptions and author bios are structured.

Blink

https://www.blinkist.com/en/nc/plans

If you don't have time to read analyze all the books in your nonfiction genre check out Blink. It's $8.34/year to get "blinks" of the book, summarized in 15-minute reads.

Book Review Targeter

Book Review Targeter can help you do research and get book reviews. See its full description in *Chapter 53, Book Review Services.*

Google Adwords Keyword Planner

adwords.google.com/home/tools/keyword-planner

Google Adwords' keyword planner is a really good research tool to figure out what keywords you should use when uploading your book for distribution. You'll need a Google account to use it.

Start by searching words or phrases related to your book. You'll see how often keywords are searched and how their search volume changes over time. Choose low to medium competition keywords. The more narrow you go, the better, because your book may get lost in a high-competition search term.

Google Cloud Vision

cloud.google.com/vision

GCV is an advanced tool for gaining insights into your images. It uses a pretrained API model or you can choose to train custom vision models.

GCV quickly classifies images into thousands of categories (such as, "sailboat"), detects individual objects and faces within images, and reads printed words contained within images.

Use it to build metadata on your image catalog, moderate offensive content, or enable new marketing scenarios through image sentiment analysis.

KDP Rocket

kdprocket.com

KDP Rocket shows you exactly what Amazon book buyers type into Amazon, as well as how many people search for these things every month. You'll learn what keywords shoppers type-in to Amazon, the number of times the keyword is typed-in, how much money books are making that rank for that keyword, and how many books are competing for that keyword.

You can also quickly find pertinent and niche categories for your books, as well as find out how many books you'd need to sell that day in order to be the new #1 bestseller.

It also shows you potential competitors, their information, reviews, book cover, and even their daily and monthly earnings. By understanding what works for your competitors, you can create book titles, subtitles, and descriptions that convert better, increase your Kindle rankings, and sell more books.

Kindle Spy

bit.ly/af-kdspy

Kindle Spy helps you figure out which Amazon Kindle categories you should choose for your book. It's a browser extension that activates when you browse Kindle books in the Amazon store.

It shows you which categories books like yours are using and what categories are too popular (saturated with so many books that yours will get lost). With that information you can place your book in a category with lower competition.

Pickfu for Surveys

www.pickfu.com

Pickfu helps you get unbiased feedback using a polling system. Use it to get feedback on your book cover, titles, graphics, marketing copies, even your book idea. It's easy to set up, they bring the responders, and you can slice and dice responses by age, gender, ethnicity, income, and education. Costs about $20/poll or discounted for bulk.

Other survey tools include:

- Facebook polls
- Google Forms to your email list
- Mturk (Amazon's artificial intelligence survey tool)

Yasiv

yasiv.com

Yasiv.com is a free tool created by Amazon that provides visual mapping of purchases made by Amazon customers. Start by searching for a book like yours to see a map of other books that readers have bought. This tool really helps you understand how people are searching on Amazon for books in your category.

51

MARKETING ADS AND APPS

DOING MARKETING FOR YOUR BOOK CAN BE OVERWHELMING. These tools help simplify the process.

Subscribe for access to updates in the *Consumer's Guide for Self-Publishers* web book:
www.selfpubbootcamp.com/readers

Amazon Advertising

advertising.amazon.com/lp/books

This is Amazon's advertising tool in the books category as described in *Chapter 33, Advertising and Giveaways.*

Author Marketing Club

bit.ly/af-ame

The Author Marketing Club ($99/yr) provides tools and resources, online learning and training to authors for marketing campaigns and launches. An author member can submit their books for promotional opportunities, as well as access to free online training and resources related to book marketing. Register to have a look around, it's free.

The premium membership offers tools that help you locate book reviewers, create compelling book descriptions, promote your books to new readers with exclusive promotions, and instantly display your books on your website with zero web design skills.

Premium members also get access to a large video learning library, mastermind groups, pre-made book covers, case studies, promotion blasts, and more. This is a great way to jumpstart your book marketing efforts and climb your way up the learning curve.

BookBub

bookbub.com

BookBub is a free service for readers that helps them discover books the editorial staff thinks they'll love through unbeatable deals, hand-picked recommendations, and updates from their favorite authors. Find out more about it in *Chapter 33, Advertising and Giveaways.*

BookFunnel

bookfunnel.com

BookFunnel delivers your books to your readers with no hassle. Upload your book to BookFunnel in PDF, MOBI, and EPUB, name your promotion, and mail your readers a link.

Your readers will be presented with a friendly menu where they'll choose their reading device (Kindle Paperwhite, etc.). Then they can download the file or email the book to themselves. This pretty much eliminates having to tutor your readers on how to download, sideload, and open your books.

Arguably, BookFunnel is the easiest way to deliver Advanced Reader Copies (ARCs) of your book for reviewers. I've used it to distribute books to beta readers, too. You can also use it to deliver free promotional books, such as the first book in a series.

Starts at $20/annually.

Book Luver

bookluver.com

Book Luver is a UK-based social sharing platform for - you guessed it - book lovers. Their Freebies Package for Authors gets your book on their Freebies page for just £30 for a month. Add a newsletter spot and other promo ops for another £10-20. You can feature your free reader magnet on Book Luver, market with your book trailer, and much more.

Bublish

bublish.com

Bublish has my vote for one of the most interesting and innovative independent author services companies of the year. They're experiencing high growth and a constantly evolving suite of hybrid solutions for developing your author platform and getting quality distribution for your book. They're affordable, charging $99/year for their distribution service, and take the standard 15% on sales.

Bublish describes itself as a "publishing technology company that offers cloud-based tools, metrics and resources to equip today's business-savvy authors for success. An innovative, award-winning platform, Bublish empowers *authorpreneurs* by providing a complete social marketing and digital publishing solution."

Here's how it works. Join (for free). Create a bio and upload your photo. Upload your ebook in EPUB format and add a synopsis, a link to your website, and at least one link to an online retailer where readers can purchase the book.

Now you create a Book Bubble, or excerpt of your book, along with an "author insight" to personalize what you shared. You can share the Book Bubble on social media and track how many people looked at it.

Bublish can help you build your platform, create Amazon and Facebook ads, and promote your book on their newsletter and by hand-selling at national (USA) book and library shows. You can bring your completed book to them or use their editing, design, and formatting services.

Independent Book Publishers Association

ibpa-online.org

IBPA members can sign up for the Books for Review catalog mailed quarterly to about 3000 reviewers, journalists, and bloggers across the United States.

Other bookstore and library mailings ($200-$400 est) will get your book in front of booksellers, libraries, and university bookstores. See this article from the IBPA for details.

Read more about the IBPA in *Chapter 62, Professional Organizations.*

eReader News Today

ereadernewstoday.com

Submit to get your book sent to over 475,000 Facebook fans and 200,000 email subscribers who are avid book readers. Pricing is $60 for a book under $2.99 and $150 for a book that costs $2.99. If you are not accepted you can still submit to their daily Bargain and Free Book promos.

Facebook Ads

facebook.com/business/products/ads

Lots of authors use Facebook Ads to identify their audience, grow their email list, and sell more books. Learn how in *Chapter 33, Advertising and Giveaways*.

Forums

reddit.com

There are a lot of different forums for a lot of different interest groups. For example, I am active on two forums for adventure travelers, Horizons Unlimited and ADV Rider. I'm also active in various forums for self-publishers, some of which live inside LinkedIn, and one of which lives in forum giant Reddit.

Reddit provides a venue for anyone who wants to create a forum on any topic. Inside Reddit there are forums for readers and authors. Choose fantasy, horror, science fiction, self-publishing, and all kinds of business topics. Plug in your genre or interest and see who wants to read your stories or connect with other authors.

Outside of Reddit and LinkedIn, seek forums in your area of expertise or genre by doing a web search for "forum <your topic>."

Figuring out where your colleagues and readers hang out online and connecting with them is half the book marketing battle.

Prolific Works

prolificworks.com

Prolific Works used to be Instafreebie. Connect with new readers and fans through your sneak peeks, advance previews, special giveaways, and/or group giveaways of your free ebook to readers. Find out more in *Chapter 33, Advertising and Giveaways*.

There's a free version with $20/mo and $50/mo premium features.

Virtual Assistants

Find virtual assistants by searching for "author assistants," or check out *The Self-Publisher's Ultimate Resource Guide* or, better yet, get a recommendation from another author.

52

SOCIAL MEDIA MARKETING TOOLS

I LOVE SOCIAL MEDIA BECAUSE IT CONNECTS ME WITH A WORLD of people I'd otherwise never meet in person. Mostly I use Facebook but I used to use Twitter a lot (and may again, soon). I share books on Goodreads or LibraryThing and I need to choose between them soon because it's too difficult to keep them both active. (Litsy is similar but, since it was purchased by LibraryThing, I predict it may be all rolled into one sometime in the future). Pinterest, Instagram, and Snapchat are image-oriented social media platforms that might interest you. Set up an account on all social media sites to make yourself more searchable. Try them all to decide where you feel most at home. Many platforms now offer business accounts that you can do a lot more with than just a personal account. Go forth and connect!

Facebook

facebook.com

Create your author page on Facebook. First you must have a personal Facebook account. Then set up your author page. There are lots of tutorials to help you. Then go learn about what Facebook offers authors, like Facebook First Reads and Facebook LIVE. Connect with me on Facebook.

Goodreads

goodreads.com

Set up your author page on Goodreads. First you must be a Goodreads member. Then you may join the author program. Do a web search to find a tutorial. Connect with me on Goodreads.

Hootsuite

hootsuite.com

Hootsuite is a social media management tool that allows you to manage multiple social media profiles from one dashboard. It will save you lots of time as you can see your posts and responses and those of whom you follow. Also great is that you can batch social media tasks by scheduling all your social media posts for the week. Free 30 day trial, limited free plan for 3 social profiles and 30 scheduled messages, then $29/mo. Buffer is a similar tool with a freemium plan but lower subscription pricing at $15/mo.

Instagram

instagram.com

Use the Instagram mobile app to create photo-centered stories for your readers who are on Instagram. Google "instagram for authors" to find ideas on how to connect.

LibraryThing

librarything.com

Set up your author page on LibraryThing. First, become a Library-Thing member. Then you may join the author program. Do a web search to find a tutorial.

Connect with me on LibraryThing. Here's my member page and here's my author page.

LinkedIn

linkedin.com

If you're a nonfiction author you need to be on LinkedIn. Present your professional persona here. Join groups and participate, helping people solve problems in your area of expertise. Everyone needs a LinkedIn account whether you're active or not. Connect with me on LinkedIn.

Litsy

litsy.com

Acquired in March 2018 by LibraryThing, Listsy describes itself as a place to share and discover your favorite books with your favorite people. Has been called a book-focused social network that goes beyond book reviews by TechCrunch. Book Riot describes Litsy as the perfect baby of Instagram and Goodreads.

Like LibraryThing, Litsy lets you import your book lists (export file) from Goodreads.

The Litsy community is full of passionate readers. You can share bookish moments with Quotes, Reviews, and Blurbs. Measure Litflu-ence to discover your "bookprint" in the world. Explore recommenda-tions from readers, not algorithms. Want to organize your reading list? Litsy has stacks for that, too.

Litsy is available on the web, for iOS, and Android. Free. Connect with me on Litsy.

Pinterest

pinterest.com

Pinterest is an image-based social media site with "boards" that's much less "social" than other social media platforms. They have now imple-mented BUY buttons directly onto pins so you can embed links to your book sales pages. Use a business account, not a personal one, because it will provide free analytics to help you figure out which pins are getting the most traffic. Search for "pinterest for authors" to find ways to use it to market your book.

Reedsy Discovery

[reedsy.com/discovery]

Reedsy describes its Discovery community as a Goodreads for indie authors. Read more about it in the Book Reviews chapter. Reedsy also provides an author marketplace and a simple EPUB creation tool.

Snapchat

snapchat.com

Snapchat is a mobile app with camera and photo-manipulation software people use to share photos in realtime. Use your snap to communicate with your followers, sharing to your public story or privately to an individual or set of individuals. Snapchat offers business accounts and ads. Find me on SnapChat to follow my stories @missadventuring.

Twitter

twitter.comTwitter is an extremely popular social networking platform with lots of opportunity to connect with readers and the media. People communicate in short messages called tweets. Tweeting is posting short messages for anyone who follows you, with the hope that your messages are useful and interesting to someone in your audience. Use hash tags (#selfpub, #romance, #amwriting, #askagent) to make your tweet visible to audiences monitoring the hashtags. Connect with me on Twitter @carlaking. Connect with my business Self-Pub Boot Camp on Twitter @selfpubbootcamp.

53

BOOK REVIEW SERVICES

GET BOOK REVIEWS SO YOUR BOOK HAS MOMENTUM RIGHT OUT of the gate. There are various ways to get reviews, the trade reviews (marked) being the most prestigious.

Subscribe for access to updates in the *Consumer's Guide for Self-Publishers* web book:
www.selfpubbootcamp.com/readers

Amazon Top Reviewers

amazon.com/review/top-reviewers

You can find the top reviewers at the URL above, but figuring out which ones read your genre and finding their email addresses is arduous. Which is why products like Book Review Targeter exist. *See below.*

Booksprout

booksprout.co

BookSprout is an app that delivers your ARC to your readers' Apple, Android, and Kindle Fire devices. Create an ARC and share a link with your readers. BookSprout sends the book to your readers and keeps track of who leaves reviews and who doesn't so you can clean your list. The app sends an alert to your readers two days before the ARC reviews are due. What's cool is that it allows you to import books you've already published on Amazon.

Book Blogger List

bookbloggerlist.com

Some avid readers have become book bloggers, taking the challenge to find and recommend great books. Find them at The Book Blogger List, a place to "help book bloggers find like-minded bloggers and help authors find book bloggers that might be interested in their book."

BookFunnel

bookfunnel.com

Delivers ARCs to reviewers in the correct formats. See *Chapter 51, Marketing Ads and Apps.*

Booklist

booklistonline.com/get-reviewed

(Trade) Booklist and Booklist Online are the American Library Association's (ALA) book review service. Send your book in advance of publication for free. They get over 60K submissions per year and will not notify publishers if their books are not selected for review. BlueInk Review is a partner and they suggest that self-publishers use that route for a chance of being included in Booklist's pages.

Book Review Targeter

bit.ly/getbookreviewsnow

Book Review Targeter is a fantastic, time-saving tool to automate the process of finding Amazon book reviewers who have listed their contact information. For both Mac and Windows at $247 but looks to be on "permanent" sale for $197. This tool finds all Amazon reviewers who have provided contact information. Just type in your keywords and search results to find relevant books. Then the tool filters out all the reviewers that do not have contact information. Export the information into a CSV file: reviewer names, email addresses, profile URL, the URL of their review, name of the book they reviewed, book author, and ASIN. The creator of this program, Debbie Drum, has also provided a contact email template with wording that works to attract reviewers, and connected it to a Google mail merge add-on called YAMM. This lets you automatically populate the email and send 50 emails per day to these reviewers (because Amazon doesn't let you send more than that). Training videos come with the tool.

BlueInk Review

blueinkreview.com

(Trade) A partner of the ALA's Booklist Review service, this company only reviews indie and self-published books and their reviews cost $395.

Booklife PW Reviews

booklife.com/about-us/review-submission-guidelines.html

(Trade) You can submit your book to unpaid book review sites like BookLife's PW Reviews, but it may be declined for review. If you get into BookLife, your book also has a chance of being reviewed by Publishers Weekly.

Foreword Reviews

publishers.forewordreviews.com/reviews

(Trade) The good news is that these reviews are free. The bad news is that it's really hard to get them to accept your book for review. Still, you should try, especially if you're confident that your book really does compete in the marketplace. Send your perfect book to them at least two months before publication. It will be evaluated and either accepted or rejected for review. To hedge your bets, I'd submit it four months before publication and, if rejected, consider a paid review service.

Foreword's Clarion Reviews

publishers.forewordreviews.com/reviews

(Trade) Foreword's Clarion Reviews charges $499 for a 450-word review, which you will receive in 4 to 6 weeks. Clarion is also associated with BlueInk Reviews, an indie and self-published book reviewer who charges $395.

Freado

freado.com

Readers sign up to get free Kindle ebooks. Authors promote free books that are already in the Kindle store. You must already have at least 10 four-star reviews on Amazon. You get a listing of your book in their free ebooks page and in Freado.com, inclusion of your book in our daily best ebooks email which goes out to 10k+ readers, a tweet with your book cover in their Twitter account, and a post in their Facebook page. They're affiliated with BookBuzzr, a marketing tool. (See also *Book Marketing Tools and Services*.)

Goodreads Giveaways

goodreads.com/genres/goodreads-giveaway

Don't do it. The algorithm favors people who have a ton of books on their reading list so eight out of 10 (est) books go to them and two go to random readers. eBay sellers have realized they can game this system, so they load up their reading list, win books, and sell them on eBay. Until Goodreads fixes this, don't use it.

Hidden Gems Books ARC Program

hiddengemsbooks.com/arc-program

The Hidden Gems ARC program sends your novel to their list of reviewers to match your type/genre of book with readers that are most likely to enjoy it for a registration cost of $20. Further costs are $2.00 per reader between 50 and 149 readers. For 150 or more, the price is capped at $300. They claim a review rate of over 80 percent, cleaning their list frequently to remove readers who ask for books but do not leave reviews.

IndieReader

indiereader.com

(Trade) IndieReader offers reviews for $225 and RUSH reviews (4-6 week turnaround) for $300. If your title earns 4 to 5 stars, it will be included in IndieReader's monthly "Best Book" roundup in the Huffington Post (from Paul Kilpatrick and Amy Edleman).

IndieView

theindieview.com/indie-reviewers

Register to see the list of book review bloggers on The IndieView. The list starts with "prolific indie reviewers."

Prolific Works

prolificworks.com

Delivers ARCs to reviewers and more. See *Chapter 33, Advertising and Giveaways.*

Kirkus Reviews

kirkusreviews.com

(Trade) Kirkus charges $425 for a review that you can expect to receive in 7 to 9 weeks or $575 for their express service that takes 4 to 6 weeks.

LibraryThing Member Giveaways Program

librarything.com

LibraryThing is a lot like Goodreads, but it's not commercial. Use their LibraryThing Member Giveaways program (LTMG) to find potential reviewers for your book on the site. This is the self-publisher option for their Early Reviewers program, which is not open to one-author publishing companies.

To enter the LTMG program you must meet the following requirements.

- You are an official LibraryThing Author
- You have at least 50 books in your LibraryThing account
- You have a paid or lifetime LibraryThing account

Winners for LTMG are picked randomly. They are encouraged but not required to review the books they receive.

Midwest Book Review

midwestbookreview.com

(Trade) The Midwest Book Review publishes Bookwatch reviews for the trade and the general public and gives priority consideration to small press publishers, self-published authors, and academic presses. Free for print and $50 for ebooks.

Publishers Weekly

publishersweekly.com/pw/diy

(Trade) PW Select ($149) is an advertisement that costs $149. Your book will appear in the magazine, the Publishers Weekly and BookLife home pages, BookLife's email newsletter, Twitter, and Facebook channels, as well as a listing in its special announcements database, and to readers who subscribe to its magazines.

NetGalley

netgally.com

NetGalley allows you to pitch your book to professional readers (media, reviewers, booksellers, librarians, bloggers, and educators) who can review and recommend your title, from one location for $399. (Get a deal on NetGalley if you're a member of IBPA.) Miral Sattar of Bibliocrunch published a useful interview with NetGalley on how self-published authors can use the service.

RT Book Reviews

rtbookreviews.com

(Trade) RT Book Reviews specializes in romance, erotica, sci fi, fantasy, inspiration, mystery, and young adult titles. Submit well in advance of publication or, if you've already published your book, use their paid service. Est $425.

San Francisco Book Review

sanfranciscobookreview.com

(Trade) You don't need to live in the city to use San Francisco Book Review's service. Sister companies are the Manhattan, Seattle, and Tulsa Book Review and Kids' BookBuzz and they are all owned by City Book Review. Submit 90 days in advance for their free service. If your book has already been published you can purchase their paid service ($199) and, for $99, cross-post it to the other book review magazines.

Redheaded Book Lover

www.redheadedbooklover.com

Freelance book reviewer Aimee Ann who offers a full refund if she can't aware your book four or five stars. Provides author spotlights. Also does editing and proofreading.

Reedsy Discovery

reedsy.com/discovery

Reedsy lists recommended book bloggers here. You can also get direct exposure to readers and reviewers by joining Reedsy Discovery, which uses machine-learning and reader communities to put your book in front of the right readers. A self-described Goodreads for indie authors, this tool was designed to create momentum for your launch. When you sign up, your book is presented to a pool of experienced and relevant reviewers. On launch date your book will be promoted to thousands of registered readers who can browse, comment, upvote, and purchase your book. $50 one-time fee.

Writers' Blog Finder

writersblogfinder.com

Check out this free search engine for finding the top blogs in your genre.

54

CROWDFUNDING SITES

YOU CAN USE CROWDFUNDING TOOLS TO PAY FOR YOUR BOOK even before you've written it. Crowdfunding is a commitment but many authors who dedicate themselves to the marketing effort it demands find the process rewarding.

Subscribe for access to updates in the *Consumer's Guide for Self-Publishers* web book:
www.selfpubbootcamp.com/readers

IndieGoGo

indiegogo.com

IndieGoGo was founded in 2007 as a place where people who want to raise money can create fundraising campaigns to tell their story and get the word out. They charge 4 percent of the money you raise if you meet your goal or 9 percent if you do not. Lots of authors have raised money for books on this platform.

Inkshares and Unbound

inkshares.com and unbound.com

Two publisher crowdfunding programs are Inkshares (San Francisco) and Unbound (in the UK). These companies host your crowdfunding site and, if you meet your goal, they will publish your book under their imprint. They offer attractive royalties and edit, design, and market your book. You are not self-publishing with these companies; they take on your project as an author publishing under their imprint.

Gumroad

gumroad.com

You can use Gumroad for crowdfunding as well as for many other things. Find out more about it in Direct Sales Tools.

Kickstarter

kickstarter.com

Since Kickstarter's launch in 2009, more than 5.2 million people have pledged more than $900 million, funding nearly 53,000 creative projects like films, games, books, music, art, design and technology. Project creators set a funding goal and deadline. If people like a project, they can pledge money to make it happen. Funding on Kickstarter is all-or-nothing. Projects must reach their funding goals to receive any money. To date, nearly 44 percent of projects have reached their funding goals. Kickstarter takes 5 percent of the funds raised. Funders pay via Amazon Payments (only), which then will apply credit card processing fees (between 3 percent and 5 percent). Check out Kickstarter Creators get started page for publishing projects.

PubLaunch

publaunch.com

PubLaunch is three things: a project management platform, a marketplace for publishing services, and a crowdfunding platform. It's run by a longtime small press and hybrid publishing service who has used crowdfunding for years and really understand the publishing universe.

Use their online marketplace to find vetted professionals. Unlink other marketplaces, these professionals are vetted based on standardized tests. In a later phase they will incorporate a rating system.

An embedded budget calculator will help you calculate how much it will cost to hire someone based on your book data (page count, images, etc.).

A crowdfunding platform is built in to PubLaunch so at the end of your budgeting process you can choose to pay directly or start a crowdfunding campaign. You can use their crowdfunding platform without using their marketplace.

Once you've put together your team and started your book, a "launch room" is created for you so everyone can communicate with private messaging and get the production process done in one space.

Authors upload your manuscript, select your publishing requirements, choose your team, get your estimate, crowdfund or pay, and manage your project through to publication with guidance at every step.

Suppliers create a profile, get tested and approved, receive submissions from authors, work on the project, and get paid via the platform.

The company is based in Toronto, Canada but services are based in US currency for now. PubLaunch makes their money from 5 percent of crowdfunding revenue and 10 percent of supplier side revenue.

Check out my talk with PubLaunch founder Greg Ioannau on the Author Friendly Podcast at www.authorfriendly.com.

Publishizer

publishizer.com

Publishizer is a crowdfunding platform that connects the author with publishers. Yep, if your goal is reached, they'll query your proposal to a targeted list of publishers. If a publisher expresses interest, you can contact them directly. Publishizer keeps 30 percent of funds raised during the campaign.

55

DIRECT SALES TOOLS

Use these direct sales tools to connect with your readers and earn more income from your book. You can sell directly at the same time you distribute your book with the distribution or direct-to-retailer services (unless contractually stated otherwise).

Subscribe for access to updates to the *Consumer's Guide for Self-Publishers* web book:
www.selfpubbootcamp.com/readers

Blockchain solutions

Blockchain offerings for publishing include:

- Alexandria
- the Authorship project
- Decent
- Gilamesh
- Po.et
- Publica

Blockchain can be used to prevent piracy issues and cryptocurrency is definitely becoming more prevalent. I suspect that services will start using blockchain and crypto eventually but if you're on the cutting edge of this kind of thing you may want to check it out.

Bookchain

scenarex.ca/en/bookchain

A distribution system built on blockchain that allows authors and publishers to configure the security, traceability, attribution, and distribution settings (including lending and reselling) of a digital document.

BundleRabbit

bundlerabbit.com/home/authors

BundleRabbit lets you bundle your own ebooks for sale or become a curator by bundling ebooks by a variety of authors. You can add your books to the site so other curators can bundle your book (with your permission) with their bundles. All authors who contribute their books are paid directly to their accounts.

All authors in a bundle receive a combined total of 70 percent for each bundle sold. Thus, if there are 10 books in a bundle, and 2 of them are yours, you receive 14 percent of the net sale. As the curator, you receive 5 percent of each bundle sold. The authors in the bundle receive a combined total of 70 percent.

Gumroad

gumroad.com

Gumroad provides widgets to embed in your site so you can sell directly to your customers with the entire experience on your site, that is, without sending them to a blank PayPal page. It is the tool I recommend most for direct sales, subscriptions, and pre-orders for digital and physical products.

Simply upload and sell your digital files–up to 4 GB–or create an order form for selling physical objects. Integrated Facebook and Twitter buttons encourage sharing with customer networks.

I like Gumroad for its ability to provide both digital downloads and order forms for physical products, as an easy shopping cart system for your site and features that help authors drum up excitement during the book launch. Gumroad competitors include Selz and Sellfy but they don't have all the features.

If you use the free version the fee is just 8.5 percent + 30 cents per transaction. If you get the premium version it's $10 (USD)/month plus 3.5 percent + 30 cents per sale.

Issuu

issuu.com

Issuu is a digital publishing platform for publishing magazines, catalogs, and booklets electronically and in print. With website embeds and social media sharing it's a great way to deliver related works and market your books. They offer free and premium programs with a 14-day trial period.

Leanpub

leanpub.com

Leanpub is a combination book writing platform, beta reader platform, and online bookstore. With Leanpub, you can quickly publish beta books, books in progress, serials, and subscriptions, updating your readers automatically when the book is updated. You can also pay a co-author automatically and set up a donation to a cause.

Create your book using simple Markdown language (an easy, plain-text format), then upload it to a connected Dropbox folder along with images and other assets. (This may sound a little complicated, but they do much of it for you automatically and provide easy instructions.)

Your book lives in the cloud so you can make it available to trusted editors, collaborators, and assistants who can edit and replace files. A publisher page holds common assets: a verso page, copyright message,

404 | CARLA KING

company logo and other elements that can be applied to more than one book. Take advantage of pay-what-you-want pricing by setting a minimum and suggested price, such as $4.99–$10.99, or even higher. Leverage your *1000 True Fans* by asking for donations up to $500. So you see it can be used as a paid blogging platform or for crowdfunding.

You can write and publish a book in several different ways on Leanpub:

- In your web browser with a visual editor (perfect for novels.).
- By uploading a Word document (.docx) that you have written according to Leanpub's formatting guidelines.
- By uploading a PDF, EPUB, or MOBI.
- In your web browser, in plain text, using Leanpub-flavored Markdown or Markup as the formatting markup syntax.
- On your computer, in plain text or Word, syncing with Dropbox.
- On your computer, in plain text or Word, syncing with Git and GitHub or Bitbucket.

Other things you can do with Leanpub include bundles, coupons, and packages.

- You can create bundles of your own books, and bundle your books with books by other authors.
- You can create coupons, which is a really useful way to promote your book.
- Using the "packages" feature, you can sell your book along with other digital content you have created, like videos or presentations.
- If you create your book using Leanpub's tools, then it is automatically available to customers to read it online and in their iOS app, as well as in PDF, EPUB, and MOBI.

Create up to 100 books or courses for free or choose their Standard or Pro plan with more features for $8.99/month and $12.99/month. You can also purchase a lifetime version and bundles with shelf spots (ad space). You get 80% royalties with each plan. They offer a 45-day happiness guarantee.

Scribd

scribd.com

Scribd is a document-sharing site and all-you-can-read book subscription service. You can sell or give away your stories, excerpts, ARCs, and ebooks in PDF and document formats. There's lots of platform-building potential here as commenting, social media and sharing widgets are everywhere. It's free to join and when you sell their take is 20 percent plus a 25¢ transaction fee. Though the social publishing features are not as prominent as they once were I still think of Scribd as kind of a Wattpad for grownups, with the bonus of being able to sell your work and distribute Advanced Reader Copies and private beta docs.

StoryBundle

https://storybundle.com/

StoryBundle can offer your book in a thematic bundle with other indie titles. They sell for $3+ for the bundle. While not the most profitable endeavor, this is a great way to introduce your writing to readers who don't know you. Look in the FAQs for their email address.

56

AFFILIATE PROGRAMS

Affiliate programs and curation tools help you make a few more pennies on each sale of your book as well as on other books and products that you recommend. You can even set up a page (or pages) on your website to "curate" a selection of affiliate books and products.

If you like and trust a product or service and you want to spread the word about it, ask the person or company if they have an affiliate program you can join. (Or just Google "affiliate program product-name.") I do this a lot. For example, I am an affiliate for many companies I recommend in this guide, including Book Design Templates, Scribd, Thrive Themes, GoDaddy, 48 Hour Books, Book Review Targeter, Legal Zoom, ProWritingAid, and Grammarly. They offer me from about 5 percent to a whopping 30 percent of sales. So when you click my link, I make a little extra money. (Thank you!)

Interested in doing this yourself? See my in-depth blog post on affiliate marketing for authors.

Subscribe for access to updates to the *Consumer's Guide for Self-Publishers* web book:

www.selfpubbootcamp.com/readers

Aerio

aer.io

Upload your own books to Aerio and choose from their inventory of 14 million print books, gifts, games, and more to create a curated storefront on your website. You'll make a small percentage of each sale you generate from your site.

Amazon Associates

affiliate-program.amazon.com

Sign up for the Amazon Affiliate program and make a few pennies on your own book and other books and products that you recommend when you use their affiliate links.

Commission Junction

cj.com

Commission Junction is one of the leading affiliate marketing services in the industry. If you have a niche market and think that you can sell products via your website and blog via recommendations and links, look here for vendors who will give you 5 percent and more for each sale. For example, I use links from CJ in reviews for travel gear. Share-ASale is another popular affiliate marketing service.

Rakutan for Kobo and Walmart Books

rakutenmarketing.com/affiliate/publishers

Like Amazon Associates, you'll get a few pennies from each sale from your links to books and other products.

Smashwords

smashwords.com/about/affiliate

Sign up for the Smashwords affiliate program and make a little extra on your own book and other books you recommend when you use affiliate links.

StreetLib

streetlib.com

StreetLib allows you to create a storefront much like the one offered by Aereo. Read more about StreetLib in *Chapter 39, Distribution Tools and Services.*

57

WEBSITE AND BLOG TOOLS

YOUR WEBSITE IS "YOU CENTRAL." SO MAKE SURE THAT everything you do is centered there. See my blog post on Website Tools to Build Your Author Email List.

Subscribe for access to updates to the *Consumer's Guide for Self-Publishers* web book:
www.selfpubbootcamp.com/readers

GoDaddy Web Hosting

godaddy.com

My WordPress blogs and websites are hosted with GoDaddy, which is where I also buy my domain names. Click here for a $2.49/mo deal on GoDaddy Web Hosting that includes one domain name through my affiliation with them. This is probably the best deal you can get. There are many other web hosting companies but I've been with GoDaddy for years. They've never let me down with their service and are available 24/7 with great phone support.

Pub Site

pubsitepro.com

I highly recommend Pub Site for any author who is timid about creating their own site using WordPress, SquareSpace, Wix, or any other website tool. The creators are John and Fauzia Burke, who are designers and marketing people from FSB Associates, an online marketing firm that has promoted books and authors online for over twenty years. They have developed over 200 author websites for such authors as Sue Grafton, Jonathan Kellerman, Gail Godwin, Tom Clancy, and Clive Cussler.

Unlike all the other website builders, Pub Site concentrates on the things that authors need and readers need to know such as ISBNs, bookseller links, tour dates, direct sales of your book, your bio, photo, and video, if you have one. You can also create new pages for media, interviews, press coverage, and anything else you like.

The interface is easy to use and, unlike WordPress, impossible to screw up. Just fill in the blanks, customize your colors and layout, and it's done.

Find out more by listening to my interview with co-founder John Burke on the Author Friendly Podcast at www.authorfriendly.com.

Sumo Plugin

sumo.com

Sumo helps you grow your email list with email signup ribbons, popup boxes, and more. I use it and love it. Alternatives include HelloBar, SleekNote, and IceGram. These and other free or inexpensive tools can put a bar or ribbon at the top of your website that invites site visitors to sign up for your email list. They connect with your email marketing service (like MailChimp) so subscribers are automatically added to your list. Some premium themes provide this feature (such as Thrive Themes).

Thrive Themes and Site Builder

bit.ly/ck-thrivethemes

I installed a Thrive Themes WordPress plugin and after using it for 10 minutes I bought the membership to get all their themes and plugins. This company is awesome and I immediately sought out an affiliate relationship with them.

You may be overwhelmed when you visit their page but remember you don't have to use all their tools right now. Just know that it makes building pages super easy with click-and-drop headings, text areas, images, offers premium themes and plugins to make so you can click and drop design elements into your web pages.

These themes include landing pages, countdown timers, credit card widgets, call to action (CTA) forms, and lots of other features that you would have to cobble together to get the same results from free Word-Press plugins. (Too many plugins can break a website.)

You don't need to know much about WordPress because the Thrive Architect interface overlays it to make it a visual and self-explanatory way to build pages and posts.

It costs $19/mo or $228/yr.

WWordPressWeb Hosting and Themes

bit.ly/WordPress-godaddy

WordPress is the most popular web software used to create websites and blogs. You need a managed, hosted WordPress website by a trusted web hosting company so you control the content and it's backed up daily, with 24/7 support. It's easy to use and if you get stuck, many consultants are available to help at all levels and reasonable prices. As mentioned above, my WordPress blogs and websites are hosted with GoDaddy, where I also buy my domain names. Through my affiliate link, you can get a $2.49/mo deal for a Managed Hosted WordPress website that includes the security features, backups, and 24/7 support you need.

Yoast SEO Plugin

yoast.com

You need this. Yoast is an SEO plugin for WordPress that helps you optimize your website for better search results. It includes real-time content analysis so you can see right away if your blog post and page titles are on target, your image tags and titles, meta descriptions, and more. It's kind of magic how it helps you choose keywords and prompts you to link to other content in your site. There's a free and premium version. This is a great marketing tool (passive marketing/metadata) and I so I recommend Yoast Premium at $89.00.

58

EMAIL MARKETING TOOLS

GETTING YOUR READERS AND WOULD-BE READERS TO SUBSCRIBE to your news via email is the number one author marketing super-power. By doing that, they give you permission to contact them directly. Don't squander this opportunity. Give them what they want–a freebie that they value–and interact with them in a human way.

Subscribe for access to updates to the *Consumer's Guide for Self-Publishers* web book:
www.selfpubbootcamp.com/readers

ConvertKit

convertkit.com

ConvertKit is a little more expensive but, in my opinion, worth it. It was created by a designer and author Nathan Barry for designers and authors. What I like about it is their visual flow. It's much easier to create automations that send subscribers the promised reward (story, worksheet, etc.) and other emails, depending on where they signed up.

You can create landing pages for your books, workshops, events... anything, and send a stream of customized, automated emails that are relevant to that subscriber. The process makes a lot of sense when you look at it this way.

MailChimp

eepurl.com/piC95

MailChimp is an email marketing service provider that helps you collect email addresses from interested website visitors, and is possibly your most important marketing tool. Other vendors that do the same sort of thing include Constant Contact, Vertical Response, AWeber, and Sendy, but MailChimp is arguably the most popular. That may be because you can use MailChimp for free if your list is under 2000 email addresses. They make it easy to place a signup form on your website and blog. MailerLite is a strong, low-cost competitor.

MotionMail

motionmailapp.com

MotionMail is an app that creates a countdown timer in your email. Create a sense of urgency with a time-limited offer. Competitors include Deadline Funnel which is a popular premium tool, but it's complicated. Another easy freebie is TickCounter.

Substack

substack.com

Substack is a free tool that makes it simple for a writer to start an email newsletter that makes money from subscriptions. See the next chapter on *Publishing by Subscription*.

59

PUBLISHING BY SUBSCRIPTION

CAN YOU CONSISTENTLY OFFER VALUABLE OR ENTERTAINING information that people will pay for? Most authors can. Here are the subscription-based publishing platforms you might use to provide written, audio, and video content to your readers.

Three of these platforms, Drip, Patreon, and Steady, do much the same thing. You create content on their site and they handle membership, subscription, delivery, and payments. Flattr is a browser extension that follows subscribers around the web and pays you based on the amount of time they spend on your website and social media properties. PayPal handles your subscription and other e-commerce but does not deliver content.

Subscribe for access to updates to the *Consumer's Guide for Self-Publishers* web book:
www.selfpubbootcamp.com/readers

Gumroad

gumroad.com

Find out more about Gumroad in *Direct Sales Tools*.

Gumroad (founded 2011) has long been one of my most highly recommended tools and they offer a subscription program as well as a sales widget you can place on your site. They charge a $10/mo hosting fee plus a per-transaction charge of 3.5 percent plus 30¢. See Gumroad's full review in *Chapter 55, Direct Sales Tools* for a complete description of all the other things Gumroad can do for you, such as preorders and physical sales of books, mugs, t-shirts, or whatever.

Leanpub

leanpub.com

Leanpub is an iterative or serial publication tool, not strictly a subscription tool, but has similarities. See more about Leanpub in *Chapter 55, Direct Sales Tools*.

Patreon

patreon.com

Patreon (founded May 2013) was the first robust subscription platform for artists. You can post blogs, audio, video, live streams on the platform and offer off-platform perks like ebooks and print books. It's an excellent way to raise money and keep in touch with your fans. I used it to fund my Baja Adventure Guide.

Patreon takes a flat fee of 5 percent of successfully-processed payments, which gives you 95 percent of earnings from the site.

PayPal

paypal.com

See more about PayPal in *Chapter 61, E-Commerce Solutions*.

In addition to using PayPal as your e-commerce system for single payments and donations, you can use it to collect a subscription fee. It's very easy to create a PayPal subscription button, customize the button text and appearance, and place it on your website.

You'll need to host your digital products elsewhere, but PayPal can take the work out of hand-creating accounts for your subscribers by automatically generating usernames and passwords for member-only content on your website. This requires writing or editing a Perl script and placing it on your website server. If you don't know how to do this, you can easily hire a web expert to do it for you on a site like UpWork or Fiverr. See *Chapter 49, Business and Productivity Tools*.

You can even offer a free or discounted trial period, have it track inventory so you don't oversell books or other products, and add a drop-down menu with prices and options.

Steady

steadyhq.com

Like Patreon, Berlin-based Steady (founded 2016) provides you with a project page on their platform where you can set prices and decide what to offer your subscribers. You promote your page to your community and they take care of the subscription process. Steady keeps a 10 percent commission and takes no fees for payment processing.

Substack

substack.com

Substack's moto is "paid newsletters made simple." Use it to start an email newsletter that makes money from subscriptions. Just sign up, connect your bank account, and get to work.

You can use it to publish your book serially for free and just collect emails for your newsletter.

Tapas Media

tapas.io

Tapas is a reading and publishing platform on the web, IOS, and Android. Create and deliver serial bite-sized stories including comics and novels. Tapas enjoys a large readership of people who want to read short, serial works, who can optionally support their favorite creators by leaving comments and tips. Partnerships with Kakao, Tencent, Hachetter, and Penguin Random House. Compare to Wattpad and Patreon.

60

COPYWRITING SERVICES

DON'T BEAT YOURSELF UP BECAUSE YOU CAN'T SEEM TO WRITE compelling, keyword-rich copy to describe your book. This is a different skillset.

Subscribe for access to updates to the *Consumer's Guide for Self-Publishers* web book:
www.selfpubbootcamp.com/readers

Best Page Forward

bestpageforward.net/blurbs

Best Page Forward is a blurb service by Bryan Cohen and team. Get a professional book description, a Facebook Ad version of the description copy, and text for your book landing page. Book descriptions are a key marketing effort and this is a good deal.

Costs $197 ($297 for a one-week turnaround, $397 for three-day turnaround).

The Blurb Bitch

blurbbitch.com

The Blurb Bitch is Carol Ann Eastman, a sassy author and copywriter who whips blurbs into shape for any genre of book. Here's her current pricing menu. Turnaround time is about a month or you can pay for a 72-hour rush job.

- Rewrite $35.00
- Rushed rewrite $45.00
- From scratch $60.00
- Rushed from scratch $70.00
- Tagline $15.00
- Promotional poetry $60.00
- Rushed Promotional Poem $70.00
- Boxed set $60.00
- Rushed boxed set $70.00

Others

The copywriting services I listed are book copywriting services specifically. You may also need a copywriter for your website and other materials. There are too many to list. Search the internet for your topic and genre and you may be surprised.

61

E-COMMERCE SOLUTIONS

IF YOU WANT TO SET UP YOUR OWN WEB STORE WITHOUT USING one of the direct sales tools I reviewed in chapter 55 you can use one of these services to set up direct payment to your own bank account instead. You'll need to find your API and other tasks that require a little tech savvy and if you can't figure it out you can easily hire it out using a service like Fiverr. These services all allow instant digital downloads and order forms for physical books. Look for pricing around 2.9 percent + 30 cents per sale.

Subscribe for access to updates to the *Consumer's Guide for Self-Publishers* web book:
www.selfpubbootcamp.com/readers

Amazon Pay

pay.amazon.com/us/merchant

Amazon Pay lets your customers use information stored in their Amazon account to pay and arrange for delivery.

Google Wallet

google.com/wallet

Similar to PayPal with credit card processing and the ability to send out invoices.

Intuit

intuit.com

If you're a small business owner, you may already use Intuit products. Besides being able to accept payments, both online and in-person with GoPayment, Intuit can also help you pay employees, calculate payroll taxes, and file payroll tax forms.

PayPal

paypal.com/us/webapps/mpp/accept-payments-online

The most common solution, convenient, and trusted. Add a checkout, donation, or subscription button to your site and start accepting payments from your readers from their own PayPal accounts or any major credit card. You can also send invoices.

Skrill

skrill.com

Free setup, low fees, and the ability to send text messages straight from your account. A popular and simple alternative to PayPal.

Stripe

stripe.com/us/payments

Like PayPal, Stripe is an e-commerce system you can use to collect payments from customers who purchase books from your website with major credit cards. Into cryptocurrency? I am. Stripe allows you to accept payment in BitCoin.

62

PROFESSIONAL ORGANIZATIONS

THERE ARE SO MANY WRITING AND PUBLISHING ORGANIZATIONS that it would be impossible to keep up with them, so I've listed a few prominent organizations here. Search the web for one near you and for genre-specific organizations as well.

Subscribe for access to updates to the *Consumer's Guide for Self-Publishers* web book:
www.selfpubbootcamp.com/readers

Alliance of Independent Authors (Alli)

allianceindependentauthors.org

ALLi, the Alliance of Independent Authors, is a non-profit professional association for authors who self-publish. The alliance offers connection and collaboration, advice and education, advocacy and representation to writers who want to self-publish well. Based in London, it is a global organization.

Members-only benefits include a closed online forum, discounts and deals, free guidebooks and booklets, seminars and events, contract and legal advice. To the wider indie author community, they run a self-publishing advice center and blog. Three times a year they host a free online conference, Indie Author Fringe.

Authors Guild

authorsguild.net

The Authors Guild is the nation's oldest and largest professional organization of writers and consists of two organizations: a membership organization that provides excellent benefits to dues-paying members, and a foundation that effectively advocates for all authors. Benefits include:

- Free legal assistance, from contract reviews to advising on and intervening in legal disputes. Joining the Authors Guild essentially provides an author with a free attorney on retainer.
- Prestigious press credentials for freelance journalists.
- Liability insurance.
- A back-in-print program and website hosting.
- A vibrant online community forum.
- Local chapters that host informal gatherings and opportunities to meet fellow authors.
- In-person and phone-in seminars on the business of publishing, tax law, self-publishing, and more.
- An annual black-tie gala and other social events.

Independent Book Publishers Assoc (IBPA)

ibpa-online.org

In a nutshell, IBPA makes it easier for independent book publishers and self-published authors to navigate the sometimes intimidating publishing process.

The Independent Book Publishers Association (IBPA) is a not-for-profit membership organization serving and leading the independent publishing community through advocacy, education, and tools for success. With over 3,000 members, IBPA is the largest publishing trade association in the US for independent publishers, self-published authors, small presses, or mid-sized publishers.

They offer a huge list of benefits, from printing to Bowker ISBNs, marketing, foreign rights, reviews, cooperative book catalogs, legal disputes, health insurance, networking, freight, and more. Not to mention the awesome print magazine that comes to your snail-mailbox every month.

The annual conference, Publishing University, roams around the US and is well worth attending.

Romance Writers of America

rwa.org

If you're a romance writer you must must must belong to the RWA. This organization is famous for the caliber of its conferences, its resources, and the enthusiasm and generosity of its members.

63

YOUR PUBLISHER'S BOOKSHELF

As in any industry, there are essential books that are worth purchasing. Got a suggestion? Let me know.

Subscribe for access to updates in the *Consumer's Guide for Self-Publishers* web book:
www.selfpubbootcamp.com/readers

Publishing

Green-Light Your Book: How Writers Can Succeed in the New Era of Publishing, Brooke Warner

Writing

Write On, Sisters! Voice, Courage, and Claiming Your Place at the Table, Brooke Warner

Finish Your Book in Three Drafts: How to Write a Book, Revise a Book, and Complete a Book While You Still Love It, Stuart Horwitz

Chicago Manual of Style: Free 30-day online subscription. This is especially helpful when you're proofread of your book.

How to Blog a Book: Write, Publish, and Promote Your Work One Post at a Time, Nina Amir

Business

Register Your Book: The Essential Guide to ISBNs, Barcodes, Copyright, and LCCNs, David Wogahn

Self-Publisher's Legal Handbook, 2nd Edition, Helen Sedwick, Attorney and Author

Business Plan in a Day, Rhonda Abrams, founder of the Planning Shop

The Business of Being a Writer, Jane Friedman

Marketing

Be the Gateway: A Practical Guide to Sharing Your Creative Work and Engaging an Audience, Dan Blank

Online Marketing for Busy Authors: A Step-by-Step Guide, Fauzia Burke

The Nonfiction Book Publishing Plan: The Professional Guide to Profitable Self-Publishing, Stephanie Chandler and Karl Palachuk (Has some overlap with this guide and a lot of great marketing ideas for nonfiction authors.)

That's it!

If you've read to the end of this guide, wow! You've digested a lot of information. You may have started to take action already, but if you haven't, you can begin with the cheatsheets and checklists you get with that readers list I keep bugging you about. :-)

I imagine you'll be diving back into the various parts of this guide you'll need these next few months during your publishing journey. Good. There are a lot of details in the guide to make sure you don't skip step.

Congratulations for making the commitment to slowing down, connecting with readers, and making sure to publish professionally. You won't be sorry!

I look forward to meeting you via email and tracking your progress. I'm always eager for feedback and I'd love to know when your book is published. I hope you'll check in with me to let me know how it's going.

Thanks!

~ Carla

FREEBIES!

These freebies are exclusive to readers of this guide.

When you sign up you'll need to double opt-in—this keeps spammers at bay. Look for an email from hello@selfpubbootcamp.com and if you don't find it, check your junk, spam, or promotions folders.

You'll get access to all these publications, cheatsheets, worksheets, and more.

A Consumer's Guide for Self-Publishers

Get free updates to *Part VII, Consumer's Guide,* forever. Change happens, so don't miss out. Publishing toolmakers and service providers are always improving to make things easier for you. On signup, I'll send you a link to the web book that you can access at any time.

www.selfpubbootcamp.com/readers

When you subscribe you'll also get links to the following documents.

What every author needs to know about Microsoft Word styles

Your most important tool as a writer is Microsoft Word and Styles is essential to making your book look great. It's very easy to learn and my little booklet makes it even easier with examples and screenshots.

Book production checklist

This checklist details all the things you need in the front matter and back matter to make your book complete, professional, and ready to print.

Book launch checklist

This checklist will help you remember all the tasks you need to do before you launch, and after launch. Use it to create your publishing calendar.

Metadata cheatsheet

You're going to be so glad you have this when it comes time to upload your book. Because you'll have less than 4,000 characters for your book description and author bio, plus the best keywords and BISAC codes. IngramSpark, Amazon KDP, Smashwords… they all have slightly different requirements. So make your life easy. Do it in advance. That's why I created the cheatsheet. It's not cheating, really!

HELPFUL LINKS

Subscribe to Reader's Updates

Author Friendly Podcast

Self-Publishing Boot Camp website

Self-Pub Boot Camp online courses

ACKNOWLEDGMENTS

Thank you to all the readers of the previous four editions of this guide for providing feedback that makes each subsequent edition so much more helpful. Based on your suggestions I divided this edition into topical parts that allow authors to focus on their current needs and find the information quickly.

For this 5th edition, I'd like to thank a great team of beta readers including Jennifer Flaig who stuck with me through to the very end checking and rechecking changes and providing the encouragement I needed to let my voice shine through. Also Sheri McGuinn, Ann Pearson, Pauline Wiles, Martha Conway, and Scott James, who went above and beyond in their feedback, identifying ways to make this guide better. Other beta team members who improved the guide are Raman Venkat, Jules Frank, Neil Dunlop, Katy Tackes, and Marla Anderson. Thank you. Any remaining errata are mine.

I owe a great debt to the founders and marketing teams of the writing and self-publishing services companies: a heartfelt thank you for checking your entries in this guide for accuracy and for everything you do for authors.

And finally, to my sister Celia Kilsby and my mom Cynthia King, avid readers who wade through all of my writing no matter the topic. I especially appreciate the beginner's eye you bring to this topic which I know will make it accessible to new authors unfamiliar with the publishing industry. I also cherish your consistent encouragement and support of everything I do. Thank you.

ABOUT THE AUTHOR

Carla King has more than twenty years experience as a writer, self-publisher, web developer, and book consultant. She started self-publishing in 1995 as a technology and travel writer. In 2010 she founded the Self-Publishing Boot Camp series of guides, workshops, and online courses. She has been connected with the Silicon Valley self-publishing technology industry from its inception, and has served as a trusted advisor to publishing companies and to authors eager to use the tools to reach readers.

Carla works for the San Francisco Writers Conference as Independent Publishing Track Leader and Director of Business Development. She contributes publishing and technology how-to articles and opinion a variety of online publications, and hosts the Author Friendly podcast. You can find her self-publishing blog and coaching services for authors at Destination Published.

Carla spent many years as a technical writer and, in the early days of portable computing, worked as a freelance writer for magazines like PC World. This experience paved the way for a career as an adventure travel writer and she has contributed hundreds of stories to magazines and anthologies.

Her first self-published book was a 1995 guidebook titled *Cycling the French Riviera*. With her writing group, the Wild Writing Women, she self-published *Wild Writing Women: Stories of World Travel* in 2001. The book was sold to a New York publishing house later that year. In 2008, Carla also produced an interactive travel magazine from the group's trip to Ireland, titled *Ireland: The Sacred and the Profane*.

The *Self-Publishing Boot Camp Guide for Authors* has been edited and expanded over 10 years. The origins of the guide was the *Self-Publishing Boot Camp Workbook*, published in 2010, from classes taught in the San Francisco Bay Area. In 2013, PBS published her columns in a book titled *How to Self-Publish*. Other books Carla has authored and self-published include *Stories from Elsewhere: Travels on Two and Three Wheels*, *American Borders: Breakdowns in Small Towns All Around the USA*, and *Motorcycling for Women: How to Choose a Beginner Bike*.

Carla is based in the San Francisco Bay Area. She is currently working on the *China Road Motorcycle Diaries*, a memoir. Wherever she is, you can find her at CarlaKing.com.

facebook.com/missadventuring

twitter.com/missadventuring

instagram.com/missadventuring

amazon.com/author/carlaking

pinterest.com/missadventuring

snapchat.com/add/missadventuring

goodreads.com/carlaking

ALSO BY CARLA KING

Consumers Guide for Self-Publishers

Reviews of writing and self-publishing companies, products, tools, and services for authors

American Borders

Breakdowns in Small Towns All Around the USA

Stories from Elsewhere

Travels on Two and Three Wheels

Motorcycling for Women

Beginner Bikes

Wild Writing Women

Stories of World Travel

Ireland

The Sacred and the Profane

Made in the USA
Monee, IL
09 September 2023

42435589R00266